CRESCENT CITY

COLLECTION

A Taste of New Orleans

⚜

The Junior League of New Orleans

This cookbook is a collection of favorite recipes, which are not necessarily original recipes.

The Junior League of New Orleans is an organization of women committed to promoting volunteerism, developing the potential of women, and improving communities through the effective action and leadership of trained volunteers. Its purpose is exclusively educational and charitable.

Copyright© 2000
Junior League of New Orleans, Inc.
4319 Carondelet Street
New Orleans, Louisiana 70115
(504) 891-5845

Library of Congress Number: 99-073485
ISBN: 0-9604774-0-3

Photographer: David G. Spielman
Introductory Text: Gene Bourg
Architectural Text: Robert J. Cangelosi, Jr., A.I.A.

Book Designers: Brad Whitfield and Susan Breining
Project Manager: Judy Jackson
Art Director: Steve Newman

Designed, edited, and manufactured by
Favorite Recipes Press
an imprint of

FRP

P.O. Box 305142
Nashville, Tennessee 37230
1-800-358-0560

Manufactured in the United States of America
First Printing: 2000   30,000 copies

Other books published by the Junior League of New Orleans, Inc.:
   The Plantation Cookbook
   Jambalaya

Contents

Appetizers 10

Soups & Salads 34

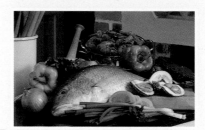

Seafood 62

Poultry 94

Preface

The members of the Junior League of New Orleans ("JLNO") welcome you to the pages of our third
cookbook, *Crescent City Collection: A Taste of New Orleans.* It was Jean Baptiste Le Moyne,
Sieur de Bienville, who christened our bend in the Mississippi "The Beautiful Crescent" in 1699,
and a unique blend of cultures and their culinary traditions has evolved since that time. Gene Bourg's
Introduction sets the tone for an adventure into the ever-unfolding cuisine of New Orleans,
while stunning color photographs by David G. Spielman create fresh angles on the past and present.
The narratives of the JLNO Show Houses by Robert J. Cangelosi, Jr., A.I.A.,
offer a glimpse into the vast architectural history of our city, as well as insights
into the colorful stories behind the homes.

No one truly owns a home or a recipe in the Crescent City; we are simply their custodians.
We hold the home or recipe for a time, perhaps adding something of our current sensibilities,
and then pass them to the next generation to preserve. *Crescent City Collection:
A Taste of New Orleans* honors these traditions: our love of good food and our respect
for our rich architectural heritage. The recipes and culinary sidebars entice the taste buds,
offering a veritable buffet of delicacies with creative ideas and preparation tips.
Enjoy the enlightening non-culinary sidebars that focus on the melange of people, events,
places, and customs that defines New Orleans.

The Decorators' Show House was selected as a distinctive fund-raiser by the JLNO almost twenty-five
years ago. It seems appropriate to feature our past Show Houses in *Crescent City Collection:
A Taste of New Orleans* because they demonstrate the theme of evolution that characterizes our city.
The JLNO selects its fund-raisers and projects to meet the changing needs of our community. Junior
League members were instrumental in the creation of the Parenting Center at Children's Hospital,
the Louisiana Nature and Science Center, the Holman Vocational Center, the Preservation Resource
Center, the New Orleans Council for Young Children, Teen Court, and many other noteworthy
programs in our city. By purchasing *Crescent City Collection: A Taste of New Orleans,* you help
to guarantee the continued success of the JLNO in training volunteers, developing the potential
of women, and improving our communities.

Cookbook Committee

Chair: Kendall Collins Gensler
Vice Chair: Lyn Hallaron

Editorial Committee: Wendy Kennedy, Chair
Cynthia Taggart Bassich, Writer
Nancy McKenzie Dupont, Writer
Jan C. Benjamin, Assistant Writer
Deborah Rhea Slattery, Assistant Writer
Laurie Ellis Doyle, Researcher

Executive Liaison: Ebie Taylor Strauss

Chapter Captains: Lesley F. Paxton, Appetizers
Lyn Hallaron, Soups & Salads
Anne Chaffe, Seafood
Mary Priestley Frank, Poultry
Pamela Lyons, Meat & Game
Michelle DeRussy Dodenhoff, Side Dishes & Sauces
Kendall Collins Gensler, Breads & Brunch
Nancy Cockrum Plough, Desserts

Executive Committee 1998-99

President: Sarah Foster "Sally" Suthon
President-elect: Melanee Gaudin Usdin
Administrative Vice President: Katherine Waters Gelderman
Communications Vice President: Ashley Simmons Bright
Community Vice President: Mimi Blessey Heebe
Recording Secretary: Jeanne LeBlanc Williams
Treasurer: Ebie Taylor Strauss
Assistant Treasurer: Holly Seavey Nalty

Board of Directors 1999-2000

President: Melanee Gaudin Usdin
President-elect: Katie Andry Crosby
Secretary: Karen Killeen Daly
Treasurer: Holly Seavey Nalty
Assistant Treasurer: Mary Gallagher Eymard
Business Council Director: Jennifer Holliday Tompkins
Community Council Director: Monique Gaudin Gardner
Membership Council Director: Elizabeth McGee Cordes
Ways and Means Council Director: Eileen Comer Gambel
Nominating Chair: Beth Talbot Dienes

Introduction

A favorite cookbook, at least on my kitchen shelves, wears its dog-eared pages and butter splats as a champion wears medals or ribbons. Every folded corner and every telltale spot memorializes a particular gustatory adventure.

No volume in my collection bears a greater number of creases and dabs than a first-edition copy of *The Plantation Cookbook*, compiled and written by members of the Junior League of New Orleans and published by Doubleday in 1972 (now published by B.E. Trice Publishing Co., Inc., of New Orleans).

The Plantation Cookbook's recipes are comparatively modest in number. Virtually every one of them is either a definitive version of a New Orleans-Creole classic or a sensible variation thereon. The Junior League's next cookbook, *Jambalaya*, dared to take a more universal approach. But it, too, was driven by the force that has always motivated New Orleans' best cooks: a profound respect for deep, full flavors that resonate with the power of judicious seasoning and the grace of simple goodness.

With *Crescent City Collection: A Taste of New Orleans*, the women of the Junior League take another step in a logical progression begun with *The Plantation Cookbook* and *Jambalaya*. This latest enterprise is as up-to-date as a fresh coat of taupe paint on a shotgun cottage.

Once again, the backdrop for the recipes is a collection of great houses, this time some of the city's handsomest old residences. The marriage is commendable: fine homes and fine food are about as ideal a pairing as voice and orchestra.

Seekers of local color can also revel in the text's celebration of a panoply of the city's cultural treasures, from the vibrant music its sons and daughters gave the world to the macabre beauty of its cities of the dead.

New Orleanians have their own scale of cultural values, but none is more deeply imbedded in the municipal psyche than food, and many ingredients in the recipes in *Crescent City Collection: A Taste of New Orleans* have become part of the city's cultural canon—shellfish, eggplant, garlic, and cayenne among them. Other recipes give long-familiar local staples a new lease on life with a contemporary twist or two:

Mascarpone and chives lend their flavors to little bundles of *roquette* (also known locally as "rocket" or "pepper grass"), the piquant leaf that generations of New Orleanians cultivated or foraged, and which now goes by the name of arugula.

Grits, another old friend, is reincarnated in these pages (as it has been in dozens of forward-looking new restaurants around the country) as polenta.

In the appetizer chapter, artichoke, whose earthy taste inspired generations of Italian cooks to create benchmark dishes, cleverly finds its way to a ramekin of flan.

In a brunch dish of glazed bacon, pecans play second fiddle to the main ingredient, but in the dessert chapter they're a star attraction in a pie with chocolate and bourbon. On another dessert page pepper jazzes up a sauté of strawberries (Louisiana strawberries, I would hope) in cabernet sauce.

Culinary Luddites may turn up their noses at such apparent challenges to the integrity of Creole tradition. They might remind themselves that a cuisine is a living thing; and, as in all living things, movement is a sign of good health.

Mainstream New Orleans cooking is still evolving after nearly three centuries. Innovation has been its lifeblood almost from the time the first French colonists started talking to the local Indians in the 1720s. In the ensuing decades, Africans, Caribbeans, Germans, Italians, and Croatians contributed to the mix. Today, Southeast Asian restaurant chefs, among others, are using the region's awesome bounty from sea and soil to add their imprint to a culinary heritage as diverse as any in the New World.

All of this may furrow the brows of Creole purists, but they can take comfort in this: If past experience is the touchstone, the cream will rise to the top.

— Gene Bourg
New Orleans, March 1999

Appetizers

Appetizers

James B. Sinnott House
5411 St. Charles Avenue

The talents of architect Allison Owen of Diboll, Owen & Goldstein
are evident in the design of this impressive Mediterranean Villa-style house,
built in 1906 for Civil War veteran James B. Sinnott.
The architectural style is one of many revival styles common in the United States
during the early twentieth century. This is not a textbook example, however,
being more picturesque than its prototype. The latter employed a cubic mass
with a symmetrical facade, arched ground-floor openings, and square second-floor
openings that disappear into the large umbrella-like tile roof.

The house is located in an Uptown faubourg once known as Rickerville.
Faubourg is a French term loosely translated as suburb. Rickerville was named
for the controversial Samuel Ricker, Jr., a native of Cincinnati who moved to
New Orleans in the 1820s. He eventually gained control of forty percent
of his wife's family plantation and amassed a fortune by using the land to
pasture up to 2,000 head of livestock for the United States government
during the Mexican-American War. In 1849 the plantation was subdivided
as Rickerville and sold off to satisfy creditors. This faubourg and six others
subsequently were incorporated as Jefferson City, which was annexed
by the City of New Orleans in 1870.

In 1918 the house was purchased by Crawford Ellis, founder of the
New Orleans-based Pan-American Life Insurance Company and a former executive
of United Fruit Company. Mr. Ellis was a civic leader who reigned as Rex,
King of Carnival, in 1914. Following a 1927 fire, the house was remodeled under
the direction of Carl Woodward. During this renovation the interior staircase
was changed, and the original porch railing was replaced with an iron one
containing Ellis's monogram. The Maurice Hartson family bought the home
in 1968, and it became the JLNO Show House VIII in 1996.
The present owners are Mr. and Mrs. Peter Koeppel.

Crab Rellenos

Yield: 12 rellenos

12	LARGE JALAPEÑO CHILES	3/4	CUP MEXICAN BEER
4	OUNCES FRESH CRAB MEAT, DRAINED, FLAKED	1/2	CUP FLOUR
			FLOUR
1/3	CUP MINCED ONION		CORN OIL
1/4	CUP MINCED BELL PEPPER	1/2	AVOCADO, PEELED, CHOPPED
1/4	CUP MAYONNAISE	1/2	CUP MILD SALSA
	SALT AND PEPPER TO TASTE	1	TABLESPOON MAYONNAISE

Cut each jalapeño in half, starting just below the stem and leaving the stem attached. Remove seeds. Bring the jalapeños and enough cold water to cover to a boil in a medium heavy saucepan over high heat; drain well. Add fresh cold water and repeat the boiling process; drain well. Pat the jalapeños dry. Combine the crab meat, onion, bell pepper and 1/4 cup mayonnaise in a small bowl. Season with salt and pepper. Fill each jalapeño cavity with crab meat mixture. Press the halves together to compress the filling. Whisk the beer gradually into 1/2 cup flour in a bowl. Let stand for 30 minutes. Coat the stuffed jalapeños with flour. Whisk the beer mixture and dip the jalapeños in the mixture. Heat the corn oil to 375 degrees in a heavy deep saucepan. Deep-fry in batches for 3 minutes or until golden brown. Remove to paper towels to drain. Mix the avocado, salsa and 1 tablespoon mayonnaise in a small bowl. Season with additional salt and pepper. Arrange the jalapeños on a serving platter and serve with avocado salsa. Note: The jalapeños can be stuffed up to 4 hours ahead. Cover and chill until needed. Since jalapeño juice can sting the skin, wear rubber gloves or wash hands thoroughly with soap and water immediately after handling jalapeños.

Crawfish Beignets with Rémoulade Sauce

Yield: 10 servings

2	CUPS FLOUR	3	TABLESPOONS CHOPPED
2	TABLESPOONS BAKING POWDER		FLAT-LEAF PARSLEY
2	TEASPOONS CAYENNE PEPPER		SALT TO TASTE
½	TEASPOON GROUND GINGER	5	DASHES OF TABASCO SAUCE
¼	CUP CHOPPED PIMENTOS	1½	CUPS WATER
1	TABLESPOON CHOPPED GARLIC		PEANUT OIL
1½	CUPS CHOPPED CRAWFISH TAILS		

Combine the flour, baking powder, cayenne pepper and ginger in a bowl. Stir in the pimentos, garlic, crawfish, parsley and salt. Stir in the Tabasco sauce and enough of the water to make a soft dough. Let dough stand for 20 minutes. Heat the peanut oil to 350 degrees in a heavy deep saucepan. Drop in teaspoonfuls of dough and fry until golden brown. Remove with a slotted spoon to paper towels to drain. Serve drizzled with Rémoulade Sauce (below).

Rémoulade Sauce

Yield: 1½ cups

2	EGG YOLKS	1	BAY LEAF, CRUMBLED
¼	CUP VEGETABLE OIL	2	TABLESPOONS WORCESTERSHIRE
½	CUP FINELY CHOPPED CELERY		SAUCE
½	CUP FINELY CHOPPED GREEN	1	TABLESPOON PREPARED MUSTARD
	ONIONS	1	TABLESPOON WHITE VINEGAR
¼	CUP CHOPPED FRESH PARSLEY	1	TABLESPOON TABASCO SAUCE
¼	CUP GRATED FRESH OR PREPARED	1	TABLESPOON MINCED GARLIC
	HORSERADISH	2	TEASPOONS SWEET PAPRIKA
¼	LEMON, SEEDED	1	TEASPOON SALT

Beat the egg yolks in a blender for 2 minutes. Add the oil in a stream, processing constantly. Add the remaining ingredients 1 at a time; beat until well mixed. Chill thoroughly.

CRAWFISH

THESE TASTY CRUSTACEANS, OFTEN REFERRED TO AS "MUDBUGS," "CRAYFISH," "CRAWDADS," AND "ÉCREVISSES," ARE SYNONYMOUS WITH LOUISIANA AND CAJUN COOKING. CRAWFISH RESEMBLE MINIATURE LOBSTERS. THE DISTINCTIVE FLAVOR OF THEIR TAIL MEAT IS ENJOYED IN RECIPES RANGING FROM SIMPLE BOILING WITH SPICY SEASONINGS TO THE HAUTE CUISINE OF CRAWFISH CARDINALE. OVER 400 SPECIES EXIST ACROSS THE WORLD, THREE-FOURTHS OF THESE IN NORTH AMERICA. LEGISLATION PASSED IN 1959 TO ALLOW CRAWFISH FARMING ENABLES US TO CONSUME AND TO EXPORT MASS QUANTITIES OF OUR BELOVED DELICACIES YEAR-ROUND, WHEREAS FORMERLY THEY WERE AVAILABLE ONLY SEASONALLY IN AREAS SUCH AS LOUISIANA'S ATCHAFALAYA BASIN. FOUND IN SONG AND LITERATURE FROM ERNEST HEMINGWAY TO NATIVE AMERICAN AND AFRICAN-AMERICAN FOLK TALES, CRAWFISH EVEN GRACED A U.S. POSTAGE STAMP HONORING THE 1984 NEW ORLEANS WORLD'S FAIR.

Crawfish Cheesecake

Yield: 8 servings

1	CUP GRATED PARMESAN CHEESE	2	TO 3 TABLESPOONS CREOLE SEASONING
1	CUP FRESH BREAD CRUMBS	2	DASHES OF WORCESTERSHIRE SAUCE
½	CUP (1 STICK) MELTED BUTTER	2	DASHES OF TABASCO SAUCE
1	TABLESPOON OLIVE OIL	2	TABLESPOONS LEMON JUICE
1	CUP CHOPPED ONION	28	OUNCES CREAM CHEESE, SOFTENED
½	CUP CHOPPED GREEN BELL PEPPER	4	EGGS
½	CUP CHOPPED RED BELL PEPPER	½	CUP HEAVY CREAM
1	POUND CRAWFISH TAILS, CHOPPED	1	CUP SHREDDED SMOKED GOUDA CHEESE
2	TEASPOONS MINCED GARLIC	2½	CUPS GREEN ONION COULIS

Mix the Parmesan cheese, bread crumbs and melted butter in a bowl. Press the mixture into the bottom of a 9-inch springform pan. Heat the olive oil in a large skillet over high heat. Add the onion and bell peppers and sauté for 2 minutes. Add the crawfish, garlic, Creole seasoning, Worcestershire sauce, Tabasco sauce and lemon juice. Sauté for 1½ minutes. Remove from the heat. Beat the cream cheese and eggs with an electric mixer for 5 minutes or until thick and frothy. Add the heavy cream, Gouda cheese and crawfish mixture. Beat for 2 minutes or until well mixed and creamy. Pour the filling into the crust and bake at 350 degrees for 1 hour or until firm. Cool to room temperature. Spoon Green Onion Coulis (below) on 8 plates. Top with a slice of Crawfish Cheesecake.

Green Onion Coulis

Yield: 2½ to 3 cups

3/4	CUP CHOPPED GREEN ONIONS	2	EGGS
½	CUP CHOPPED FRESH PARSLEY	1	TEASPOON SALT
1	TABLESPOON CHOPPED SHALLOTS	6	TURNS FRESHLY GROUND PEPPER
1	TABLESPOON CHOPPED GARLIC	1½	CUPS VEGETABLE OIL

Purée the green onions, parsley, shallots and garlic in a blender or food processor. Add the eggs, salt and pepper and process until mixed. Add the oil in a stream with the machine running. Process until well mixed.

Thai Crawfish Noodle Nests

YIELD: 6 SERVINGS

12	OUNCES COOKED ANGEL HAIR PASTA, CUT INTO 3-INCH THREADS	½	TEASPOON CAYENNE PEPPER
12	OUNCES COOKED CRAWFISH TAILS OR SHRIMP, CHOPPED	2	EGGS, BEATEN
1	TABLESPOON DRY MUSTARD	¾	CUP FLOUR
1½	TEASPOONS SALT	½	CUP CHOPPED GREEN ONIONS
		2	QUARTS VEGETABLE OIL
		2	CUPS GARLIC MAYONNAISE

Combine the cooked pasta, crawfish, mustard, salt, cayenne pepper and eggs in a bowl and mix well. Stir in the flour and green onions. Roll the mixture into slightly firm balls about the size of a golf ball. Heat the oil to 350 degrees in a 4-quart deep-fryer or heavy saucepan. Fry the balls in batches of 3 for about 3 minutes or until golden brown. Remove with a slotted spoon and drain on paper towels. Spread Garlic Mayonnaise (below) on each of 6 plates. Top with 3 nests on each plate.

Garlic Mayonnaise

YIELD: 2 CUPS

3	EGG YOLKS	5	TABLESPOONS KETCHUP
1	CUP OLIVE OIL	5	TEASPOONS CHOPPED FRESH PARSLEY
1	CUP VEGETABLE OIL		SALT AND PEPPER TO TASTE
2	TABLESPOONS MINCED GARLIC		

Beat the egg yolks in a large bowl at medium speed with an electric mixer. Add the olive oil and vegetable oil in a stream with the mixer running and beat until all the oil is incorporated. Whisk in the garlic, ketchup, parsley, salt and pepper. Cover and chill for up to 2 days.

Hollandaise Sauce

8 egg yolks
2 tablespoons lemon juice
2 tablespoons tarragon vinegar
2 cups (4 sticks) melted butter, warm
3/4 teaspoon paprika
Salt and cayenne pepper to taste

Beat the egg yolks, lemon juice and vinegar in a bowl. Pour into the top of a double boiler. Cook over hot water until thickened. Remove from the heat and beat in the warm melted butter gradually. Season with the paprika, salt and cayenne pepper. Keep warm but not hot.
Yield: 2 cups

Huitres à la Foch

Yield: 6 servings

1½ cups Tomato Sauce (below)	6 slices toast, crusts trimmed
2/3 cup sherry	36 raw oysters
1½ cups warm Hollandaise Sauce (at left) Kitchen Bouquet	1 cup finely ground yellow cornmeal
6 tablespoons canned pâté de fois gras	2 teaspoons salt
	½ teaspoon ground white pepper

Cook the Tomato Sauce and sherry in a saucepan over medium heat until reduced to 2/3 cup. Let cool slightly. Blend in the Hollandaise Sauce. Add enough Kitchen Bouquet to produce a nice brown color. Set aside and keep warm. Spread 1 tablespoon fois gras on each toast slice. Coat the oysters with a mixture of cornmeal, salt and pepper. Heat oil to 375 degrees in a heavy deep saucepan. Fry oysters for 4 minutes or until cooked. Remove with a slotted spoon; drain. Place 6 oysters on each toast. Top each with some of the sauce mixture.

Recipe provided by Antoine's Restaurant

Tomato Sauce

Yield: 2 cups

3/4 cup chopped onion	2 garlic cloves, minced
3 tablespoons butter	½ rib celery, chopped
2 tablespoons flour	2 sprigs of fresh parsley
2 cups chicken broth	1 bay leaf
1½ cups chopped tomatoes	Salt and white pepper to taste
¼ teaspoon dried thyme	

Sauté the onion in 2 tablespoons of the butter in a saucepan until beginning to brown. Add remaining butter and flour. Cook until golden brown, stirring frequently. Add the remaining ingredients. Simmer for 30 minutes. Press the sauce through a strainer.

Jazz Fest Oysters

Yield: 8 servings

24	OYSTERS, DRAINED, THEIR LIQUOR RESERVED	1	TABLESPOON CRUSHED RED PEPPER
2	TABLESPOONS LEMON JUICE	¼	CUP CRYSTAL HOT SAUCE
¼	CUP PREPARED BASIL PESTO	2	EGGS
1	TEASPOON CORNSTARCH	3	TABLESPOONS WATER
2	TEASPOONS COLD WATER	1	EGGPLANT, CUT INTO 8 (¼-INCH) SLICES
10	GARLIC CLOVES, MINCED	4	CUPS ITALIAN BREAD CRUMBS
1	CUP (2 STICKS) BUTTER, SOFTENED		VEGETABLE OIL
1	TABLESPOON CHOPPED PARSLEY		SALT AND PEPPER TO TASTE

Poach the oysters in just enough water to cover in a saucepan for 1 to 2 minutes. Remove the oysters with a slotted spoon. Add the lemon juice, oyster liquor and the pesto to the poaching liquid. Bring to a boil and cook until reduced by ½. Dissolve the cornstarch in 2 teaspoons water in a cup. Stir the cornstarch into the pesto mixture and remove from the heat. Mix the garlic and butter in a large bowl. Stir in the parsley, red pepper and hot sauce. Beat the eggs and water in a small bowl until blended. Dip the eggplant slices into the bread crumbs, then into the egg mixture and back into the crumbs. Heat the oil in a skillet and fry the eggplant until golden brown. Drain on paper towels. Add the garlic butter and poached oysters to the oyster liquid. Heat until the mixture registers 140 degrees on a candy thermometer. Set one eggplant slice on each of 8 plates. Top with oysters and sauce.

Recipe provided by Nanci Easterling, Food Art

JAZZ AND STORYVILLE

JAZZ, THAT NEBULOUS DESIGNATION ASSOCIATED WITH A CONGLOMERATION OF MUSICAL STYLES AND SOUNDS, IS SAID TO HAVE EVOLVED IN NEW ORLEANS AT THE TURN OF THE TWENTIETH CENTURY. ITS EARLY ORIGINS WERE THE CENTURIES-OLD AFRICAN TRIBAL CHANTS. JAZZ WAS A SECULAR MUSIC OF AFRICAN-AMERICANS AND GREW TO ENCOMPASS OTHER IDIOMS SUCH AS RAGTIME AND BLUES. LOCALLY, IT WAS PERFORMED IN THE RED-LIGHT DISTRICT KNOWN AS STORYVILLE, NAMED AFTER ALDERMAN SIDNEY STORY IN 1898. LOUIS ARMSTRONG, ONE OF THE MOST FAMOUS JAZZ PERFORMERS, WAS BORN IN NEW ORLEANS. OTHER RENOWNED ARTISTS WHO PLAYED HERE INCLUDE FERDINAND "JELLY ROLL" MORTON AND COUNT BASIE. TODAY, EVENTS SUCH AS THE NEW ORLEANS JAZZ AND HERITAGE FESTIVAL PROMOTE THE CONTINUED DEVELOPMENT AND ENJOYMENT OF THIS UNIQUE MUSICAL FORM.

Spicy Rémoulade Sauce

2 TABLESPOONS YELLOW MUSTARD
⅓ CUP CREOLE MUSTARD
⅓ CUP KETCHUP
2 TABLESPOONS WHITE VINEGAR
2 TABLESPOONS HORSERADISH
2 TABLESPOONS WORCESTERSHIRE SAUCE
½ TEASPOON PAPRIKA
½ RIB CELERY, MINCED
1 TABLESPOON CHOPPED PARSLEY
½ TEASPOON GROUND BAY LEAF
1 TEASPOON SALT
1 TEASPOON HOT SAUCE
1 TEASPOON MINCED GARLIC
1 TEASPOON LEMON JUICE
1 EGG
½ CUP VEGETABLE OIL

COMBINE ALL THE MUSTARD, KETCHUP, VINEGAR, HORSERADISH, WORCESTERSHIRE SAUCE, PAPRIKA, CELERY, PARSLEY, BAY LEAF, SALT, HOT SAUCE, GARLIC, LEMON JUICE, EGG AND OIL IN A BLENDER. PROCESS UNTIL PURÉED.
YIELD: 1 SERVING

Shrimp Rémoulade Napoleon

YIELD: 1 SERVING

2	EGGS	4	OUNCES MEDIUM SHRIMP, BOILED, PEELED, DEVEINED
¼	CUP MILK		SPICY RÉMOULADE SAUCE (AT LEFT)
3	(¼-INCH-THICK) SLICES GREEN TOMATO	1	COOKED HEAD-ON SHRIMP FOR GARNISH
1	CUP FLOUR		
1	CUP BREAD CRUMBS	1	TEASPOON SLICED GREEN ONIONS FOR GARNISH
	VEGETABLE OIL		

Combine eggs and milk in a bowl. Dip each tomato slice in the flour, then the egg mixture and then the bread crumbs. Heat the oil in a skillet to 350 degrees and deep-fry the tomatoes for 2 minutes. Drain on paper towels for 1 minute. Mix the medium shrimp with the Spicy Rémoulade Sauce. Place 1 fried tomato slice on a plate. Top with half of the shrimp mixture. Top with another tomato slice and the remaining shrimp mixture. Top with the remaining tomato slice. Garnish with the head-on shrimp and green onions.

Recipe provided by Devlin Roussel, Ralph Brennan's Red Fish Grill

Escargots Esplanade

YIELD: 4 SERVINGS

20	MEDIUM MUSHROOMS	1	TABLESPOON CHOPPED GARLIC
½	CUP (1 STICK) BUTTER	½	CUP CHOPPED FRESH PARSLEY
20	SMALL SNAILS	2	TEASPOONS LEMON JUICE
2	TABLESPOONS CHOPPED SUN-DRIED TOMATOES		BLACK PEPPER TO TASTE

Remove the stems from the mushrooms. Wash and dry the caps. Melt the butter in a large skillet. Sauté the mushroom caps for 5 minutes; remove with a slotted spoon. Add the remaining ingredients to the skillet. Sauté for 5 minutes. Serve the sautéed escargots in the caps. Spoon the tomato mixture over the top.

Citrus-Cured Salmon

Yield: 10 to 12 servings

1	SIDE OF SALMON WITH SKIN	½	CUP GRATED ORANGE ZEST
⅔	CUP COARSE SALT	½	CUP SUGAR
½	CUP GRATED LEMON ZEST	3	TABLESPOONS BLACK
½	CUP GRATED LIME ZEST		PEPPERCORNS

Sprinkle the salmon with the salt, lemon zest, lime zest, orange zest, sugar and peppercorns. Wrap in plastic wrap and then in foil. Chill for 2 days, turning every 12 hours. Remove the wrappings. Rinse the salmon and pat dry. Cut into paper-thin slices to serve.

Chicken and Cognac Pâté

Yield: 4 cups

1	POUND CHICKEN LIVERS	⅛	TEASPOON GROUND
½	CUP (1 STICK) BUTTER		BLACK PEPPER
¾	TO 1 CUP SLICED FRESH	⅛	TEASPOON CAYENNE PEPPER
	MUSHROOMS	¼	TEASPOON GROUND ALLSPICE
¼	CUP CHOPPED GREEN ONIONS	⅛	TEASPOON GROUND THYME
¼	CUP COGNAC		SPRIGS OF FRESH PARSLEY
1	TEASPOON SALT		FOR GARNISH

Wash, dry and chop chicken livers. Melt the butter in a skillet and add the mushrooms. Sauté for 5 minutes and remove with a slotted spoon. Add the green onions to the skillet and sauté for 5 minutes. Add the chicken livers and sauté for 5 minutes or until barely pink.

Combine the chicken liver mixture, mushrooms, Cognac, salt, black pepper, cayenne pepper, allspice and thyme in a blender. Blend until smooth. If the mixture is too thick, add additional melted butter. Pour into a bowl or mold. Chill until set. Garnish with fresh parsley sprigs. Note: This pâté freezes well.

Pimm's Cup

¼ CUP PIMM'S #1
2 TABLESPOONS FROZEN LEMON JUICE CONCENTRATE, THAWED, SWEETENED
LEMON-LIME SODA
CUCUMBER SLICE FOR GARNISH

Fill a tall glass with ice. Add the Pimm's and lemon juice concentrate. Fill with the soda. Garnish with a cucumber slice.
Yield: 1 serving

Artichoke Flan

YIELD: 10 TO 12 SERVINGS

3	TABLESPOONS FINE DRY BREAD CRUMBS	1/8	TEASPOON DRIED THYME, CRUMBLED
16	OUNCES CREAM CHEESE, SOFTENED	1/8	TEASPOON DRIED MARJORAM, CRUMBLED
2/3	CUP SOUR CREAM		
1/4	CUP CRUMBLED BLEU CHEESE, SOFTENED	1	CUP CANNED OR FRESH ARTICHOKE HEARTS, CUT INTO QUARTERS
3	TABLESPOONS BUTTER, SOFTENED		
3	EGGS	2/3	CUP SOUR CREAM
2	TABLESPOONS CHOPPED FRESH PARSLEY	6	TO 12 CANNED OR FRESH ARTICHOKE HEARTS, CUT INTO QUARTERS
1	TABLESPOON CHOPPED FRESH DILLWEED		

Coat a buttered 9-inch pie plate evenly with the bread crumbs. Shake out any excess. Place in the refrigerator until needed. Combine the cream cheese, 2/3 cup sour cream, bleu cheese and butter in a food processor container or large mixer bowl and blend well. Mix in the eggs, parsley, dillweed, thyme and marjoram. Fold in 1 cup artichoke hearts. Spread the cream cheese mixture in the prepared pie plate, distributing the artichoke hearts evenly. Bake at 375 degrees for 30 to 35 minutes or until puffed and light brown. Let stand until cool. The flan will settle some as it cools. Spread 2/3 cup sour cream over the cooled flan. Top with the remaining artichoke hearts. Cut the flan into wedges and serve at room temperature.

SAZERAC

1/4 teaspoon Pernod
1/2 teaspoon sugar
2 dashes of Peychaud bitters
Water
2 ice cubes
2 ounces bourbon
Lemon peel for garnish

Pour the Pernod into an old-fashioned glass and swirl until the glass is coated. Add the sugar and bitters. Barely cover with water and swirl to mix. Add the ice cubes and bourbon and stir well. Garnish with a twist of lemon peel.
Yield: 1 serving

Layered Polenta Torte with Montrachet Sauce

Yield: 8 servings

4	OUNCES PANCETTA OR BACON, CHOPPED	½	CUP FRESHLY GRATED PARMESAN CHEESE
1	(10-OUNCE) PACKAGE FROZEN CHOPPED	½	CUP CHOPPED DRAINED ROASTED RED
	SPINACH, THAWED, DRAINED		BELL PEPPERS OR IMPORTED PIMENTOS
4	CUPS WATER		FLOUR
1	TEASPOON SALT	2	TABLESPOONS OLIVE OIL
1½	CUPS YELLOW CORNMEAL		

Cook the pancetta in a medium heavy skillet until crisp. Remove to a bowl with a slotted spoon. Stir in the spinach and set aside. For the polenta, bring the water and salt to a boil in a heavy saucepan. Add the cornmeal gradually, whisking constantly. Reduce the heat to low. Cook for 5 minutes or until tender and very thick, stirring frequently. Stir in the cheese. Spoon 2 cups of the polenta into a buttered 9-inch deep-dish glass pie plate or quiche pan. Smooth the top. Cover with the spinach mixture. Spoon 1 cup of the polenta over the spinach mixture and smooth the top. Sprinkle with the bell pepper. Spoon the remaining polenta over the bell peppers and spread evenly. Chill, covered, for 3 to 12 hours. Cut the polenta into 8 wedges. Dust each wedge with flour. Heat 1 tablespoon of the olive oil in a large heavy nonstick skillet over medium-high heat. Working in batches, cook the polenta in the olive oil for 8 minutes per side or until brown and heated through, adding additional olive oil as needed. Remove the polenta to individual plates. Bring the Montrachet Sauce (below) to a simmer in a saucepan. Spoon over the polenta.

Montrachet Sauce

Yield: about 2 cups

1	CUP HEAVY CREAM	SALT AND WHITE PEPPER TO TASTE
2	TABLESPOONS BUTTER	
4	OUNCES MONTRACHET OR OTHER MILD	
	WHITE GOAT CHEESE, CRUMBLED	

Bring the cream and butter to a simmer in a large heavy saucepan. Add the cheese, whisking until blended and smooth. Season with salt and white pepper.

Arugula Bundles with Mascarpone and Chives

Yield: 24 bundles

12	TABLESPOONS MASCARPONE CHEESE	12	LARGE THIN SLICES PROSCIUTTO
2	TABLESPOONS MINCED CHIVES	1	BUNCH ARUGULA
1	TABLESPOON CAPERS		

Mix cheese, chives and capers in a bowl. Lay a slice of prosciutto on a work surface. Spread with 1 tablespoon of the cheese mixture. Arrange a few leaves of arugula on top so that the leaves slightly hang over the edge. Roll the prosciutto up like a jelly roll. Cut the roll in half and stand on the flat end so that the arugula leaves show on top. Repeat with the remaining prosciutto, cheese mixture and arugula. Arrange on a serving platter.

Curried Crab Pirogues

Yield: 24 servings

¼	CUP MAYONNAISE		BLACK PEPPER TO TASTE
2	TABLESPOONS MINCED CELERY	4	SMALL OR 2 LARGE HEADS BELGIAN
2	TABLESPOONS MINCED ONION		ENDIVE, SPEARS SEPARATED
1	TEASPOON CURRY POWDER	2	TABLESPOONS MINCED FRESH CILANTRO
1	CUP CRAB MEAT		

Combine mayonnaise, celery, onion and curry powder in a small bowl. Stir in the crab meat and season with pepper. Place 1 heaping teaspoon of the crab meat mixture on the base of an endive spear. Sprinkle with minced cilantro. Repeat with the remaining spears and crab mixture. Arrange on a serving platter in a spoke pattern. Note: The crab meat mixture can be prepared up to 8 hours ahead. Cover and chill.

Soft-Shell Crabs with Asian Dipping Sauce

2	EGG WHITES	2	TEASPOONS KOSHER SALT
2	TABLESPOONS CORNSTARCH	6	JUMBO SOFT-SHELL CRABS, CLEANED
2	TABLESPOONS DRY WHITE WINE	1	CUP CORNSTARCH
1	TABLESPOON HOT SAUCE	3	CUPS VEGETABLE OIL

Stir egg whites, 2 tablespoons cornstarch, wine, hot sauce and salt in a large shallow dish. Add the crabs and turn to coat thoroughly. Arrange the crabs snugly in the dish. Cover and chill for up to 2 hours. Spread 1 cup cornstarch on a large plate. Remove the crabs 2 at a time from the marinade and dredge in the cornstarch. Shake off any excess. Heat the oil to 375 degrees in a large deep saucepan. Add the crabs to the hot oil using tongs. Fry for 4 minutes or until cooked through and very crisp, turning once. Remove to a wire rack to drain. Cut the crabs at their natural separations into pieces that can be easily handled. Serve crab bites hot with Asian Dipping Sauce (below) on the side.

Asian Dipping Sauce

¼	CUP LOW-SODIUM SOY SAUCE	1	TEASPOON FINELY GRATED GINGER
1	GREEN ONION, THINLY SLICED	½	TEASPOON SUGAR
1	TABLESPOON RICE VINEGAR	2½	TABLESPOONS WATER
1½	TEASPOONS ASIAN SESAME OIL		

Combine the soy sauce, green onion, vinegar, sesame oil, ginger, sugar and water in a small serving bowl and mix well.

CLARIFYING BUTTER

CLARIFYING BUTTER SEPARATES THE BUTTER FROM THE MILK SOLIDS, WHICH CAN BURN DURING COOKING. TO CLARIFY BUTTER, MELT UNSALTED BUTTER SLOWLY OVER LOW HEAT TO ALLOW MOST OF THE WATER TO EVAPORATE. WHEN MELTED, LET STAND FOR 5 MINUTES. SKIM THE SOLIDS OFF THE TOP, THEN POUR THE CLEAR BUTTER INTO A BOWL OR JAR. DISCARD THE WATER AND OTHER SOLIDS. THE BUTTER MAY BE COVERED AND STORED IN THE REFRIGERATOR FOR UP TO 1 MONTH. CLARIFIED (CLEAR) BUTTER IS ESPECIALLY GOOD FOR FRYING BECAUSE IT HAS A HIGHER SMOKE POINT. WHEN READY TO USE, MELT OVER LOW HEAT.

Triple Cheese Triangles

YIELD: 42 TRIANGLES

1	CUP (2 STICKS) UNSALTED BUTTER, CLARIFIED (SEE SIDEBAR)	¼	CUP FLOUR
8	OUNCES FETA CHEESE	2	EGGS, LIGHTLY BEATEN
1	CUP PLUS 1 TABLESPOON COTTAGE CHEESE	¼	TEASPOON WHITE PEPPER
⅓	CUP FRESHLY GRATED PARMESAN CHEESE	1	(1-POUND) PACKAGE PHYLLO DOUGH

Line 2 baking sheets with parchment paper. Melt the butter and set aside. Combine the feta cheese, cottage cheese and Parmesan cheese in a medium bowl. Stir in the flour, eggs and pepper. Place 1 sheet of phyllo dough on a work surface. Cover remaining phyllo with waxed paper topped with a damp towel. Position the sheet of phyllo so that the long side is facing you. Brush with some of the melted butter. Top with a second sheet of phyllo and brush with more butter. Cut into 4 strips, each 12 inches long. Mound a scant tablespoon of the cheese mixture in the center of one end of each strip. Working with one strip at a time, fold the bottom edge up to meet the left edge to form a triangle. Continue folding, keeping the triangle shape. Brush the top of the finished triangle with melted butter and place it on one of the baking sheets. Continue with remaining phyllo and filling. Bake at 400 degrees for 16 minutes or until crisp and golden brown. Switch the position of the baking sheets halfway through baking. Let the triangles cool slightly. Serve warm. Note: The unbaked triangles can be frozen for up to one week. Thaw before baking.

Creole Croquettes with
Orange Honey Mustard Dipping Sauce

YIELD: 18 CROQUETTES

1½ CUPS FINELY SHREDDED CHEDDAR CHEESE	1½ CUPS FRESH WHITE BREAD CRUMBS
¾ CUP RICOTTA CHEESE	½ CUP FLOUR
2 TABLESPOONS CHOPPED FRESH THYME	½ CUP MILK
SALT AND PEPPER TO TASTE	1 EGG
	VEGETABLE OIL

Purée the Cheddar cheese, ricotta cheese and thyme in a food processor. Season with salt and pepper. Place the bread crumbs and flour in separate bowls. Mix the milk and egg in another bowl. Form the cheese mixture into 18 walnut-size balls. Coat the balls with flour, then dip in the egg mixture, then coat completely with the bread crumbs. Place the balls on a large baking sheet lined with foil. Pour the oil into a large heavy skillet to a depth of 1 inch. Heat the oil to 350 degrees. Fry the croquettes in batches for 1 minute or until golden brown. Remove with a slotted spoon to paper towels to drain. Arrange croquettes on a serving platter and serve with Orange Honey Mustard Dipping Sauce (below). Note: The croquettes can be made up to 4 hours before frying. Cover and chill until ready to fry.

Orange Honey Mustard Dipping Sauce

YIELD: ⅔ CUP

1 SMALL GARLIC CLOVE, MINCED	¼ TEASPOON COARSE SALT
2 TABLESPOONS FRESH ORANGE JUICE	½ CUP OLIVE OIL
1½ TEASPOONS CREOLE OR DIJON MUSTARD	FRESHLY GROUND BLACK PEPPER
1 TEASPOON HONEY	TO TASTE

Process the garlic, orange juice, mustard, honey and salt in a food processor until well mixed. Add the olive oil in a slow stream, processing constantly. Process until mixture is thickened. Season with pepper. Note: This sauce can be made 2 days ahead. Cover and chill. Bring to room temperature before serving.

Frico

Yield: 25 to 30 chips

4	ounces Parmigiano-Reggiano or grana cheese, rind removed	Chopped walnuts or chopped fresh rosemary for garnish

Grate the cheese into a bowl. Spoon 6 evenly spaced tablespoons of cheese onto a nonstick baking sheet. Pat each mound into a 2$\frac{1}{2}$- to 3-inch round. Garnish with a few chopped walnuts or rosemary. Bake at 400 degrees for 3 minutes or until golden brown and bubbly. Remove the chips immediately to a wire rack to cool. Let baking sheet cool before next batch and repeat with remaining cheese. Store the chips in an airtight container for up to 1 week.

Jalapeño Cheese Squares

Yield: 50 squares

4	cups shredded Cheddar cheese	4	whole jalapeño chiles, sliced, patted dry
4	eggs, beaten		
1	teaspoon minced onion		

Combine the cheese, eggs, onion and jalapeños in a bowl and mix well. Pour into an 8x8-inch baking pan. Bake at 350 degrees for 30 minutes. Cut into small squares and serve at room temperature.

French-Fried Eggplant

YIELD: 4 SERVINGS

1	LARGE EGGPLANT, PEELED		WHITE PEPPER TO TASTE
	SALT TO TASTE	1	CUP FLOUR
1	EGG, LIGHTLY BEATEN	3	CUPS PEANUT OIL
¼	CUP MILK	¼	CUP CONFECTIONERS' SUGAR

Cut the eggplant into thick strips. Soak in salted water in a bowl for 30 minutes. Rinse and pat dry. Mix the egg and milk in a bowl. Season generously with additional salt and white pepper. Dip the eggplant into the egg mixture, then coat with flour. Deep-fry in the peanut oil in a skillet or deep-fryer until golden brown. Sprinkle with additional salt and confectioners' sugar

Pecans Diablo

YIELD: 10 TO 12 SERVINGS

2¼	TEASPOONS SWEET PAPRIKA	1	POUND EXTRA-LARGE PECAN
1½	TEASPOONS SALT		HALVES
1½	TEASPOONS CAYENNE PEPPER	1	CUP CONFECTIONERS' SUGAR
1½	TEASPOONS BLACK PEPPER	1	QUART CANOLA OIL

Mix the paprika, salt, cayenne pepper and black pepper in a large bowl. Set aside. Boil the pecans in enough water to cover in a saucepan for 5 minutes; drain well. Coat the pecans with confectioners' sugar. Heat the canola oil to 350 degrees in a large saucepan over medium-high heat. Add the pecans and fry for 4 minutes or until golden brown. Remove the pecans with a slotted spoon. Add the pecans to the spice mixture and toss until coated. Let cool completely before serving.

ROQUEFORT PECAN GRAPES

4 OUNCES BLEU CHEESE, CRUMBLED
3 OUNCES CREAM CHEESE, SOFTENED
24 SEEDLESS GREEN GRAPES
1 CUP FINELY CHOPPED PECANS, TOASTED

Beat the bleu cheese and cream cheese at medium speed with an electric mixer until smooth. Chill for at least 1 hour. Remove and discard grape stems. Wash grapes, drain and pat completely dry. Wrap enough cheese mixture around each grape to cover. Roll in pecans and chill for at least 1 hour.
YIELD: 2 DOZEN

Mushroom Turnovers

Yield: 50 turnovers

3	OUNCES CREAM CHEESE, SOFTENED	¼	TEASPOON DRIED THYME
½	CUP (1 STICK) BUTTER, SOFTENED	½	TEASPOON SALT
1½	CUPS FLOUR		PEPPER TO TASTE
3	TABLESPOONS BUTTER	2	TABLESPOONS FLOUR
1	ONION, MINCED	¼	CUP SOUR CREAM
8	OUNCES FRESH MUSHROOMS, FINELY CHOPPED		

*F*or the pastry, mix the cream cheese and ½ cup butter in a bowl. Stir in 1½ cups flour and mix well. Chill for 1 hour or longer. For the filling, melt 3 tablespoons butter in a skillet. Add the onion and sauté until softened. Add the mushrooms and sauté for 3 minutes. Stir in the thyme, salt and pepper. Sprinkle 2 tablespoons flour over the mixture and add the sour cream. Stir over medium heat until thickened. Do not boil. Remove from the heat. Roll out the chilled dough out on a floured board until very thin. Cut out 3-inch rounds. Place 1 teaspoon of filling on each round. Fold dough over filling and press edges with a fork to seal. Prick each turnover with a fork. Place on ungreased baking sheets. Bake at 450 degrees for 15 minutes. Remove to wire rack to cool slightly. Serve warm.
Note: The unbaked turnovers can be frozen for up to 2 weeks. Allow additional time in the oven if baked frozen.

JEFFERSON CITY

JEFFERSON CITY WAS ORIGINALLY PART OF THE LARGE PLANTATION OWNED BY JEAN BAPTISTE LE MOYNE, SIEUR DE BIENVILLE, FOUNDER OF NEW ORLEANS. THE LAND INITIALLY WAS USED FOR PASTURING CATTLE AND FOR VEGETABLE GARDENING. THE ECONOMY WAS BASED PRIMARILY ON LIVESTOCK OPERATIONS, INCLUDING BUTCHERING. AFTER THE CIVIL WAR, NEW ORLEANS ANNEXED JEFFERSON CITY AS THE SIXTH DISTRICT, AND THE LIVESTOCK OPERATIONS THAT HAD EXISTED PRIOR TO THAT TIME WERE MOVED DOWNRIVER. JEFFERSON CITY FELL INTO DISUSE UNTIL THE STREETCAR LINE WAS EXTENDED AT THE TURN OF THE CENTURY. THE STREETCAR LINE BROUGHT NEW ORLEANIANS TO THE AREA IN ORDER TO ESTABLISH FASHIONABLE NEW RESIDENCES.

Prosciutto Pinwheels

YIELD: 40 PINWHEELS

1	SHEET PUFF PASTRY	3/4	CUP FINELY SHREDDED GRUYÈRE
1	EGG, LIGHTLY BEATEN		CHEESE (ABOUT 3 OUNCES)
2	OUNCES THINLY SLICED PROSCIUTTO	4	TEASPOONS CHOPPED FRESH SAGE LEAVES

Lay the sheet of pastry on a work surface with the short side facing you. Cut the sheet in half crosswise. Turn a half sheet so that the long side is facing you. Brush the edge of the far side with some of the beaten egg. Arrange half the prosciutto evenly on the sheet, avoiding the edge brushed with egg. Mix the cheese and sage in a bowl. Sprinkle half the cheese mixture on top of the prosciutto. Starting at the edge closest to you, roll it up to make a log. Wrap the log in waxed paper. Make another log with the remaining pastry, egg, prosciutto and cheese mixture. Chill with the seam side down for 3 hours or up to 3 days. Cut the logs into ½-inch pinwheels and place 1 inch apart on lightly greased baking sheets. Bake at 400 degrees for 14 to 16 minutes. Remove to a wire rack to cool slightly. Serve warm.

Marinated Shrimp, Mushrooms and Artichoke Hearts

YIELD: 8 SERVINGS

1	PACKAGE GOOD SEASONS ITALIAN SALAD DRESSING MIX	2	(4-OUNCE) CANS WHOLE BUTTON MUSHROOMS, DRAINED
1	PACKAGE GOOD SEASONS CHEESE AND GARLIC SALAD DRESSING MIX	2	(14-OUNCE) CANS ARTICHOKE HEARTS, DRAINED
	VINEGAR	1	RED ONION, THINLY SLICED
½	TEASPOON SALT	1	WHITE ONION, THINLY SLICED
	JUICE OF 2 LEMONS	1	BUNCH GREEN ONIONS, CHOPPED
2	TEASPOONS CREOLE MUSTARD	1	BOTTLE CAPERS, DRAINED
2	TO 3 POUNDS FRESH SHRIMP, BOILED, PEELED, DEVEINED		

Prepare the dressing mixes according to package directions, substituting vinegar for the water. Mix the salad dressings, salt, lemon juice, Creole mustard, shrimp, mushrooms, artichoke hearts, all the onions and capers in a deep bowl. Marinate, covered, in the refrigerator overnight, stirring occasionally. Serve chilled.

Parsley Herb Dip

Yield: 2 cups

1	SMALL GARLIC CLOVE	1	CUP MAYONNAISE
½	TEASPOON SALT	½	CUP SOUR CREAM
1	CUP PACKED FRESH PARSLEY	1	TEASPOON CHOPPED FRESH THYME
1	GREEN ONION, WHITE AND GREEN PARTS, CUT INTO 1-INCH PIECES	¼	TEASPOON FRESHLY GROUND PEPPER

Place the garlic and salt in a food processor and process until the garlic is minced. Add the parsley and green onion and process until finely chopped. Add the mayonnaise, sour cream, thyme and pepper and process until well mixed. Cover and chill until ready to serve. Serve with bite-size fresh vegetables.

Barefoot Boursin

Yield: 3 cups

16	OUNCES CREAM CHEESE, SOFTENED	¼	TEASPOON DRIED BASIL
1	CUP (2 STICKS) UNSALTED BUTTER, SOFTENED	¼	TEASPOON DRIED DILL
3	GARLIC CLOVES, PRESSED	¼	TEASPOON DRIED MARJORAM
½	TEASPOON DRIED OREGANO	¼	TEASPOON BLACK PEPPER

Mix the cream cheese and butter in a bowl until blended. Add the garlic, oregano, basil, dill, marjoram and pepper and mix well. Chill overnight to blend the flavors. Serve with crackers.

Hot Spinach and Oyster Dip

Yield: 20 to 30 servings

2	TABLESPOONS OLIVE OIL	8	OUNCES CREAM CHEESE, SOFTENED
½	CUP FINELY CHOPPED ONION	¼	CUP SKIM MILK
½	CUP MINCED CELERY	1	PINT OYSTERS WITH THEIR
2	TABLESPOONS MINCED GARLIC		LIQUOR, COARSELY CHOPPED
1	(10-OUNCE) PACKAGE FROZEN		SALT, PEPPER AND HOT SAUCE
	CHOPPED SPINACH, COOKED,		TO TASTE
	DRAINED		

Heat the olive oil in a nonstick skillet. Add the onion, celery and garlic and sauté until soft but not browned. Place the mixture in a blender or food processor along with the spinach, cream cheese and milk. Process until smooth. Pour into a saucepan. Cook over medium heat until heated through, stirring constantly. Add the oysters and their liquor. Cook for 10 minutes or until the oysters are cooked through, stirring constantly. Season with salt, pepper and hot sauce. Spoon into a heated serving dish. Surround with toasted slices of French bread or crackers.

Santa Fe Spread

Yield: 4 cups

16	OUNCES CREAM CHEESE, SOFTENED	1	TABLESPOON GROUND CUMIN
¼	CUP LIME JUICE	½	TEASPOON SALT
¼	CUP VEGETABLE OIL		DASH OF PEPPER
1	TABLESPOONS GROUND RED	1¼	CUPS WHOLE KERNEL CORN
	CHILES	1	CUP CHOPPED WALNUTS
2	JALAPEÑO CHILES, SEEDED,	1	SMALL ONION, CHOPPED
	CHOPPED		

Combine the cream cheese, lime juice, oil, ground red chiles, chopped jalapeños, cumin, salt and pepper. Beat at medium speed with an electric mixer or process in a food processor until smooth. Stir in the corn, walnuts and chopped onion. Spoon into a serving dish and serve with tortilla chips.

SALMON CAVIAR SPREAD

1 CUP SOUR CREAM
2 GREEN ONIONS, VERY
THINLY SLICED
1 TABLESPOON FRESH
LEMON JUICE
1 TABLESPOON CHOPPED
FRESH CHIVES
6 TABLESPOONS SALMON
CAVIAR, GENTLY RINSED,
DRAINED
1 TEASPOON CHOPPED FRESH
CHIVES FOR GARNISH
1 TABLESPOON CAVIAR
FOR GARNISH

MIX THE SOUR CREAM, GREEN ONIONS, LEMON JUICE AND 1 TABLESPOON CHIVES IN A MEDIUM BOWL. GENTLY FOLD IN 6 TABLESPOONS CAVIAR. SPOON INTO A SERVING BOWL. COVER AND CHILL FOR 6 HOURS OR LONGER. GARNISH THE DIP WITH 1 TEASPOON CHOPPED CHIVES AND 1 TABLESPOON CAVIAR. SERVE WITH TOAST POINTS, CRACKERS OR BITE-SIZE FRESH VEGETABLES.

YIELD: 1 CUP

Soups & Salads

Soups & Salads

Cornelius Payne House
1604 Fourth Street

The present appearance of this house conceals its 1859 construction date. Only the surviving elliptical openings, large panes of glass, and Ionic columns hint at its original Italianate style. Old photographs show that the porch railing, now cast iron, was formerly a heavy, turned wood balustrade in the Italianate taste.

❧

The house is situated in the Garden District, part of the former City of Lafayette, which was incorporated in 1833. Lafayette served as the parish seat of Jefferson until annexation by New Orleans in 1852 as the Fourth Municipal District. In 1850, nine years before 1604 Fourth Street was built, a writer for the *Daily Delta* observed: "We took a ramble a few days ago in the suburbs of Lafayette and were no less surprised than delighted with the view of so many pretty villas and beautiful gardens which abound in that part of our vicinity… Charming are the residences in the rear of Lafayette." Growth of the City of Lafayette, as well as the cities of Jefferson and Carrollton, was accelerated by the New Orleans & Carrollton Rail Road. It commenced operation in 1835 and eventually evolved into the present-day St. Charles Avenue streetcar.

❧

In two separate purchases in 1857 and 1858, Cornelius Payne, steamboat agent and real estate speculator, purchased four and one-half lots on which he subsequently built this house. Local directories first list Payne at this address in 1860. In 1861 he sold the house for $18,000 to Thomas Clarke, in whose family it remained until 1890 when noted attorney Alfred Grima purchased it. Grima commissioned architect Paul Andry and builder John McNally to remodel the house in the then-popular Renaissance Revival style in 1891. During the Grima family ownership, further alterations and additions were made to the house in the 1920s, including a formal side garden and trellis. 1604 Fourth Street became the JLNO Show House V in 1987. Mr. and Mrs. Walter C. Flower, III, are the current owners.

Crawfish Bisque

Yield: 12 servings

1	CUP BACON DRIPPINGS (SEE NOTE)	1	(28-OUNCE) CAN CHOPPED ITALIAN-STYLE TOMATOES
2	CUPS FLOUR		
1	CUP FINELY CHOPPED ONION	¼	CUP WORCESTERSHIRE SAUCE
1	CUP FINELY CHOPPED CELERY		SALT AND PEPPER TO TASTE
1	GARLIC CLOVE, PRESSED	3	QUARTS WATER
1	BUNCH PARSLEY, FINELY CHOPPED		STUFFED CRAWFISH
2	BAY LEAVES		

Make a roux from the bacon drippings and flour in a very large stockpot. Cook until deep brown, stirring constantly. Add the onion, celery, garlic, parsley, bay leaves, tomatoes, Worcestershire sauce, salt, pepper, and water. Simmer for 1 hour. Add the stuffed crawfish. Simmer for 1 hour or longer. Discard the bay leaves. Remove the crawfish to individual bowls. Ladle the bisque over the crawfish to serve.

Note: One pound of bacon will yield approximately 1 cup drippings.

Stuffed Crawfish

Yield: 12 servings

3	POUNDS CRAWFISH TAILS (SEE NOTE)	24	OUNCES ITALIAN BREAD CRUMBS
4	CUPS FINELY CHOPPED ONIONS	6	EGGS, LIGHTLY BEATEN
3	CUPS FINELY CHOPPED BELL PEPPERS	½	CUP WORCESTERSHIRE SAUCE
2	CUPS FINELY CHOPPED CELERY		SALT AND PEPPER TO TASTE
1	GARLIC CLOVE, PRESSED	1½	TEASPOONS FRESH OREGANO
1	BUNCH PARSLEY, FINELY CHOPPED	1½	TEASPOONS BASIL
¾	CUP FINELY CHOPPED GREEN ONIONS		

Peel the crawfish, reserving the tails and fat for flavor. Clean out crawfish cavity and clip off front of head (feelers and eyes). Rinse in hot water and set aside. Chop each tail in half. Combine the onions, bell peppers, celery, garlic, parsley and green onions in a large bowl and mix well. Add the crawfish tails. Add the bread crumbs, eggs, Worcestershire sauce, salt, pepper, oregano and basil and mix well. Stuff each cleaned crawfish shell generously with the vegetable mixture. Store in the refrigerator until needed or freeze for later use.

Note: Ten pounds whole boiled crawfish yield about 1 pound of crawfish tails. Prepackaged crawfish tails may be used to supplement.

Spinach Oyster Bisque

YIELD: 8 SERVINGS

36	SHUCKED OYSTERS, WITH THEIR LIQUOR	1	CUP PACKED SPINACH LEAVES, WASHED, DRAINED WELL, FINELY SHREDDED
2	TABLESPOONS UNSALTED BUTTER		SALT AND PEPPER TO TASTE
2	LARGE SHALLOTS, FINELY CHOPPED		SMALL SPINACH LEAVES FOR GARNISH
½	CUP MEDIUM-DRY SHERRY		
1½	CUPS MILK	¼	CUP FINELY CHOPPED RED BELL PEPPER FOR GARNISH
1	CUP HEAVY CREAM		
1½	CUPS MILK		

Drain the oysters in a fine sieve and reserve the liquor. Add enough water to the reserved liquor to measure 1 cup and set aside. Rinse the oysters with cold water and drain. Place drained oysters in a bowl, cover and chill. Melt the butter in a large saucepan over medium heat. Add the shallots when the foam subsides and sauté until soft. Stir in the sherry and cook until most of the liquid evaporates. Stir in the oyster liquor mixture and 1½ cups milk and bring to a simmer. Do not boil. Stir in 12 oysters and poach for 2 minutes or until the edges start to curl. Remove from the heat. Purée in batches in a blender. Strain mixture back into the saucepan and skim off the foam. Stir in the cream and 1½ cups milk. Bring to a simmer. Add the remaining 24 oysters and spinach and season with salt and pepper. Simmer for 2 minutes or until the edges of the oysters start to curl. Ladle the bisque into 8 heated soup bowls and garnish with spinach leaves and chopped bell pepper.

Serve with Corn Bread Croutons (at right).

CORN BREAD CROUTONS

1 TABLESPOON OLIVE OIL
1 CORN MUFFIN OR FROZEN TOAST CAKE, CUT INTO CROUTON-SIZE PIECES
SALT AND PEPPER TO TASTE

HEAT THE OLIVE OIL IN A NONSTICK SKILLET OVER MEDIUM-HIGH HEAT UNTIL HOT BUT NOT SMOKING. ADD THE CORN BREAD AND COOK UNTIL GOLDEN BROWN AND CRISP, TOSSING FREQUENTLY. SEASON WITH SALT AND PEPPER.

NOTE: THE CROUTONS CAN BE MADE 1 DAY AHEAD. STORE IN A PLASTIC FOOD STORAGE BAG AT ROOM TEMPERATURE.

YIELD: 8 SERVINGS

Crab and Leek Bisque

Yield: 2 quarts

3	LEEKS (ABOUT 1½ POUNDS)	2	CUPS HALF-AND-HALF
½	CUP (1 STICK) BUTTER OR MARGARINE	8	OUNCES FRESH CRAB MEAT, DRAINED,
1	GARLIC CLOVE, MINCED		FLAKED
½	CUP FLOUR	¼	TEASPOON SALT
4	CUPS CHICKEN BROTH	¼	TEASPOON GROUND WHITE PEPPER
½	CUP DRY WHITE WINE		

Remove the roots, tough outer leaves and green tops from the leeks. Split the white portion in half and wash. Thinly slice halves. Melt the butter over medium-high heat in a large heavy saucepan. Add the leeks and garlic and sauté for 3 minutes or until tender. Add the flour and sauté for 1 minute. Stir in the broth and wine gradually. Cook over medium heat for 4 minutes or until thickened, stirring constantly. Add the half-and-half, crab meat, salt and pepper. Cook until heated through, stirring constantly.

Shrimp and Corn Chowder

Yield: 8 to 10 servings

⅓	CUP VEGETABLE OIL	1	CAN WHOLE PEELED TOMATOES
3	TABLESPOONS FLOUR	1	CAN WHOLE KERNEL CORN, HALF
2	MEDIUM ONIONS, CHOPPED		DRAINED
1	BELL PEPPER, SEEDED, CHOPPED	1	CAN CREAMED CORN
1	POUND PEELED UNCOOKED SHRIMP	1	CUP WATER
2	TABLESPOONS CHOPPED PARSLEY		
	SALT, BLACK PEPPER AND CAYENNE		
	PEPPER TO TASTE		

For the roux, combine the oil and flour in a saucepan. Cook over low heat until the mixture is a medium brown color, stirring constantly. Add the onions and sauté for 10 to 15 minutes. Add the bell pepper, shrimp and parsley and season with salt, black pepper and cayenne pepper. Simmer for 5 minutes. Add the tomatoes, whole kernel corn, creamed corn and water and simmer for 1 hour.

Seafood Okra Gumbo

YIELD: 6 ENTRÉE SERVINGS OR 10 TO 12 APPETIZER SERVINGS

2	POUNDS FRESH OR FROZEN UNCOOKED HEAD-ON SHRIMP (ABOUT 40 TO 50 COUNT PER POUND)	2	CUPS CHOPPED ONIONS
		1	CUP CHOPPED GREEN BELL PEPPER
		½	CUP CHOPPED CELERY
2	QUARTS WATER	1	TEASPOON MINCED GARLIC
2	SMALL FRESH OR FROZEN BLUE CRABS	1	(16-OUNCE) CAN CHOPPED TOMATOES
1	QUART WATER	2	BAY LEAVES
2	TABLESPOONS VEGETABLE OIL	2	TEASPOONS SALT, OR TO TASTE
1	QUART FRESH OR FROZEN OKRA, CUT INTO ½-INCH SLICES	½	TEASPOON BLACK PEPPER, OR TO TASTE
		½	TEASPOON WHITE PEPPER, OR TO TASTE
⅔	CUP VEGETABLE OIL	¼	TEASPOON CAYENNE PEPPER, OR TO TASTE
½	CUP FLOUR		

Peel, devein and remove heads from the shrimp, reserving shells and heads. Cover and chill the shrimp. Rinse the shells and heads and place in a large nonreactive saucepan with 2 quarts water. Bring to a boil, reduce the heat and simmer for 30 to 45 minutes. Strain the stock and reserve. Discard the shells and heads. Rinse the crabs well and place in a non-reactive saucepan with 1 quart water. Bring to a boil, reduce the heat and simmer for 20 to 30 minutes. Strain and reserve stock and crabs. When the crabs are cool enough to handle, snap off both claws and break the body in half. Set aside. Heat 2 tablespoons oil in a heavy skillet over medium-high heat. Add the okra and sauté for 10 to 20 minutes or until all "stringiness" is gone. Heat ⅔ cup oil in an 8-quart heavy saucepan over medium-high heat. Add the flour and stir until the roux is a dark brown color. Add the onions, bell pepper, celery and garlic and sauté until the vegetables are tender. Allow the vegetables to stick to the bottom of the pan occasionally so that they caramelize. Add the tomatoes, bay leaves, black pepper, white pepper and cayenne pepper. Sauté for 10 minutes, allowing the tomatoes to stick to the bottom of the pan occasionally so that they caramelize. Add the cooked okra and cook for 10 minutes, stirring constantly. Add the crab stock and half the shrimp stock. Bring the mixture to a boil, stirring constantly. Reduce the heat, cover partially and simmer for 30 minutes, stirring occasionally. Add additional shrimp stock if the gumbo is too thick. Season with salt and pepper. Add the broken crabs and simmer for 10 minutes. Add the peeled shrimp. Return to a boil, reduce the heat and simmer for 5 minutes or until the shrimp are firm and pink. Discard the bay leaves. Serve over rice in large bowls. Note: As with most gumbos, this one also benefits by being made early in the day or the day before to allow time for the flavors to blend. Cover and chill. Reheat gently before serving.

Recipe provided by The Gumbo Shop

Spicy Thai Lobster Soup

2	FRESH LOBSTER TAILS	6	LARGE FRESH MUSHROOMS, SLICED
1	TABLESPOON GROUND GINGER		
½	TEASPOON GROUND RED PEPPER	½	CUP CHOPPED ONION
1	TABLESPOON PEANUT OIL	1	TABLESPOON CHOPPED FRESH CILANTRO
5	CUPS CHICKEN BROTH		
1	TABLESPOON COARSELY GRATED LIME ZEST	2	TABLESPOONS LIME JUICE
⅓	CUP UNCOOKED LONG-GRAIN RICE		Chopped green onions for GARNISH
1'	CUP UNSWEETENED COCONUT MILK		Sprigs of fresh cilantro FOR GARNISH

Remove the lobster meat from the shell. Slice and set aside. Combine the ground ginger, cayenne pepper and peanut oil in a large saucepan. Cook over medium heat for 1 minute. Stir in the chicken broth and lime zest and bring to a boil. Stir in the rice, reduce the heat and simmer for 15 to 20 minutes. Add the coconut milk, mushrooms, onion and cilantro and cook for 5 minutes, stirring occasionally. Add the lobster meat and cook for 3 to 5 minutes. Remove from the heat and stir in the lime juice. Spoon into 6 bowls and garnish with chopped green onions and fresh sprigs of cilantro. Note: One pound of peeled and deveined uncooked medium shrimp can be substituted for the lobster.

CANAL STREET

CANAL STREET IS ONE OF THE WIDEST STREETS IN THE WORLD. THE FIFTY-FOOT CANAL PROPOSED FOR THIS SITE WAS NEVER DUG ON ITS TERRE COMMUNE (PUBLIC GROUND), SO SHOPS, HOTELS, AND PRIVATE HOMES WERE BUILT. IT BECAME A MAJOR THOROUGHFARE IN THE EARLY 1800S, ALSO EVOLVING INTO ONE OF THE FRENCH QUARTER'S BOUNDARIES. JUDAH TOURO, A PROMINENT JEWISH MERCHANT AND PHILANTHROPIST, ONCE OWNED A BLOCK OF STORES ON CANAL STREET. FOLLOWING HIS DEATH IN 1854, THE STREET WAS BRIEFLY RENAMED TOURO BOULEVARD, BUT CANAL STREET SOON BECAME THE PERMANENT NAME. THIS STREET

(CONTINUED ON NEXT PAGE)

Turtle Soup

Yield: 6 servings

1	CUP (2 STICKS) UNSALTED BUTTER	½	TEASPOON FRESHLY GROUND
¾	CUP FLOUR		BLACK PEPPER
¼	CUP (½ STICK) UNSALTED BUTTER	1½	CUPS TOMATO PURÉE
1	POUND TURTLE MEAT, CUT INTO	1	QUART BEEF STOCK OR BROTH
	½-INCH CUBES		SALT AND FRESHLY GROUND
1	CUP MINCED CELERY		BLACK PEPPER TO TASTE
1¼	CUPS MINCED ONIONS	½	CUP LEMON JUICE
1½	TEASPOONS MINCED GARLIC	5	HARD-COOKED EGGS, FINELY
3	BAY LEAVES		CHOPPED
1	TEASPOON DRIED OREGANO	1	TABLESPOON MINCED PARSLEY
½	TEASPOON DRIED THYME	6	TEASPOONS DRY SHERRY

Melt 1 cup butter in a heavy saucepan. Add the flour and cook over medium heat until the roux is a light brown color, stirring constantly. Set aside. Melt ¼ cup butter in a 5-quart saucepan. Add the turtle meat and sauté until browned. Add the celery, onions, garlic, bay leaves, oregano, thyme and pepper. Cook until the vegetables are translucent. Add the tomato purée, reduce the heat and simmer for 10 minutes. Add the beef stock. Simmer for 30 minutes. Add the roux and cook over low heat until the soup is smooth and thickened, stirring constantly. Season with salt and pepper. Stir in the lemon juice, eggs and parsley. Remove the bay leaves. Spoon into 6 bowls. Top each with 1 teaspoon sherry.

Recipe provided by Jamie Shannon, Commander's Palace

REPRESENTED A LINE OF DEMARCATION BETWEEN THE CREOLES, WHOSE ROOTS WERE WELL PLANTED IN THE VIEUX CARRÉ (THE OLD PART OF TOWN), AND THE NEWLY ARRIVING ANGLO-AMERICANS, WHO SETTLED UPTOWN. THE CREOLES WERE PROUD OF THEIR PREDOMINANTLY FRENCH HERITAGE AND OFFERED "INTRUDERS" NO ENTRY INTO THEIR TIGHTLY KNIT SOCIETY. THEY REFUSED TO SPEAK ENGLISH, WHILE THE AMERICANS REFUSED TO SPEAK FRENCH AND MOCKED THE FRIVOLOUS LIFESTYLE OF THE CREOLES. FINALLY, IN 1852, THE SEPARATE MUNICIPALITIES WERE UNITED AS ONE.

Chicken and Andouille Gumbo

YIELD: 6 SERVINGS

1	CUP VEGETABLE OIL		2	TEASPOONS MINCED GARLIC
1	CUP FLOUR		1	TEASPOON DRIED BASIL
3	QUARTS CHICKEN STOCK OR BROTH		1	TEASPOON DRIED OREGANO
1	WHOLE CHICKEN, CUT INTO PIECES		4	BAY LEAVES
				SALT AND PEPPER TO TASTE
2	CUPS CHOPPED ONIONS		12	SLICES BACON, CHOPPED
1	CUP CHOPPED GREEN BELL PEPPER		2	POUNDS ANDOUILLE SAUSAGE, CHOPPED
3/4	CUP CHOPPED CELERY			FLOUR

Heat the oil in a heavy saucepan over medium-high heat. Add
1 cup flour and cook until the roux is a dark brown color, stirring
constantly. Remove from the heat and set aside. Combine chicken
stock, chicken pieces, onions, bell pepper, celery, garlic, basil,
oregano and bay leaves in a large saucepan. Season with salt and
pepper. Bring to a boil, reduce the heat and simmer for 1 hour or until
the chicken is cooked through. Fry the bacon in a skillet until
crisp. Add the sausage and cook until browned. Stir in enough flour
to absorb the excess drippings. Remove the chicken from the gumbo.
Remove and discard the bones. Chop the chicken. Stir the roux
into the gumbo gradually. Add the chopped chicken, bacon and
sausage mixture and cook for 15 minutes. Remove the bay leaves.
Add additional beef stock or water if the gumbo is too thick.

Recipe provided by Randy Barlow, Kelsey's Restaurant

Brie and Roasted Garlic Soup

Yield: 6 servings

2	TABLESPOONS OLIVE OIL	1	TEASPOON CHOPPED
2	HEADS GARLIC, SEPARATED INTO		FRESH OREGANO
	CLOVES, UNPEELED	½	TEASPOON CHOPPED
¼	CUP OLIVE OIL		FRESH THYME
1	MEDIUM ONION, FINELY CHOPPED	7	OUNCES BRIE CHEESE, RIND
2	RIBS CELERY, FINELY CHOPPED		REMOVED, CHEESE CUT
1	CARROT, FINELY CHOPPED		INTO PIECES
¼	CUP FLOUR		SALT AND GROUND WHITE
6	CUPS CHICKEN STOCK OR CANNED		PEPPER TO TASTE
	LOW-SODIUM BROTH		

Drizzle 2 tablespoons olive oil over garlic cloves in a glass baking dish. Bake, covered with foil, at 325 degrees for 30 minutes or until golden brown and tender. Remove garlic to a wire rack to cool. Heat ¼ cup olive oil in a large heavy saucepan over medium heat. Add the onion and sauté for 10 minutes or until translucent. Add the celery and carrot and sauté for 10 minutes or until tender. Add the flour and sauté for 3 minutes. Stir in the chicken stock gradually. Bring to a boil, stirring constantly. Reduce the heat to medium-low. Simmer for 15 minutes or until slightly thickened, stirring occasionally. Peel the garlic and combine with 1 cup of the soup in a food processor. Process until smooth. Return the mixture to the saucepan. Stir in the oregano and thyme and bring to a simmer over medium-low heat. Stir in the Brie in batches, melting the cheese before adding the next batch. Season with salt and white pepper. Note: This soup can be partially made 1 day ahead. Cover and chill before adding the herbs and Brie. Reheat gently and stir in the herbs and cheese as directed.

CHICKEN STOCK

2 QUARTS UNCOOKED AND/OR
COOKED CHICKEN BONES
AND SCRAPS
2 TEASPOONS SALT
½ CUP CHOPPED ONION
½ CUP CHOPPED CELERY
½ CUP CHOPPED CARROT
1 BAY LEAF (OPTIONAL)
8 SPRIGS FRESH PARSLEY
(OPTIONAL)

CHOP THE BONES AND SCRAPS INTO 1-INCH PIECES. COMBINE WITH THE SALT AND WATER TO COVER BY 1 INCH IN A 3-QUART STAINLESS STEEL SAUCEPAN. BRING TO A SIMMER, SKIMMING OFF ANY FOAM THAT FORMS. ADD THE VEGETABLES, BAY LEAF AND PARSLEY. SIMMER, LOOSELY COVERED, FOR 1½ HOURS, ADDING ADDITIONAL WATER IF NEEDED TO KEEP THE INGREDIENTS COVERED. STRAIN THROUGH A FINE SIEVE; DISCARD BONES AND COOKED VEGETABLES. CHILL THE STOCK UNTIL FAT RISES AND SOLIDIFIES. SKIM OFF FAT. CHILL OR FREEZE THE STOCK. NOTE: ONION, CELERY, CARROT, BAY LEAF AND/OR PARSLEY MAY BE OMITTED.
YIELD: 2 QUARTS

Sweet Red Pepper Soup with Cucumber Salsa

YIELD: 4 SERVINGS

6	MEDIUM RED BELL PEPPERS	2	TABLESPOONS FINELY CHOPPED
1	TABLESPOON OLIVE OIL		PEELED SEEDED CUCUMBER
1	MEDIUM YELLOW ONION, COARSELY CHOPPED	1	SMALL JALAPEÑO CHILE, SEEDED, FINELY CHOPPED
1	GARLIC CLOVE, COARSELY CHOPPED	1	TABLESPOON FINELY CHOPPED RED ONION
4	CUPS VEGETABLE STOCK OR VEGETABLE BROTH, OR 3 CUPS WATER	2	TABLESPOONS FINELY CHOPPED FLAT-LEAF PARSLEY
1	TEASPOON CORIANDER SEEDS	4½	TEASPOONS FRESH LIME JUICE
1	TEASPOON CUMIN SEEDS	¼	CUP FRESH ORANGE JUICE
1	TEASPOON FENNEL SEEDS	¼	CUP CRÈME FRAÎCHE OR SOUR CREAM
	SALT AND FRESHLY GROUND PEPPER TO TASTE	2	TABLESPOONS RED WINE VINEGAR

Roast the bell peppers over a gas flame or under a broiler until evenly charred. Place peppers in a bowl; cover with plastic wrap. Let stand for 15 minutes. Peel and seed the peppers over a bowl to catch the juice. Coarsely chop the peppers. Strain the juice and reserve. Heat the olive oil in a medium saucepan over medium-high heat. Add the yellow onion and garlic. Sauté for 3 minutes or until translucent. Stir in the vegetable stock, bell peppers and reserved pepper juice. Bring to a boil; reduce the heat. Simmer for 20 minutes. Pour the mixture into a blender; purée until smooth. Pour into a bowl; let cool. Cook the coriander seeds, cumin seeds and fennel seeds in a skillet over high heat for 2 minutes or until the seeds are fragrant, shaking the skillet constantly. Grind the seeds to a powder in a spice grinder. Reserve a pinch of the ground seeds. Stir the remaining seeds into the soup. Season with salt and pepper. Cover and chill for 2 hours or up to 3 days. Mix the cucumber, jalapeño, red onion, parsley, lime juice and reserved ground seeds in a bowl. Cover and chill. Stir the remaining ingredients into the soup just before serving. Ladle into bowls. Garnish with cucumber salsa.

GREEK REVIVAL

THE GREEK REVIVAL period of the nineteenth century first appeared in NEW ORLEANS around 1830. INSPIRED BY THE buildings of ancient GREECE, it exerted a great influence on the local architecture. MAJOR CHARACTERISTICS OF GREEK REVIVAL ARE MONUMENTAL PROPORTIONS, USE OF CLASSICAL DETAILS, AND SYMMETRICAL FACADES. A FULL ENTABLATURE SUPPORTED BY GREEK COLUMNS (DORIC, IONIC, OR CORINTHIAN) IS ALSO TYPICAL OF THE STYLE, AS ARE THE GREEK KEY DOORWAY, A LOW-PITCHED ROOF, AND EGG-AND-DART MOLDING.

Potage Petits Pois with Chive Oil

Yield: 8 servings

2	TABLESPOONS UNSALTED BUTTER		SALT AND FRESHLY GROUND
4	MEDIUM LEEKS, WHITE PART		PEPPER TO TASTE
	ONLY, COARSELY CHOPPED	1/4	CUP CHOPPED FRESH CHIVES
5	CUPS CHICKEN STOCK OR CANNED	1/3	CUP CANOLA OIL
	LOW-SODIUM BROTH	6	SLICES BACON, CUT INTO
2	(10-OUNCE) PACKAGES FROZEN		1/2-INCH PIECES (OPTIONAL)
	BABY PEAS (ABOUT 4 CUPS)		
1	SMALL IDAHO POTATO, PEELED,		
	COARSELY GRATED		

Melt the butter in a large saucepan over low heat. Add the leeks and sauté for 5 minutes or until barely softened. Add the chicken stock, peas and potato and bring to a boil over high heat. Cover partially and boil for 10 minutes or until the vegetables are tender but the peas are still bright green. Remove the soup in batches to a blender and purée until smooth. Season with salt and pepper. Return the soup to the pan and keep warm over low heat. Rinse and dry the blender container. Add the chives and canola oil and purée for 4 minutes or until smooth. Pour into a small bowl and season with salt. Cook the bacon over medium heat in a small skillet for 6 minutes or until crisp. Drain on paper towels and crumble. Ladle the soup into shallow soup plates and drizzle with the chive oil. Top with crumbled bacon. Note: The soup and chive oil can be made up to 2 days ahead. Cover and chill separately. Reheat the soup gently before serving.

ITALIANATE STYLE

THE ITALIANATE STYLE EVOLVED LOCALLY IN THE 1850S AS A REACTION TO THE SYMMETRY OF THE GREEK REVIVAL. BASED ON THE RURAL ARCHITECTURE OF NORTHERN ITALIAN FARMHOUSES, IT IDEALLY FEATURES ASYMMETRICAL FACADES. THE SCALE IS STILL BIG IN PROPORTION LIKE THE GREEK REVIVAL, BUT THE CLASSICAL DETAILS BECOME MORE MANNERISTIC OR ARE COMPLETELY DROPPED LATER IN THE PERIOD. THE MACHINE PLAYS A GREATER ROLE IN MILLWORK, AND LACY CAST IRON REPLACES CLASSICAL PORCHES AND COLUMNS IN NEW ORLEANS. OTHER COMMON FEATURES OF THE ITALIANATE STYLE ARE BRACKETED CORNICES WITH PAIRED BRACKETS IN THE ENTABLATURE ALIGNED OVER THE COLUMNS, SEGMENTAL ARCHES, STILTED ARCHES, AND DECORATIVE PARAPETS.

FOUR-VEGETABLE CHOWDER

½ cup (1 stick) butter
2 large tomatoes, unpeeled, coarsely chopped
2 Irish potatoes, unpeeled, coarsely chopped
2 large yellow onions, peeled, coarsely chopped
Kernels of 2 ears fresh corn (about 1 cup kernels)
4 cups half-and-half
Salt and pepper to taste

Melt the butter in a saucepan over medium heat. Add the tomatoes, potatoes, onions and corn and sauté for 10 minutes. Stir in the half-and-half and season with salt and pepper. Bring to a boil, reduce the heat and simmer for 25 to 30 minutes.
Yield: 4 servings

Bucktown Black-Eyed Pea Soup

Yield: 6 servings

2   tablespoons olive oil
2¾ cups finely chopped onions
1   tablespoon minced garlic
2   (15-ounce) cans black-eyed peas, drained
2¼ cups low-sodium chicken broth or stock
2   (8-ounce) cans tomato sauce

2½ teaspoons dried oregano
    Large pinch of cayenne pepper
1   teaspoon red wine vinegar
    Salt and pepper to taste
    Freshly grated Parmesan cheese

Heat the olive oil in a heavy saucepan over medium heat. Add the onions and garlic and sauté for 8 minutes or until golden brown and tender. Add the black-eyed peas, chicken broth, tomato sauce, oregano and cayenne pepper. Simmer for 15 minutes. Stir in the vinegar. Season with salt and pepper. Ladle into bowls and sprinkle with Parmesan cheese.

Pumpkin Orange Soup

Yield: 6 servings

2   tablespoons butter or margarine
1   onion, chopped
1¼ cups orange juice
2   cups puréed pumpkin

1½ cups chicken broth
1½ cups water
    Salt and pepper to taste
1   cup light cream
    Sour cream for garnish

Melt the butter in a saucepan over medium heat. Add the onion and sauté until translucent. Stir in the orange juice, pumpkin, chicken broth and water and season with salt and pepper. Bring to a simmer. Stir in the cream and heat through but do not boil. Ladle into bowls and garnish with a dollop of sour cream.

Chilled Sweet Corn Broth with Crab and Avocado Salad

YIELD: 6 SERVINGS

¼	CUP OLIVE OIL		SALT AND FRESHLY GROUND WHITE
1	CUP FINELY CHOPPED WHITE ONION		PEPPER TO TASTE
½	CUP FINELY CHOPPED CELERY		CHOPPED FRESH CHIVES FOR GARNISH
	KERNELS OF 4 EARS FRESH CORN		FRESHLY GROUND WHITE PEPPER FOR
	(ABOUT 2 CUPS KERNELS)		GARNISH
4	SPRIGS OF FRESH THYME		EXTRA-VIRGIN OLIVE OIL
4½	CUPS WATER		FOR GARNISH

Heat the olive oil in a saucepan over medium heat. Add the onion and celery and sauté for 5 minutes. Stir in the corn, thyme and water and season with salt and white pepper. Bring to a boil, reduce the heat and simmer for 15 minutes. Remove the thyme sprigs. Remove the soup in batches to a blender and purée until smooth. Strain the soup through a fine sieve. Season with salt and white pepper. Add slightly more salt than needed to compensate for the cold serving temperature. Cover and chill for 3 hours or longer. Divide the Crab and Avocado Salad (below) between 6 chilled bowls. Arrange the salad in a ring in each bowl. Spoon the soup into the center. Garnish with chopped fresh chives, freshly ground white pepper and a drizzle of extra-virgin olive oil.

Recipe provided by John Harris, Gautreau's Restaurant

Crab and Avocado Salad

YIELD: 6 SERVINGS

	JUICE OF 2 ORANGES, 1 LIME AND	1	POUND JUMBO LUMP OR LUMP CRAB
	1 LEMON		MEAT, FLAKED
½	CUP EXTRA-VIRGIN OLIVE OIL	3	AVOCADOS, PEELED, COARSELY CHOPPED
	SALT AND FRESHLY GROUND WHITE		
	PEPPER TO TASTE		

Whisk the orange juice, lime juice, lemon juice and olive oil in a bowl. Season with salt and white pepper. Fold in the crab meat and avocados. Adjust seasonings. Cover and chill.

Crab Meat Caribe

Yield: 4 servings

1	POUND LUMP CRAB MEAT, FLAKED	1/4	CUP FRESH LIME JUICE
4	GREEN ONIONS, CUT DIAGONALLY INTO 1-INCH PIECES	1/2	CUP OLIVE OIL
1/2	TEASPOON FINELY CHOPPED JALAPEÑO CHILE		SALT AND FRESHLY GROUND BLACK PEPPER TO TASTE
2	PLUM TOMATOES, SEEDED, CHOPPED	2	RIPE AVOCADOS, HALVED, PITTED
1/4	CUP SLICED FRESH BASIL		SLICED FRESH BASIL FOR GARNISH

Combine the crab meat, green onions, jalapeño, tomatoes and 1/4 cup basil in a bowl. Add the lime juice and olive oil and season with salt and pepper. Toss gently to mix. Spoon into the avocado halves. Garnish with fresh basil.

Godchaux Salad

Yield: 6 servings

1	HEAD ICEBERG LETTUCE, CORED, COARSELY CHOPPED	2/3	CUP VEGETABLE OIL
2	LARGE TOMATOES, CHOPPED	1/3	CUP RED WINE VINEGAR
1	POUND BACKFIN LUMP CRAB MEAT, FLAKED	1/2	CUP CREOLE MUSTARD
		3	HARD-COOKED EGGS, FINELY CHOPPED
30	TO 35 LARGE SHRIMP, BOILED, PEELED, DEVEINED	12	ANCHOVIES

Combine the lettuce, tomatoes, crab meat and shrimp in a large salad bowl. Whisk the oil, vinegar and mustard in a small bowl. Pour the dressing over the salad and toss to mix. Divide the salad between 6 chilled plates. Top each with chopped hard-cooked egg and 2 anchovies.

Recipe provided by Galatoire's Restaurant

Orzo Orleans

Yield: 8 servings

2	GARLIC CLOVES, MINCED	2	MEDIUM TOMATOES, CHOPPED
1½	TABLESPOONS FRESH LEMON JUICE	6	GREEN ONIONS, WHITE AND PALE
¼	CUP OLIVE OIL		GREEN PARTS, THINLY SLICED
1	TABLESPOON MINCED FRESH	1	CUP PACKED FINELY CHOPPED
	OREGANO		FRESH FLAT-LEAF PARSLEY
	SALT AND PEPPER TO TASTE	½	GARLIC CLOVE, COARSELY
1½	POUNDS MEDIUM UNCOOKED		CHOPPED
	SHRIMP, PEELED, DEVEINED	2	TABLESPOONS FRESH LEMON
	(ABOUT 50)		JUICE
11	OUNCES ORZO PASTA (ABOUT 1½	¼	CUP CHOPPED FRESH FLAT-LEAF
	CUPS)		PARSLEY
½	POUND SUGAR SNAP PEAS,	2	TEASPOONS MINCED FRESH
	TRIMMED		OREGANO
⅓	CUP CRUMBLED FETA CHEESE	¼	CUP OLIVE OIL

For the shrimp, whisk 2 garlic cloves, 1½ tablespoons lemon juice, ¼ cup olive oil and 1 tablespoon oregano in a bowl. Season with salt and pepper. Add the shrimp and stir to coat. Cover and marinate in the refrigerator for 1 hour. Soak 8 wooden skewers in warm water for 30 minutes. Heat the grill. Thread the shrimp onto the skewers and discard the marinade. Grill the shrimp 5 to 6 inches from the heat source for 1 to 2 minutes per side or until just cooked through. Remove the shrimp from the skewers and keep warm. For the salad, fill a 6-quart saucepan ¾ full with salted water. Bring to a boil and stir in the orzo. Cook until orzo is al dente, stirring frequently. Add the snap peas and cook for 15 seconds. Drain orzo and snap peas for 5 minutes and place in a large bowl. Stir in the cooked shrimp, feta cheese, tomatoes, green onions and 1 cup parsley. For the dressing, place ½ garlic clove, 2 tablespoons lemon juice, ¼ cup parsley, 2 teaspoons oregano and ¼ cup olive oil in a blender container. Blend until dressing is emulsified. Add to the salad and toss well. Season with salt and pepper.

CITRUS PEPPERCORN VINAIGRETTE

½ CUP FRESH GRAPEFRUIT JUICE
2 TABLESPOONS FRESH LIME JUICE
2 TABLESPOONS CHOPPED SHALLOTS
1 TABLESPOON DIJON MUSTARD
1 TABLESPOON EXTRA-VIRGIN OLIVE OIL
2 TABLESPOONS CHOPPED FRESH CHIVES OR GREEN ONION TOPS
1 TABLESPOON COARSELY GROUND DRIED PINK OR BLACK PEPPERCORNS

COMBINE THE GRAPEFRUIT JUICE, LIME JUICE, SHALLOTS AND MUSTARD IN A BLENDER OR FOOD PROCESSOR CONTAINER. BLEND FOR 30 SECONDS. ADD THE OLIVE OIL IN A SLOW STREAM, PROCESSING UNTIL EMULSIFIED. STIR IN THE CHIVES AND PEPPERCORNS.
YIELD: ¾ CUP

Shrimp Salad Wraps

YIELD: 4 SERVINGS

2	TEASPOONS OLIVE OIL	1	TABLESPOON FRESH LIME JUICE
1½	POUNDS UNCOOKED MEDIUM-LARGE SHRIMP, PEELED, DEVEINED, HALVED LENGTHWISE	1	TEASPOON TABASCO SAUCE
		¼	TEASPOON SALT
		¼	TEASPOON FRESHLY GROUND BLACK PEPPER
¼	CUP MINCED RED ONION		
1	LARGE RIB CELERY, FINELY CHOPPED	8	(7-INCH) FLOUR TORTILLAS
		8	LARGE SPEARS BELGIAN ENDIVE OR SMALL ROMAINE LETTUCE LEAVES (OPTIONAL)
½	CUP MAYONNAISE		
2	TABLESPOONS PLUS 1½ TEASPOONS KETCHUP		
		1	(3¼-OUNCE) PACKAGE ALFALFA SPROUTS
4½	TEASPOONS FINELY CHOPPED FRESH TARRAGON		

Heat the olive oil in a large nonstick skillet over medium-high heat. Add the shrimp and sauté for 4 to 5 minutes or until just opaque throughout. Remove to a plate to cool. Chop the shrimp coarsely and place in a large bowl. Add the onion and celery and toss to mix. Mix the mayonnaise, ketchup, tarragon, lime juice, Tabasco sauce, salt and pepper in a bowl. Fold the mayonnaise mixture into the shrimp mixture. Wrap the tortillas in foil and heat at 350 degrees for 5 minutes or until softened. Lay the tortillas on a work surface. Place 1 spear of endive in the center of each tortilla. Spoon ⅓ cup of the shrimp salad over each spear. Top each with ¼ cup of alfalfa sprouts. Roll up the tortilla and cut in half, if desired. Serve immediately. Note: The shrimp salad can be made 1 day ahead. Cover and chill.

Smoked Trout with Lentils

Yield: 4 servings

1	cup French green lentils (about ½ pound)	6	ounces skinless smoked trout fillets, coarsely flaked
1	tablespoon olive oil	½	cup Tarragon Shallot Vinaigrette (below)
1	small onion, finely chopped	4	ounces frisée, torn into bite-size pieces
1	small carrot, finely chopped		
1	small rib celery, finely chopped		
2	cups water		
	Salt and freshly ground pepper to taste		

Rinse and sort the lentils. Heat the olive oil in a heavy medium saucepan over medium heat. Add the onion, carrot and celery and sauté for 5 minutes or until soft. Add the lentils and water and season with salt and pepper. Bring to a boil over high heat. Reduce the heat to medium-low and cover partially. Simmer for 1 hour or until the lentils are tender and the liquid is absorbed, stirring occasionally. Stir the trout and Tarragon Shallot Vinaigrette gently into the lentils and season with salt and pepper. Arrange the frisée on 4 plates and spoon the warm lentil mixture on top.

Tarragon Shallot Vinaigrette

Yield: 1 cup

2	tablespoons tarragon vinegar	6	tablespoons olive oil
1½	teaspoons minced shallots		Salt and freshly ground pepper to taste
1	teaspoon Dijon mustard		

Combine the vinegar, shallots and mustard in a bowl. Whisk in the olive oil and season with salt and pepper. Note: The vinaigrette can be made up to 1 day ahead. Cover and chill. Whisk before serving.

Sizzling Steak Salad

Yield: 4 servings

8	LARGE GARLIC CLOVES, UNPEELED	6	CUPS TORN ASSORTED SALAD GREENS
1	TABLESPOON OLIVE OIL		(SUCH AS GREEN LEAF, RADICCHIO AND
1	LARGE RED BELL PEPPER		ARUGULA)
8	TEASPOONS STEAK BLACKENING MIX	1	SMALL SWEET ONION, THINLY SLICED
4	(4-OUNCE) TOP SIRLOIN STEAKS,	1	LARGE TOMATO, CUT INTO WEDGES
	3/4 INCH THICK	1	CUP GORGONZOLA DRESSING

Mix the garlic cloves with olive oil in a bowl. Place the garlic on a baking sheet. Bake at 400 degrees for 10 minutes or until garlic is soft. Let cool. Press the cloves with fingers to release the garlic from the skins. Slice the garlic and set aside. Roast the bell pepper directly over a gas flame or under a broiler until evenly charred. Wrap in a paper bag and let stand for 10 minutes. Peel and seed the pepper and cut into strips. Heat a large cast-iron skillet over high heat for 10 minutes. Rub 1 teaspoon blackening mix on each side of each steak. Add the steaks to the skillet and cook for 3 minutes per side for rare. Remove steaks to a cutting board and let stand for 5 minutes. Divide the greens among 4 plates. Cut the steaks diagonally into thin slices and arrange on the greens. Top with roasted peppers, onion slices and tomato wedges. Spoon Gorgonzola Dressing (below) over the salads. Top with roasted garlic and serve.

Gorgonzola Dressing

Yield: 1 cup

6	TABLESPOONS VEGETABLE OIL	1	TABLESPOON COARSE-GRAINED MUSTARD
4	OUNCES GORGONZOLA CHEESE	2	LARGE GARLIC CLOVES, PRESSED
2	TABLESPOONS PLUS 1½ TEASPOONS RED	2	TEASPOONS DRIED BASIL, CRUMBLED
	WINE VINEGAR		SALT AND PEPPER TO TASTE

Combine the oil, cheese, vinegar, mustard, garlic and basil in a food processor or blender. Season with salt and pepper. Blend until well mixed. Cover and chill.

Curried Chicken Salad

Yield: 6 servings

4	CHICKEN BREASTS, BONE IN	½	CUP MAYONNAISE
6	RIBS CELERY, FINELY CHOPPED	¼	CUP SOUR CREAM
6	GREEN ONIONS, THINLY SLICED	½	TO 1 TEASPOON SALT
1½	POUNDS SEEDLESS RED GRAPES, HALVED	20	TURNS FRESHLY GROUND PEPPER
	LENGTHWISE	1	TABLESPOON LEMON JUICE
¾	CUP CHOPPED PECANS, TOASTED	1	HEAD ROMAINE LETTUCE, THINLY
1	TABLESPOON CURRY POWDER		SLICED OR SHREDDED

Cover the chicken with water in a saucepan and simmer for 1½ hours or until the meat is falling from the bones. Remove the chicken and let cool. Remove and discard the bones. Chop the chicken. Combine the chicken, celery, green onions, grapes, pecans, curry powder, mayonnaise, sour cream, salt, pepper and lemon juice in a bowl; mix well. Cover and chill thoroughly. Arrange the lettuce on a large round serving platter. Pack the chicken salad into a small bowl. Unmold the salad in the center of the platter. Note: For individual servings, arrange the lettuce on 6 dinner plates. Pack the chicken salad in coffee cups and unmold in the center of each plate.

Apple, Endive and Stilton Salad

Yield 4 to 6 servings

2	TABLESPOONS UNSALTED BUTTER	½	CUP CRUMBLED STILTON CHEESE
1	CUP COARSELY CHOPPED WALNUTS	2	TABLESPOONS CHOPPED FRESH
½	TEASPOON SUGAR		TARRAGON
2	LARGE BELGIAN ENDIVES, CUT		SALT AND FRESHLY GROUND WHITE
	LENGTHWISE INTO JULIENNE STRIPS		PEPPER TO TASTE
2	GRANNY SMITH APPLES, CORED,	⅓	CUP DIJON VINAIGRETTE
	HALVED, CUT INTO JULIENNE STRIPS		

Melt the butter in a small saucepan over medium heat. Add the walnuts and sugar and cook for 2 minutes or until golden brown, stirring constantly. Combine the endives, apples, walnuts, cheese, tarragon and Dijon Vinaigrette (below) in a large bowl. Toss gently to mix. Season with salt and white pepper.

Dijon Vinaigrette

Yield: ⅓ cup

2	TABLESPOONS WHITE WINE VINEGAR	1	SMALL SHALLOT, MINCED
1	TABLESPOON RED WINE VINEGAR	⅛	TEASPOON SALT
½	TEASPOON DIJON MUSTARD		FRESHLY GROUND BLACK PEPPER
¼	TEASPOON SUGAR		TO TASTE
2	TABLESPOONS EXTRA-VIRGIN OLIVE OIL		

Whisk the white wine vinegar, red wine vinegar, mustard and sugar in a small bowl. Add the olive oil in a stream and continue whisking until emulsified. Stir in the shallot and salt and season with black pepper.

Spring Melon Salad with Feta

Yield: 8 servings

1	TABLESPOON VEGETABLE OIL		1	TABLESPOON FRESH LIME JUICE
2	RED ONIONS, SLICED ¼-INCH THICK			PEPPER TO TASTE
2	CANTALOUPES		½	CUP CRUMBLED FETA CHEESE
1	HONEYDEW MELON		½	CUP PINE NUTS, TOASTED
¼	CUP CHOPPED FRESH MINT			

*H*eat the oil in a large skillet over medium heat until hot but not smoking. Add the onions and sauté just until softened. Let cool. Cut a slice from the top to bottom of each melon with a sharp knife. Set the melons on the cut end. Remove the rinds by cutting from top to bottom. Cut melons in half and discard the seeds. Cut half of 1 cantaloupe and half of the honeydew into 1-inch wedges. Arrange the wedges on a serving platter. Cut the remaining melon into ¾-inch chunks and place in a bowl. Add the mint and lime juice and season with pepper. Toss to mix. Spoon the melon chunks over the wedges on the platter. Top with the feta cheese, cooked onions and pine nuts. Toss again just before serving.

Bayou Bean Salad

Yield: 4 servings

8	OUNCES DRIED GREAT NORTHERN BEANS (ABOUT 1⅓ CUPS)	½	CUP KALAMATA OLIVES
2	TEASPOONS SALT	¼	CUP OLIVE OIL
1	LARGE RED BELL PEPPER	2	TABLESPOONS RED WINE VINEGAR
8	OUNCES GREEN BEANS, TRIMMED, CUT INTO THIRDS	1	TABLESPOON BALSAMIC VINEGAR
1	LEMON	1	TABLESPOON GARLIC POWDER
		1	TEASPOON WHITE PEPPER
		½	TEASPOON SALT

Place the dried beans in a medium saucepan. Add enough cold water to cover by 3 inches and let stand overnight. Drain the dried beans and add enough cold water to cover by 3 inches. Bring to a boil and reduce the heat. Simmer, covered partially, for 40 minutes or until the beans are tender. Remove from the heat and add 2 teaspoons salt. Let stand for 15 minutes. Drain and let beans cool. Roast the bell pepper directly over a gas flame or under a broiler until evenly charred. Wrap in a paper bag and let stand for 10 minutes. Peel, seed and cut into julienne strips. Cook the green beans in boiling salted water in a saucepan for 4 minutes or just until tender. Drain the beans and plunge into ice water to stop the cooking process. Drain again. Remove the peel from the lemon in long strips with a vegetable peeler. Cut into thin strips. Combine the great Northern beans, bell pepper, green beans, lemon peel and olives in a large bowl. Whisk the olive oil, red wine vinegar, balsamic vinegar, garlic power, white pepper and ½ teaspoon salt in a bowl and pour over the bean mixture. Toss to coat.

STORING OLIVE OIL

Store olive oil in an airtight container in a cool dark place, such as a cupboard. When stored in the refrigerator, olive oil will become cloudy and will eventually solidify. This will not affect the quality and flavor; just bring the oil to room temperature when ready to use. Properly stored, olive oil will keep its optimum flavor up to 2 years, which is longer than vegetable oil or salad oil.

Madras Salad

YIELD: 8 SERVINGS

1⅓	CUPS WHITE RICE	1	TEASPOON SALT
3	TABLESPOONS CHOPPED ONION	1	CUP CHOPPED CELERY
1	TABLESPOON VINEGAR	1	(16-OUNCE) PACKAGE FROZEN GREEN
2	TABLESPOONS CORN OIL		PEAS, THAWED, DRAINED
1	TEASPOON CURRY POWDER	¾	CUP MAYONNAISE

Cook the rice according to package directions. Add the onion, vinegar, corn oil, curry powder and salt to the warm rice and mix well. Cover and chill for 3 hours. Add the celery, peas and mayonnaise to the rice mixture and stir to combine.

Thai Peanut Slaw

YIELD: 8 SERVINGS

½	CUP SALTED PEANUTS, VERY FINELY GROUND	1	TABLESPOON SOY SAUCE
1½	TEASPOONS SUGAR	4	CUPS SHREDDED CABBAGE OR COLESLAW MIX
¼	TEASPOON RED PEPPER FLAKES	½	CUP COARSELY CHOPPED CUCUMBER
1	TEASPOON MINCED GARLIC	⅓	CUP SLICED GREEN ONIONS
3	TABLESPOONS PEANUT OR VEGETABLE OIL	¼	CUP SALTED PEANUTS
3	TABLESPOONS RICE VINEGAR OR VINEGAR	¼	CUP FINELY CHOPPED RED BELL PEPPER

Combine the ground peanuts, sugar, red pepper flakes, garlic, peanut oil, vinegar and soy sauce in a small bowl; mix well. Combine the cabbage, cucumber, green onions, ¼ cup peanuts and bell pepper in a large bowl. Add the dressing and toss to coat. Serve immediately.

MARDI GRAS

IBERVILLE REDISCOVERED THE MISSISSIPPI RIVER ON SHROVE TUESDAY IN 1699 AND DUBBED HIS CAMPSITE BAYOU DU MARDI GRAS. EARLY CARNIVAL CELEBRATIONS INCLUDED CREOLE BALLS, MASKING, THROWING FLOUR, AND PARADING A BOEUF GRAS (FAT OX) THROUGH THE STREETS THE DAY BEFORE ASH WEDNESDAY. IN 1857 THE COMUS ORGANIZATION PRESENTED THE FIRST NIGHT PARADE, WHICH CONSISTED OF ONLY TWO FLOATS. THE FLOATS, AS WELL AS THE MASKERS WHO WALKED IN THE PARADE, WERE ILLUMINATED WITH FLAMBEAUX, OR TORCHLIGHTS. COMUS WAS THE SPRINGBOARD FOR CARNIVAL PARADES AND BALLS TO FOLLOW, INCLUDING REX AND MOMUS IN 1872. THE CUSTOM OF MASKERS ON FLOATS THROWING BEADS AND TRINKETS TO THE SPECTATORS BEGAN IN 1881, WHEN MEMBERS OF REX THREW CANDY AND PEANUTS. THE "GREATEST FREE SHOW ON EARTH" HAS STOPPED ONLY FOR MAJOR WARS AND A POLICE STRIKE IN 1979. MARDI GRAS IS THE FINAL MERRIMENT BEFORE LENT.

1	TEASPOON SALT	½	YELLOW BELL PEPPER, CHOPPED
½	MEDIUM HEAD GREEN CABBAGE, CHOPPED	1	CUP WHITE VINEGAR
½	MEDIUM HEAD PURPLE CABBAGE, CHOPPED	2	CUPS SUGAR
		1	TEASPOON CELERY SEEDS
3	RIBS CELERY, CHOPPED	1	TEASPOON MUSTARD

Sprinkle the salt over the chopped green and purple cabbage in a bowl. Let stand for 1 hour. Squeeze out all liquid. Mix the cabbage, celery and bell pepper in a bowl. Combine the vinegar, sugar, celery seeds and mustard in a saucepan. Bring to a boil and boil for 1 minute. Let cool. Pour over cabbage mixture and mix well. Place in an airtight container and place in the freezer for 30 to 45 minutes. Remove from the freezer and let stand at room temperature to thaw. The slaw will be crisp when thawed.

Salsa Salad

YIELD: 8 SERVINGS

3½	CUPS COOKED FRESH CORN KERNELS, OR 2 CANS CORN KERNELS
1	RED BELL PEPPER, CHOPPED
1	GREEN BELL PEPPER, CHOPPED
2	JALAPEÑO CHILES, SEEDED, FINELY CHOPPED
½	CUP CHOPPED FRESH CILANTRO

	JUICE OF 2 LIMES
	OLIVE OIL
	SALT AND PEPPER TO TASTE
1	CAN BLACK BEANS, RINSED, DRAINED
1	YELLOW ONION, CHOPPED, AND/OR ½ CUP CHOPPED GREEN ONIONS

Combine the corn, bell peppers, jalapeños, cilantro and lime juice in a bowl. Drizzle with olive oil and toss to coat. Season with salt and pepper. Fold in the black beans and onion gently. Serve chilled or at room temperature.

Spinach and Strawberry Salad

YIELD: 6 SERVINGS

1	EGG YOLK
¼	CUP SUGAR
2	TABLESPOONS FRESH LEMON JUICE
¼	TEASPOON SALT
6	TABLESPOONS SAFFLOWER OIL

10	OUNCES FRESH SPINACH LEAVES, RINSED WELL, DRIED
1	PINT FRESH STRAWBERRIES, HULLED

Combine the egg yolk, sugar, lemon juice and salt in a bowl. Whisk in the safflower oil 1 tablespoon at a time. Chill the dressing. Place the spinach in a bowl. Top with the strawberries. Pour on the dressing and toss to coat.

LENT

LENT IS THE PERIOD OF FASTING AND PENITENCE TRADITIONALLY OBSERVED BY CHRISTIANS IN PREPARATION FOR EASTER. THE LENGTH OF THE LENTEN FAST, DURING WHICH OBSERVANTS EAT SPARINGLY, WAS ESTABLISHED IN THE FOURTH CENTURY AS FORTY DAYS. THE FORTY-DAY PERIOD BEGINS ASH WEDNESDAY AND EXTENDS, WITH THE OMISSION OF SUNDAYS, TO THE DAY BEFORE EASTER. THE ROMAN CATHOLIC CHURCH HAS IN RECENT YEARS RELAXED ITS LAWS ON FASTING. ACCORDING TO AN APOSTOLIC CONSTITUTION ISSUED BY POPE PAUL VI IN FEBRUARY 1966, FASTING AND ABSTINENCE DURING LENT IS OBLIGATORY ONLY ON ASH WEDNESDAY AND GOOD FRIDAY. FRIDAYS DURING LENT WERE CONSIDERED "MEATLESS" DAYS FOR CATHOLICS. HOWEVER, THEY COULD EAT ANY TYPE OF SEAFOOD THAT THEY WISHED. THIS TRADITION IS STILL OBSERVED BY MOST NEW ORLEANS CATHOLICS.

Seafood

Seafood

Nathaniel Wilkinson House
1015 S. Carrollton Avenue

Nathaniel Wilkinson, an exchange broker, commission merchant, and officer of the Canal Bank, purchased this site for $4,000 on February 19, 1849, from Laurent Millaudon, one of the developers of the area. Wilkinson likely had the house built shortly thereafter. He sold it the following year to his brother-in-law, Alfred Hurtubise, with eight other squares in Carrollton and seven lots in New Orleans for $31,000. Six days after Hurtubise purchased the house, he donated it and the other property to his sister, Angele Hurtubise Wilkinson. While residing in Paris in 1851, Angele sold the house and lot to Rachel Martin for $8,500.

An advertisement for the sale of the house in the *New Orleans Daily Crescent* of November 29, 1859, described it as "that elegantly newly built Gothic Mansion situated on the Carrollton Avenue." The Gothic style, popularized nationwide by such architectural pattern books as Andrew Jackson Downing's *Villas and Cottage Residences*, was rarely used in the Deep South, where homeowners preferred the Greek Revival style. In New Orleans, the Gothic style generally was employed for religious architecture, St. Patrick's Church on Camp Street being one such example.

The house has had numerous owners and was the JLNO Show House III in 1979. It now is owned by Mr. and Mrs. Joseph M. Bruno, who retained Trapolin Architects to restore the home and enlarge it with a major rear addition. Rene Fransen served as landscape architect for the project. The lush vegetation of the site hints at the suburban nineteenth-century character that Carrollton once had, when the St. Charles streetcar was a railroad line.

Grilled Amberjack with Tapenade

Yield: 4 servings

4   (6- to 7-ounce) amberjack fillets
2   teaspoons olive oil

Salt and pepper to taste
Cucumber Salsa

Prepare the grill at medium-high heat or preheat the broiler. Brush the fillets with olive oil and season with salt and pepper. Grill or broil for 4 minutes per side or just until opaque in the center. Serve with Tapenade and Cucumber Salsa (below).

Tapenade

Yield: 4 servings

½   cup oil-cured black olives, pitted, finely chopped
2   tablespoons finely chopped pine nuts
½   small garlic clove, minced
1   tablespoon finely chopped fresh Italian parsley

½   teaspoon finely chopped fresh rosemary
6   cherry tomatoes, cut into ¼-inch wedges
1   tablespoon grated lemon zest
4½ teaspoons olive oil

Combine the olives, pine nuts, garlic, parsley, rosemary, cherry tomatoes, lemon zest and olive oil in a small bowl and mix well. Serve at room temperature.

Cucumber Salsa

Yield: 4 servings

1½ cups chopped seeded peeled cucumbers
⅓   cup chopped red onion
2   tablespoons white wine vinegar

6   tablespoons chopped fresh mint
4½ teaspoons olive oil
3   teaspoons sugar
Salt and pepper to taste

Combine cucumbers, onion, vinegar, mint, olive oil and sugar in a bowl. Toss to blend. Season with salt and pepper. Serve at room temperature.

Catfish with Spinach Salad and Creole Andouille Vinaigrette

Yield: 6 servings

1	CUP CIDER VINEGAR	6	(5 TO 6-OUNCE) CATFISH FILLETS
1/3	CUP HONEY		FLOUR
2/3	CUP OLIVE OIL	2	EGGS, LIGHTLY BEATEN
2 1/2	TABLESPOONS CREOLE MUSTARD OR	3	CUPS FRESH BREAD CRUMBS
	WHOLE-GRAIN DIJON MUSTARD	3	TABLESPOONS OLIVE OIL
	SALT AND PEPPER TO TASTE	2	(6-OUNCE) PACKAGES BABY SPINACH
2	TEASPOONS CIDER VINEGAR		LEAVES
8	OUNCES FULLY COOKED ANDOUILLE	1	CUP CRUMBLED ROQUEFORT CHEESE
	SAUSAGE, CHOPPED		

Boil 1 cup cider vinegar and honey in a small saucepan for 10 minutes or until reduced to 1/3 cup. Pour into a small bowl. Whisk in 2/3 cup olive oil and mustard. Season with salt and pepper. Whisk in 2 teaspoons cider vinegar. Sauté the sausage in a skillet over medium heat for 10 minutes or until browned and heated through. Drain on paper towels and stir into the dressing. Season the fillets with salt and pepper. Place the flour, eggs and bread crumbs in separate shallow bowls. Dip the fillets into the flour, then the eggs and then the bread crumbs to coat. Heat 3 tablespoons olive oil in a large heavy skillet over medium-high heat. Add the fillets and fry for 3 minutes per side or until golden brown on the outside and opaque in the center. Remove from the skillet and keep warm. Place the spinach in a large bowl. Add enough dressing to coat and toss to mix. Divide the salad among 6 plates. Place one fillet on each salad and top with Roquefort cheese. Drizzle with additional dressing, if desired.

Recipe provided by Greg Piccolo, Bistro at the Maison de Ville

Poisson en Papillote

Yield: 2 servings

1	(8-ounce) skinless fish fillet	2	cups sliced fresh mushrooms
4	ounces bay scallops	4	teaspoons chopped fresh dill
½	teaspoon salt	2	tablespoons fresh lemon juice
½	teaspoon pepper	2	tablespoons butter
3	tablespoons finely chopped green onions		Lemon wedges for garnish

Cut two 12x16-inch pieces of foil or parchment paper. Fold each in half to form two 8x12-inch rectangles. Open the rectangles on a work surface. Cut the fillet crosswise into ½-inch wide strips. On half of each piece of foil, overlap the fish strips. Top with the scallops and season with the salt and pepper. Top with the green onions and mushrooms. Add the dill and lemon juice. Dot with butter. Fold over the other half of the foil and crimp the edges to seal. Bake at 475 degrees for 10 minutes or until packages are puffed and the seafood is just cooked through. Remove the packages to plates and cut open with a small knife. Garnish with lemon wedges.

En Papillote

Pompano en Papillote was created by Jules Alciatore in honor of the balloonist Alberto Santos-Dumont. Jules, son of the original proprietor of Antoine's Restaurant, referred to his father's Pompano Montgolfier (named for the brothers who invented the first hot air balloon) in which the fish was cooked and served in a paper bag. This method sealed in the juices as well as provided a decorative presentation resembling a balloon. Jules's signature dish is a favorite of New Orleanians and tourists to this day.

Flounder Stuffed with Shrimp and Pecans

Yield: 2 servings

1	TABLESPOON BUTTER	½	CUP CHOPPED PECANS
1	POUND UNCOOKED SHRIMP, PEELED,	1	TABLESPOON BUTTER
	DEVEINED	1	WHOLE FLOUNDER
1	GARLIC CLOVE, MINCED		SALT AND PEPPER TO TASTE
¼	CUP FINELY CHOPPED CELERY	1	TABLESPOON BUTTER

Melt 1 tablespoon butter in a skillet. Add the shrimp and sauté until they are pink. Add the garlic and celery and sauté for 1 minute. Add the pecans and sauté for 1 minute. Turn off the heat but leave the skillet on the burner. Place 1 tablespoon butter in a roasting pan. Place the pan in a 400-degree oven until the butter is melted. Tilt the pan to coat evenly with butter. Place the flounder in the pan. Cut a cross in the flounder and pull back the skin and meat to expose the bones. Season the cavity with salt and pepper. Close the skin and dot the flounder with 1 tablespoon butter. Bake at 400 degrees for 5 minutes. Open up the flounder and spoon the shrimp mixture into the cavity. Bake at 400 degrees for 10 to 15 minutes or until the meat is white and flakes easily. Serve hot.

Mahi Mahi with Sun-Dried Tomatoes

Yield: 4 servings

⅓	CUP CHOPPED SUN-DRIED TOMATOES (NOT PACKED IN OIL)	4	(4 TO 6-OUNCE) MAHI MAHI FILLETS SALT AND PEPPER TO TASTE
2	CUPS FRESH BREAD CRUMBS	1	TABLESPOON FINELY CHOPPED FRESH
2	GARLIC CLOVES, MINCED		ITALIAN PARSLEY
1	EGG WHITE, LIGHTLY BEATEN		LEMON WEDGES
½	CUP BUTTERMILK		

Place the tomatoes in a microwave-safe bowl and cover with water. Cover loosely with plastic wrap and microwave for 1 minute or longer to soften. Drain and place in a sealable plastic bag with the bread crumbs and garlic. Shake the bag to mix. Remove the mixture to a bowl. Whisk egg white and buttermilk in a small bowl. Season the fillets with salt and pepper. Dip each into the buttermilk mixture and then coat in the bread crumbs. Place on a greased baking sheet. Bake at 425 degrees for 12 to 15 minutes or until the meat is white and flakes easily. Sprinkle with the parsley and serve with lemon wedges.

Salmon Encrusted with Basil and Pistachios

Yield: 6 servings

¼	CUP SHELLED PISTACHIOS (ABOUT 1 OUNCE)			SALT AND PEPPER TO TASTE
10	LARGE FRESH BASIL LEAVES		6	(6-OUNCE) SALMON FILLETS
1	GARLIC CLOVE, MINCED		½	CUP DRY WHITE WINE
½	CUP (1 STICK) BUTTER, SOFTENED			FRESH BASIL LEAVES FOR
1	TEASPOON LIME JUICE			GARNISH

Place pistachios, 10 basil leaves and garlic in a food processor. Process until finely chopped. Add the butter and lime juice and process until well mixed. Season with salt and pepper. Pour into a bowl. Cover and chill thoroughly. Place the fillets in a single layer in a buttered 9x13-inch baking dish. Pour the wine over the fillets and season with salt and pepper. Bake at 400 degrees for 10 minutes or until fillets are almost opaque on top. Place 2 tablespoons of the pistachio mixture on top of each fillet. Bake at 400 degrees for 5 minutes or just until the fillets are opaque in the center. Garnish with fresh basil leaves and serve immediately.

SIMPLE SALMON MARINADE

JUICE OF 1 LEMON
¼ CUP SOY SAUCE
¼ CUP SUNFLOWER OIL
2 TEASPOONS GROUND GINGER
¼ TEASPOON SALT
¼ TEASPOON PEPPER
4 (6 TO 8-OUNCE) SALMON STEAKS

COMBINE THE LEMON JUICE, SOY SAUCE, SUNFLOWER OIL, GINGER, SALT AND PEPPER IN A 9X12-INCH GLASS BAKING DISH. ADD THE SALMON. COVER AND CHILL OVERNIGHT. TURN THE SALMON OCCASIONALLY WHILE MARINATING. GRILL FOR 5 TO 8 MINUTES PER SIDE.
YIELD: 4 SERVINGS

Red Snapper Bienville

YIELD: 6 SERVINGS

2	QUARTS COLD WATER	2	TABLESPOONS CHOPPED FRESH THYME, OR 1 TABLESPOON DRIED THYME
1	BAG CRAB BOIL SEASONING		
2	TABLESPOONS SALT		
2	TABLESPOONS LEMON JUICE	1	TABLESPOON MINCED GARLIC
3	DROPS OF TABASCO SAUCE	1½	TEASPOONS CAYENNE PEPPER
1	POUND UNCOOKED MEDIUM SHRIMP	8	OUNCES FRESH LUMP CRAB MEAT, FLAKED
4	OUNCES SLICED BACON, CHOPPED		SALT TO TASTE
1	CUP (2 STICKS) BUTTER		BLACK PEPPER AND CAYENNE PEPPER TO TASTE
½	CUP FLOUR		
¼	CUP (½ STICK) BUTTER	6	(4-OUNCE) RED SNAPPER FILLETS
1	CUP MINCED SHALLOTS	¼	CUP GRATED PARMESAN CHEESE
1	CUP CHOPPED CELERY	2	TABLESPOONS BREAD CRUMBS
½	CUP CHOPPED FRESH PARSLEY		FRESH PARSLEY SPRIGS AND LEMON WEDGES FOR GARNISH
2	TABLESPOONS SALT		

Combine the water, crab boil seasoning, 2 tablespoons salt, lemon juice and Tabasco in a large stockpot. Bring to a boil over high heat. Add the shrimp and boil for 5 minutes. Drain, reserving cooking liquid. Let shrimp cool. Peel, devein and chop the shrimp. Cook the bacon in a saucepan over medium-low heat until the fat is rendered. Remove the bacon with a slotted spoon to paper towels to drain. Add 1 cup butter to the bacon drippings in the saucepan. Heat until the butter melts. Stir in the flour. Cook for 8 minutes or until golden brown, stirring constantly. Stir in 3 cups of the shrimp liquid gradually. Stir until smooth and thickened; set aside. Melt ¼ cup butter in a skillet over medium heat. Add the bacon, shallots, celery, parsley, 2 tablespoons salt, thyme, garlic and 1½ teaspoons cayenne pepper. Sauté for 5 minutes. Stir in the chopped shrimp and crab meat. Stir in the sauce. Remove from the heat and season with salt and pepper. Pour the remaining shrimp liquid into a large baking dish. Arrange the fillets in the baking dish. Bake at 425 degrees for 10 minutes. Drain well. Cover the fillets with the shrimp mixture. Sprinkle with a mixture of the cheese and bread crumbs. Bake at 425 degrees for 5 minutes. Garnish with parsley and lemon wedges.

BIENVILLE

JEAN BAPTISTE LE MOYNE, SIEUR DE BIENVILLE, IS THE FATHER OF NEW ORLEANS, HAVING DISCOVERED IT IN 1718. HE AND HIS BROTHER, PIERRE LE MOYNE, SIEUR D'IBERVILLE, HAD BEEN SENT TO THE NEW WORLD IN 1699 BY KING LOUIS XIV TO FIND AND CHART THE MISSISSIPPI RIVER. THEY FOUND THE RIVER, AND ON THEIR WAY UPSTREAM STOPPED BESIDE A BEND, WHICH BIENVILLE DUBBED "THE BEAUTIFUL CRESCENT." YEARS LATER, BIENVILLE ORDERED A GROUP OF ENGINEERS TO PLOT THE TOWN. THE STREETS THEY LAID OUT BECAME THE WORLD-FAMOUS FRENCH QUARTER.

Snapper and Pesto Pinwheels

Yield: 6 servings

6	(6-ounce) red snapper fillets	½	cup (1 stick) butter
12	tablespoons Parmesan Pesto (below)	½	cup vegetable oil
		12	sheets phyllo dough

Cut each fillet crosswise into 4 pieces. Spread 1 tablespoon pesto on a piece of fillet. Top with another piece of fillet. Repeat the process with remaining fillet pieces and pesto, making 12 "sandwiches." Heat the butter and oil in a saucepan over medium heat until the butter melts. Remove 1 sheet of phyllo dough to a work surface. Cover remaining phyllo with waxed paper topped with a damp towel. Position the sheet of phyllo so that the long side is facing you. Brush lightly with the butter mixture. Fold the sheet in half as for a book. Brush with the butter mixture. Place 1 fillet sandwich 2 inches from the bottom short side. Fold the bottom 2 inches of phyllo over the fillet. Fold the long sides of phyllo in. Roll up like a jelly roll. Place the packet seam side down on a large baking sheet. Brush with the butter mixture. Repeat with remaining phyllo and fillet sandwiches. Bake at 425 degrees for 15 minutes or until the snapper is firm and the pastry is golden brown.

Parmesan Pesto

Yield: 2 cups

1½	cups olive oil	⅔	cup freshly grated Parmesan cheese
2	garlic cloves		
2	tablespoons pine nuts	1	teaspoon lemon juice
½	teaspoon salt	8	cups fresh basil leaves

Process the olive oil, garlic, pine nuts, salt, Parmesan cheese and lemon juice in a food processor until smooth. Add the basil and process until it becomes a fine paste.

BASIL AND OREGANO PESTO

2 cups fresh basil leaves
1 cup freshly grated Parmesan cheese
¼ cup olive oil
3 garlic cloves
2 tablespoons pine nuts
1 tablespoon finely chopped fresh oregano leaves
1 tablespoon fresh lime juice
Salt and pepper to taste

Combine the basil, Parmesan cheese, olive oil, garlic, pine nuts, oregano and lime juice in a food processor. Process until it becomes a fine paste. Stop to scrape the sides as needed. Season with salt and pepper. Yield: 1 cup

Trout Pecan

YIELD: 4 SERVINGS

1	TABLESPOON FRESH LEMON JUICE	2	TEASPOONS DRIED ROSEMARY
4	LARGE TROUT FILLETS	1/3	CUP FLOUR
	SALT AND PEPPER TO TASTE	1	EGG
2	TABLESPOONS BREAD CRUMBS	2	TEASPOONS WATER
1	CUP TOASTED PECANS	2	TABLESPOONS VEGETABLE OIL
6	TABLESPOONS BREAD CRUMBS	2	TABLESPOONS BUTTER

Sprinkle the lemon juice over the fillets. Season with salt and pepper and let stand at room temperature for 10 minutes. Combine 2 tablespoons bread crumbs and the pecans in a food processor. Process until pecans are finely ground. Mix with 6 tablespoons bread crumbs and the rosemary. Remove the mixture to a plate. Beat the egg and water in a shallow dish. Dredge the fillets in flour and then dip in the egg mixture. Press the fillets skin side up into the crumb mixture to coat. Heat half the oil and half the butter in a large skillet over medium-high heat. Fry two fillets skin side up for 3 minutes or until golden brown. Flip the fillets carefully and fry for 3 minutes or until no longer transparent in the center. Remove to a plate and keep warm. Repeat with the remaining oil, butter and fillets.

SUN-DRIED TOMATO PESTO

1 CUP DRAINED OIL-PACKED
SUN-DRIED TOMATOES
2 LARGE GARLIC
CLOVES, MINCED
1/2 TEASPOON FINELY CHOPPED
FRESH OREGANO, OR
1/4 TEASPOON DRIED OREGANO
1/8 TEASPOON CRUSHED
RED PEPPER
1/2 CUP EXTRA-VIRGIN OLIVE OIL
1/4 CUP FINELY CHOPPED FRESH
FLAT-LEAF PARSLEY
2 TABLESPOONS FRESHLY GRATED
PECORINO ROMANO CHEESE

PROCESS THE SUN-DRIED TOMATOES, GARLIC, OREGANO, RED PEPPER, OLIVE OIL, PARSLEY AND CHEESE IN A FOOD PROCESSOR UNTIL IT BECOMES A FINE PASTE. STOP TO SCRAPE THE SIDES AS NEEDED.
NOTE: SUBSTITUTE 2/3 CUP DRY-PACKED SUN-DRIED TOMATOES FOR THE OIL-PACKED TOMATOES IF DESIRED.
YIELD: 1 CUP

Trout Bon Homme

Yield: 6 servings

¼	CUP (½ STICK) BUTTER	1	TEASPOON DRY MUSTARD
¼	CUP FLOUR	1	POUND COOKED SHRIMP,
1½	CUPS HALF-AND-HALF		PEELED, DEVEINED
6	TROUT FILLETS	1	POUND CRAB MEAT, FLAKED
	SALT AND PEPPER TO TASTE	3	TABLESPOONS LEMON JUICE
2	TABLESPOONS BUTTER	1½	TEASPOONS WORCESTERSHIRE SAUCE
8	OUNCES SLICED MUSHROOMS		TABASCO SAUCE TO TASTE
3	TABLESPOONS DRY SHERRY		BREAD CRUMBS

Melt ¼ cup butter in a saucepan over medium heat. Add the flour and cook for 3 minutes, stirring constantly. Add the half-and-half gradually, stirring until smooth and thickened. Set aside. Place the fillets in a buttered baking dish. Season with salt and pepper. Bake at 350 degrees until opaque. Melt 2 tablespoons butter in a skillet over medium heat. Add the mushrooms and sauté until cooked. Add the mushrooms and next 6 ingredients to the white sauce. Mix well and season with Tabasco sauce. Pour over the fillets. Sprinkle with bread crumbs. Bake at 350 degrees for 10 to 12 minutes or until hot.

Rosemary Tuna Kabobs

Yield: 4 servings

1	TABLESPOON OLIVE OIL	1	LARGE ORANGE, PEELED, CUT INTO
2	TEASPOONS MINCED GARLIC		8 PIECES
1¾	TEASPOONS GRATED ORANGE ZEST	8	CHERRY TOMATOES
1½	TEASPOONS MINCED FRESH ROSEMARY	1	ONION, CUT INTO 1-INCH
1½	POUNDS TUNA STEAKS, CUT INTO		WEDGES
	16 (1-INCH) CUBES	½	TEASPOON EACH SALT AND PEPPER

Soak 8 wooden skewers in water for 30 minutes. Combine the olive oil, garlic, orange zest and rosemary in a bowl. Add the tuna cubes and stir to coat. Marinate for 1 hour at room temperature or up to 8 hours, covered, in the refrigerator. Thread 2 cubes of tuna alternately with 1 orange piece, 1 cherry tomato and 1 onion wedge onto each skewer. Prepare the grill or preheat the broiler. Rub any remaining marinade on the kabobs. Season with the salt and pepper. Grill or broil the kabobs for 6 minutes or just until the tuna is opaque in the center, turning frequently.

Seared Yellowfin Tuna

Yield: 8 servings

2	POUNDS YELLOWFIN TUNA	1	TEASPOON POMEGRANATE
	SALT TO TASTE		MOLASSES
	PEPPER TO TASTE	2	TEASPOONS GROUND CUMIN
	GROUND FENNEL SEEDS TO TASTE	2	TEASPOONS MINCED GARLIC
	OLIVE OIL TO TASTE	1/4	CUP OLIVE OIL
	SOY SAUCE TO TASTE		JUICE OF 2 LEMONS
3	RED BELL PEPPERS	1/8	TEASPOON RED PEPPER FLAKES
1/2	CUP CHOPPED TOASTED WALNUTS	1/4	CUP OLIVE OIL

Remove the skin from the tuna; trim the blood line. Cut the tuna into 8 pieces. Season with salt, pepper, fennel seeds, olive oil to taste and soy sauce. Marinate in a shallow glass dish for up to 1 hour. Roast the bell peppers at 350 degrees until charred. Let cool. Peel, seed and finely chop. For the pesto, combine the chopped bell peppers, walnuts, molasses, cumin, garlic, 1/4 cup olive oil, lemon juice and red pepper flakes in a bowl and mix well. Season with salt and pepper. Heat 1/4 cup olive oil in a medium skillet. Sear the tuna on each side. Cook to medium rare. Serve with the walnut pepper pesto.

Recipe provided by Susan Spicer, Bayona

MARINATED TUNA

2 TABLESPOONS SOY SAUCE

2 TABLESPOONS BROWN SUGAR

1 TABLESPOON SHERRY

1 TABLESPOON RICE VINEGAR

1 TABLESPOON VEGETABLE OIL

1 TEASPOON ASIAN
SESAME OIL

3 GARLIC CLOVES, MINCED

1 (1-INCH) PIECE OF
GINGERROOT, PEELED,
FINELY CHOPPED

2 GREEN ONIONS,
FINELY CHOPPED

1/2 TEASPOON RED PEPPER FLAKES

4 (8-OUNCE) TUNA OR
SWORDFISH STEAKS

COMBINE THE SOY SAUCE, BROWN SUGAR, SHERRY, VINEGAR, VEGETABLE OIL, SESAME OIL, GARLIC, GINGERROOT, GREEN ONIONS AND RED PEPPER FLAKES IN A LARGE BOWL. ADD THE TUNA. MARINATE, COVERED, IN THE REFRIGERATOR FOR 2 HOURS OR LONGER. DRAIN THE TUNA AND DISCARD THE MARINADE. PREPARE THE GRILL OR PREHEAT THE BROILER. GRILL OR BROIL FOR 3 MINUTES PER SIDE FOR MEDIUM RARE.

Yield: 4 servings

Caribbean Bouillabaisse

Yield: 6 servings

12	SPINY LOBSTERS	1	BOUQUET GARNI
2	TABLESPOONS UNSALTED BUTTER	12	SMALL RED SNAPPER FILLETS
3	TABLESPOONS EXTRA-VIRGIN		OLIVE OIL
	OLIVE OIL	1	TABLESPOON UNSALTED BUTTER
12	SHALLOTS, MINCED	2	TABLESPOONS CHOPPED GARLIC
4	LIMES, PEELED, SEEDED, CHOPPED	12	VERY LARGE GULF SHRIMP, PEELED
4	WHOLE CLOVES	3	POUNDS FRESH MUSSELS
1/3	CUP HERBSAINT OR PERNOD	1	TEASPOON TABASCO SAUCE
1/4	TEASPOON SAFFRON		SALT, PEPPER AND TABASCO
1	CUP TOMATO PASTE		SAUCE TO TASTE
1	GALLON FISH BROTH		CHOPPED FLAT-LEAF PARSLEY
2	TEASPOONS SALT		FOR GARNISH

Bring water to a boil in a large stockpot. Add 6 lobsters and boil for 9 minutes. Remove cooked lobsters; repeat with the remaining 6 lobsters. Separate the heads and set aside. Remove the meat from the tails; set aside. Melt 2 tablespoons butter with 3 tablespoons olive oil in a large saucepan. Add the shallots and sauté just until soft. Remove the shallots. Add the lobster heads to the saucepan. Sauté for 10 minutes. Add the limes, cloves and liqueur and flambé. Add the saffron and wait 1 minute. Stir in the tomato paste, fish broth, 2 teaspoons salt and bouquet garni. Bring to a boil, skimming the foam frequently. Reduce the heat; simmer until reduced by 1/3 to make lobster stock. Fry the snapper fillets in olive oil in a skillet until crispy. Melt 1 tablespoon butter in a large stockpot. Add the garlic, lobster tail meat, shrimp and mussels. Sauté for 4 minutes. Stir in 1 teaspoon Tabasco sauce. Strain the stock through wet cheesecloth. Bring the stock to a gentle boil and season with salt, pepper and Tabasco sauce. Place 1 snapper fillet in each of 12 warmed large soup bowls. Top with the shallots. Divide the seafood evenly among the bowls. Pour the stock over the seafood. Garnish with parsley.

Recipe provided by Hubert Sandot, Martinique Bistro

Crab Meat and Artichoke Carrollton

YIELD: 8 SERVINGS

½   CUP (1 STICK) BUTTER
½   CUP FLOUR
¼   CUP CHOPPED GREEN ONIONS
2   TABLESPOONS CHOPPED PARSLEY
2   CUPS HEAVY CREAM
¾   CUP DRY WHITE WINE
2   TEASPOONS SALT
¼   TEASPOON CAYENNE PEPPER

½   TEASPOON WHITE PEPPER
2   TABLESPOONS LEMON JUICE
2   POUNDS CRAB MEAT, FLAKED
1   (14-OUNCE) CAN ARTICHOKE
    HEARTS, DRAINED, SLICED
8   OUNCES FRESH MUSHROOMS,
    SLICED

Melt the butter in a medium saucepan over medium heat. Add the flour and cook for 5 minutes, stirring constantly. Add the green onions and parsley. Cook for 2 minutes, stirring constantly. Stir in the cream gradually. Add the wine, salt, cayenne pepper and white pepper, stirring until smooth and thickened. Remove from heat and let cool to lukewarm. Stir in the lemon juice. Spread the crab meat in a baking dish. Spoon ⅓ of the sauce on top. Layer with the artichokes. Cover with another ⅓ of the sauce. Layer with the mushrooms and top with the remaining sauce. Bake at 350 degrees for 35 minutes. Serve by itself or over pasta.

CARROLLTON

THE AREA THAT BECAME THE TOWN OF CARROLLTON WAS NAMED AFTER GENERAL WILLIAM CARROLL, WHO FOUGHT IN THE WAR OF 1812. CARROLLTON WAS PART OF THE LAND GRANTED TO JEAN BAPTISTE LE MOYNE, BIENVILLE, THE FOUNDER OF NEW ORLEANS, IN 1719. THE AREA WAS ORIGINALLY MILES OF PLANTATIONS AND GARDENS, AS WELL AS SWAMPLAND. THE TOWN OF CARROLLTON DEVELOPED ALONG WITH THE CARROLLTON RAILROAD IN 1835 AND WAS INCORPORATED IN 1845. IT SERVED AS THE PARISH SEAT OF JEFFERSON PARISH FROM 1852 UNTIL 1874. IN 1874, CARROLLTON WAS ANNEXED BY NEW ORLEANS TO BECOME THE SEVENTH DISTRICT.

Crab Cakes with Basil Aïoli

1	POUND FRESH LUMP CRAB MEAT, FLAKED	1	TABLESPOON MILK
1⅓	CUPS SOFT BREAD CRUMBS	1	TEASPOON HOT SAUCE
⅓	CUP FINELY CHOPPED GREEN ONIONS	½	TEASPOON SALT
⅓	CUP FINELY CHOPPED FRESH PARSLEY	½	TEASPOON PEPPER
		4	EGG WHITES, LIGHTLY BEATEN
2	TABLESPOONS LEMON JUICE	1⅓	CUPS SOFT BREAD CRUMBS
		2	TABLESPOONS VEGETABLE OIL
			LEMON WEDGES

Mix first 10 ingredients in a bowl. Shape into 8 patties. Coat the patties with 1⅓ cups bread crumbs. Heat half the oil in a skillet and fry 4 patties for 3 minutes per side or until golden brown. Repeat process. Serve with Basil Aïoli (at left) and lemon wedges.

Eggplant Beauvoir

YIELD: 6 TO 8 SERVINGS

2	EGGS	½	CUP VEGETABLE OIL
1	CUP MILK	1	POUND LUMP CRAB MEAT, FLAKED
2	CUPS FLOUR		
	SALT AND PEPPER TO TASTE	24	SLICES PROVOLONE CHEESE
2	LARGE EGGPLANT, SLICED INTO THIN ROUNDS	6	CUPS SPICY TOMATO SAUCE
		4	CUPS HOLLANDAISE SAUCE

Beat the eggs and milk in a bowl. Mix the flour, salt and pepper in a shallow dish. Dip the eggplant in the egg mixture, then the flour. Fry the eggplant in the oil in a skillet just until soft and golden brown; do not overcook. Overlap half the slices in a single layer in a greased 10x14-inch baking dish. Sprinkle with half the crab meat and top with half the cheese slices. Cover with half the tomato sauce. Repeat the layers. Bake at 400 degrees for 45 minutes. Cut into squares and place on serving plates. Top with the hollandaise sauce.

BASIL AÏOLI

¾ CUP HOMEMADE MAYONNAISE
⅓ CUP MINCED FRESH BASIL LEAVES
1 TABLESPOON LEMON JUICE
1½ TEASPOONS MINCED GARLIC
1½ TEASPOONS GRATED LEMON ZEST
SALT AND PEPPER TO TASTE

COMBINE THE MAYONNAISE, BASIL, LEMON JUICE, GARLIC AND LEMON ZEST IN A BOWL AND MIX WELL. SEASON WITH SALT AND PEPPER. COVER AND CHILL FOR 1 HOUR OR LONGER.
YIELD: 1 CUP

Tempura Soft-Shells with Oriental Salad

Yield: 4 servings

1	CUP SUGAR		1	TABLESPOON OLIVE OIL
½	CUP RICE WINE VINEGAR		2	TABLESPOONS SESAME OIL
¼	CUP FRESH ORANGE JUICE		1	TABLESPOON SOY SAUCE
¼	CUP FRESH LEMON JUICE		2	TABLESPOONS CHOPPED FRESH
1	TABLESPOON OLIVE OIL			CILANTRO
½	CUP THINLY SLICED RED BELL PEPPER		¼	CUP CHOPPED PEANUTS
½	CUP THINLY SLICED YELLOW BELL PEPPER		4	LARGE SOFT-SHELL CRABS
¼	CUP CHOPPED RED ONION			VEGETABLE OIL
	SALT AND FRESHLY GROUND PEPPER TO		⅔	CUP FLOUR
	TASTE		⅓	CUP CORNSTARCH
½	CUP THINLY SLICED CHINESE CABBAGE		1	EGG
2	TEASPOONS CHOPPED GARLIC		2	TABLESPOONS CLUB SODA
4	OUNCES ANGEL HAIR PASTA, COOKED,			PARSLEY FOR GARNISH
	DRAINED			

Bring the sugar, vinegar, orange juice and lemon juice to a boil in a nonreactive saucepan. Boil until reduced by ¾ or until the mixture is syrupy. Pour into a bowl and let cool completely; set aside. Heat 1 tablespoon olive oil in a skillet over medium heat. Add the bell peppers and onion. Season with salt and pepper. Sauté for 2 minutes. Add the cabbage and sauté for 2 minutes. Season with salt and pepper. Remove from the heat and stir in the garlic. Remove the mixture to a medium bowl; let cool. Toss the hot cooked pasta with 1 tablespoon olive oil. Add to the cabbage mixture; toss well. Add the sesame oil, soy sauce, cilantro and peanuts. Season with salt and pepper; toss well. Cut the crabs across the face with kitchen shears. Remove the eye sockets and lower mouth. Season with salt and pepper. Heat 6 inches of vegetable oil to 360 degrees in a large heavy deep stockpot or deep fryer. Blend the flour, cornstarch, egg and club soda in a bowl. Season with salt and pepper. Dip each crab in the batter; shake off any excess. Hold the top of each crab with tongs and drag the legs through the hot oil for 5 seconds to allow the individual legs to fry separately. Turn the crabs over carefully and allow the tops to fry for 2 to 3 minutes or until golden brown. Turn the crabs over and fry for 2 to 3 minutes. Drain on paper towels. Adjust seasonings. Mound the cabbage mixture in the center of a serving platter. Arrange the crabs around the cabbage. Drizzle with the citrus mixture and garnish with parsley.

Recipe provided by Emeril Lagasse, Delmonico Restaurant and Bar

Crab Meat Ravioli with Lemon Basil Butter

YIELD: 5 SERVINGS

LEMON BASIL BUTTER

¼ CUP WHITE WINE
¼ CUP SEASONED RICE VINEGAR
2 TABLESPOONS FRESH
LEMON JUICE
1 SHALLOT, MINCED
2 TABLESPOONS HEAVY CREAM
2 CUPS (4 STICKS) BUTTER,
CUT INTO CUBES
2 TABLESPOONS SLICED
FRESH BASIL LEAVES
SALT AND PEPPER TO TASTE

COOK THE WINE, VINEGAR, LEMON JUICE AND SHALLOT IN A SAUCEPAN OVER MEDIUM HEAT UNTIL THE LIQUID IS REDUCED AND THE MIXTURE IS SYRUPY, STIRRING CONSTANTLY. ADD THE CREAM. COOK UNTIL REDUCED BY ½. REDUCE THE HEAT TO LOW. WHISK IN THE BUTTER A FEW CUBES AT A TIME, MELTING THE BUTTER BEFORE ADDING MORE. STRAIN THE SAUCE. STIR IN THE BASIL. SEASON WITH SALT AND PEPPER.
YIELD: 5 SERVINGS

¼	CUP OLIVE OIL	1	POUND LUMP CRAB MEAT, FLAKED
1	YELLOW ONION, FINELY CHOPPED		
1	SUMMER SQUASH, CHOPPED	½	CUP DRY BREAD CRUMBS
1	ZUCCHINI, FINELY CHOPPED	6	EGGS, LIGHTLY BEATEN
1	BUNCH GREEN ONIONS, CHOPPED	4	POUNDS SEMOLINA FLOUR
2	TEASPOONS CHOPPED MIXED FRESH HERBS	1	POUND ALL-PURPOSE FLOUR
		1	TEASPOON SALT
1	TEASPOON CREOLE SEASONING	1	EGG
	SALT AND WHITE PEPPER TO TASTE	2	TEASPOONS WATER
			CORNMEAL

For the filling, heat the olive oil in a saucepan over medium heat. Add the onion and sauté for 5 minutes or until translucent. Add the squash and zucchini and sauté for 5 to 7 minutes. Add the green onions, mixed herbs and Creole seasoning. Season with salt and white pepper to taste. Sauté for 5 minutes. Pour the mixture into a colander; drain well. Remove to a bowl; cool. Stir in the crab meat and bread crumbs. Season with salt and white pepper to taste. For the ravioli, place 6 eggs in a measuring cup and add enough water to measure 2 cups. Combine all the flour, 1 teaspoon salt and egg mixture in a bowl. Mix to form a dough. Process the dough through a pasta machine or roll out on a floured surface until thin. Cut the dough into 2 equal sheets. Mix 1 egg with 2 teaspoons water. Brush 1 sheet of dough with the egg mixture. Place balls of filling 2½ inches apart on top of the sheet. Cover with the other sheet of dough. Cut through the layers between the filling to make filling-enclosed squares. To seal, press the edges of each square, removing any air pockets. Place the ravioli on a baking sheet dusted with cornmeal. Sprinkle cornmeal on the ravioli. Add the ravioli to salted boiling water in a stockpot and boil for 4 minutes; drain well. Toss the ravioli and Lemon Basil Butter (at left) in a bowl.

Recipe provided by Haley Gabel, Bacco

Crawfish Ravioli

Yield: 6 servings

1½	TEASPOONS UNSALTED BUTTER	1	TEASPOON MINCED FRESH TARRAGON
1½	TEASPOONS FLOUR	½	TEASPOON DIJON MUSTARD
½	CUP HALF-AND-HALF OR WHOLE MILK		SALT AND PEPPER TO TASTE
8	OUNCES FROZEN CRAWFISH TAILS, THAWED, SHELLED, CHOPPED	48	WONTON WRAPPERS
			FLOUR
1	LARGE SCALLION, WHITE PART ONLY, MINCED	1⅓	CUPS SHALLOT CREAM

Melt the butter in a medium saucepan over medium-high heat. Add the flour and whisk for 30 seconds. Add the half-and-half gradually. Whisk for 1 minute or until very thick. Remove from the heat and let cool. Fold in the crawfish, scallion, tarragon and mustard. Season with salt and pepper. Place 1 wonton wrapper on a flour-dusted work surface. Place a dollop of the crawfish filling in the center. Cover with another wonton wrapper. Pinch the edges with wet fingers to seal. Repeat with remaining wonton wrappers and filling. Add the ravioli to a saucepan of boiling salted water. Boil for 5 to 7 minutes; drain well. Place 4 ravioli on each of 6 serving plates. Pour the Shallot Cream (below) over the ravioli and serve.

Shallot Cream

Yield: 1⅓ cups

2	TABLESPOONS UNSALTED BUTTER	2	TEASPOONS DIJON MUSTARD
1	LARGE SHALLOT, MINCED	1	TABLESPOON MINCED FRESH
1	CUP HEAVY CREAM		FLAT-LEAF PARSLEY
⅓	CUP SHRIMP OR CLAM BROTH		SALT AND WHITE PEPPER TO TASTE

Melt the butter in a medium saucepan. Add the shallot and sauté for 5 minutes or until soft. Stir in the cream and shrimp broth gradually. Add the mustard and stir for a few minutes to mix well. Stir in the parsley and season with salt and pepper.

Fried Crawfish Rémoulade on the Half-Shell

YIELD: 6 SERVINGS

3	BAKING POTATOES, BAKED, COOLED TO ROOM TEMPERATURE	1	POUND CRAWFISH TAILS, SHELLED, DRAINED
	VEGETABLE OIL		CHOPPED FRESH PARSLEY AND LEMON WEDGES FOR GARNISH
	FLOUR		
	SALT AND PEPPER TO TASTE		HORSERADISH RÉMOULADE

Slice the potatoes and place in a bowl. Microwave on Medium-High for 2 minutes. Heat the oil in a deep skillet and add the potato slices. Fry until lightly browned. Drain on paper towels. Season flour with salt and pepper in a bowl. Coat the crawfish tails in the flour and shake to remove any excess. Heat additional oil in the skillet. Fry the crawfish, in 4 batches, for 45 seconds or until golden brown. Drain on paper towels. Arrange the potatoes on 6 serving plates. Top with the crawfish. Spoon the Horseradish Rémoulade (below) over the crawfish. Garnish with chopped parsley and lemon wedges.

Horseradish Rémoulade

YIELD: 6 SERVINGS

3	TABLESPOONS PREPARED HORSERADISH, DRAINED	1	TEASPOON CAYENNE PEPPER
		1	TEASPOON CHILI SAUCE (OPTIONAL)
3	TABLESPOONS CREOLE MUSTARD	2/3	CUP VEGETABLE OIL
6	TABLESPOONS VINEGAR	4	GREEN ONIONS, FINELY CHOPPED
2	TEASPOONS PAPRIKA	2	RIBS CELERY, FINELY CHOPPED
1½	TEASPOONS SALT		

Combine the horseradish, mustard, vinegar, paprika, salt, cayenne pepper and chili sauce in a food processor. Process until mixed. Add the oil in a stream, processing constantly until mixed. Pour into a bowl and stir in the green onions and celery. Cover and chill for up to 24 hours.

Crawfish and Caramelized Onions

YIELD: 4 SERVINGS

1	TABLESPOON OLIVE OIL	1	TEASPOON HERBES DE PROVENCE
1	LARGE YELLOW ONION, THINLY SLICED		SALT AND BLACK PEPPER TO TASTE
2	GARLIC CLOVES, MINCED		CRUSHED RED PEPPER TO TASTE
1	POUND CRAWFISH TAILS, SHELLED		GRATED PARMESAN CHEESE
2	TABLESPOONS SHERRY		TO TASTE
1	TOMATO, CHOPPED		FRESH PARSLEY SPRIGS
½	CUP CLAM JUICE OR FISH STOCK		FOR GARNISH
½	CUP CHOPPED FRESH PARSLEY		

Heat the olive oil in a large skillet. Add the onion and cook over low heat for 10 minutes or until deep golden brown, stirring occasionally. Add the garlic, crawfish, sherry and tomato and simmer for 3 minutes, stirring occasionally. Stir in the clam juice and parsley. Simmer for 1 minute or until heated through. Add the herbes de Provence and season with salt, black pepper and crushed red pepper. Serve on Grilled Parmesan Polenta (at right) and sprinkle with Parmesan cheese. Garnish with fresh parsley sprigs.

GRILLED PARMESAN POLENTA

2¾ CUPS WATER
¾ CUP YELLOW CORNMEAL
½ TEASPOON SALT
½ CUP SHREDDED PART-SKIM MOZZARELLA CHEESE
2 TABLESPOONS GRATED PARMESAN CHEESE

COMBINE THE WATER, CORNMEAL AND SALT IN A 2-QUART MICROWAVE-SAFE DISH. COVER AND MICROWAVE ON HIGH FOR 6 MINUTES. STIR ONCE, COVER AND MICROWAVE ON HIGH FOR 6 MORE MINUTES. STIR IN THE MOZZARELLA CHEESE, COVER AND LET STAND FOR 2 MINUTES. SPREAD IN A LIGHTLY GREASED 9-INCH ROUND PAN. LET COOL SLIGHTLY. COVER AND CHILL FOR 1 TO 8 HOURS. CUT THE POLENTA INTO 4 WEDGES AND REMOVE FROM THE PAN. PREPARE THE GRILL. GRILL THE WEDGES OVER MEDIUM HEAT FOR 15 MINUTES OR UNTIL BROWNED AND HEATED THROUGH. SPRINKLE WITH THE PARMESAN CHEESE. YIELD: 4 SERVINGS

Shrimp and Shiitake Cakes

Yield: 8 servings

1	TABLESPOON OLIVE OIL	6	TABLESPOONS CHICKEN BROTH
¼	CUP CHOPPED ONION	3	DASHES OF WORCESTERSHIRE SAUCE
¼	CUP BUTTON MUSHROOMS	2	TABLESPOONS CHOPPED GREEN ONIONS
¼	CUP SHIITAKE MUSHROOMS	4	CUPS COOKED BASMATI RICE
1	TABLESPOON MINCED GARLIC	1	CUP BREAD CRUMBS
1	POUND UNCOOKED MEDIUM SHRIMP, PEELED, DEVEINED	2	EGGS, LIGHTLY BEATEN
			FLOUR
2	TEASPOONS SALT	1	EGG
½	TEASPOON BLACK PEPPER	2	TEASPOONS WATER
½	TEASPOON ONION POWDER		BREAD CRUMBS
½	TEASPOON GARLIC POWDER		VEGETABLE OIL
½	TEASPOON DRIED BASIL		MIXED GREENS
⅛	TEASPOON DRIED OREGANO, OR TO TASTE		CHOPPED GREEN ONIONS
⅛	TEASPOON DRIED THYME, OR TO TASTE		FOR GARNISH
⅛	TEASPOON PAPRIKA, OR TO TASTE		

Heat the olive oil in a large skillet. Add the onion and sauté until golden brown. Add all the mushrooms and garlic and sauté until the garlic is soft. Add the shrimp and sauté until pink. Stir in the salt, black pepper, onion powder, garlic powder, basil, oregano, thyme, paprika and broth. Cook until the liquid is reduced by ⅓ to ½, stirring constantly. Stir in Worcestershire sauce and 2 tablespoons green onions. Remove from the heat and add the rice. Toss to mix. Allow the mixture to cool to room temperature and then coarsely chop by hand or in a food processor. Remove to a large bowl. Stir in 1 cup bread crumbs and 2 eggs. Form into 3-ounce patties. Place flour in a bowl. Mix 1 egg and the water in a separate bowl. Place bread crumbs in another bowl. Coat the patties in the flour, then dip in the egg mixture and then coat in the bread crumbs. Heat vegetable oil to 350 degrees in a large skillet. Fry the patties until golden brown. Serve on a bed of mixed greens and top with Roasted Pepper and Cilantro Mayonnaise (page 91). Garnish with chopped green onions.

Recipe provided by Randy Barlow, Kelsey's Restaurant

Roasted Pepper and Cilantro Mayonnaise

1	RED BELL PEPPER	1/4	TEASPOON PAPRIKA, OR TO TASTE
4	EGGS	1/4	CUP CHOPPED GREEN ONIONS
1/2	TEASPOON MINCED GARLIC	2	TABLESPOONS LEMON JUICE
3	TEASPOONS SALT	3	DASHES OF WORCESTERSHIRE SAUCE
3/4	TEASPOON BLACK PEPPER	1	BUNCH CILANTRO, CHOPPED
3/4	TEASPOON ONION POWDER	1/4	CUP CREOLE MUSTARD
3/4	TEASPOON GARLIC POWDER	1/8	TEASPOON SUGAR, OR TO TASTE
3/4	TEASPOON DRIED BASIL	1	TEASPOON RED WINE VINEGAR
1/4	TEASPOON DRIED OREGANO, OR TO TASTE		OLIVE OIL OR CANOLA OIL
1/4	TEASPOON DRIED THYME, OR TO TASTE	1	CUP BUTTERMILK

Roast the bell pepper directly over a gas flame or under the broiler until evenly charred. Wrap in a paper bag and let stand for 10 minutes. Peel, seed and chop. Combine the bell pepper, eggs, garlic, salt, black pepper, onion powder, garlic powder, basil, oregano, thyme, paprika, green onions, lemon juice, Worcestershire sauce, cilantro, mustard, sugar and vinegar in a food processor. Process until well mixed. Add the oil in a stream, processing constantly until the mixture thickens and is the consistency of mayonnaise. Pour into a bowl and stir in the buttermilk.

Seafood St. Louis

YIELD: 8 SERVINGS

4	MEDIUM EGGPLANT, SPLIT LENGTHWISE (ABOUT 1 POUND EACH)	1/4	TEASPOON CAYENNE PEPPER
2	CUPS WATER	1	CUP BREAD CRUMBS
1	TEASPOON SALT	2	TO 3 TROUT FILLETS, COOKED, FLAKED
4	TABLESPOONS VEGETABLE OIL		SALT AND BLACK PEPPER TO TASTE
2	ONIONS, CHOPPED (ABOUT 2 CUPS)	2	TABLESPOONS DRY BREAD CRUMBS
1	POUND UNCOOKED LARGE SHRIMP, PEELED, DEVEINED, COARSELY CHOPPED		

Arrange the eggplant on a large baking sheet and pierce with a fork. Place under a preheated broiler and broil for 4 minutes. Turn over and broil for another 4 minutes. Scoop out the pulp, leaving a 1/2-inch thick shell. Purée the pulp in a food processor. Combine the pulp, water and salt in a saucepan. Bring to a boil; reduce the heat. Simmer, covered, for 15 minutes. Uncover and simmer for 5 minutes or until the liquid has evaporated. Set aside. Brush the inside of the eggplant shells with 1 tablespoon of the oil and place on a baking sheet. Bake at 375 degrees for 20 minutes or until the shells are tender but still hold their shape. Heat the remaining 3 tablespoons oil in a skillet over medium-high heat. Add the onions and sauté for 5 minutes or until soft. Add the eggplant pulp, shrimp and cayenne pepper and cook for 4 minutes or until the shrimp are cooked through. Remove from the heat and stir in 1 cup bread crumbs and the cooked trout. Season with salt and black pepper. Fill the eggplant shells with the seafood mixture. Sprinkle with 2 tablespoons bread crumbs. Bake at 375 degrees for 30 minutes or until heated through. Let stand for 5 minutes before serving.

The Royal Meal

YIELD: 4 TO 6 SERVINGS

4	OUNCES SMOKED CRAWFISH	¼	CUP FLOUR
4	OUNCES SMOKED SHRIMP	2	CUPS HALF-AND-HALF
2	TABLESPOONS OLIVE OIL		GRATED PARMESAN CHEESE
1	CUP FINELY CHOPPED		TO TASTE
	WHITE ONION	2	TABLESPOONS CHOPPED
2	GARLIC CLOVES, MINCED		FRESH PARSLEY
1	TO 2 CUPS DRY WHITE WINE	2	TABLESPOONS CHOPPED
1	TABLESPOON TOMATO PASTE		GREEN ONIONS
4	OUNCES SKINLESS BONELESS	1	POUND GNOCCHI OR
	CHICKEN BREAST, CUT		BOW TIE PASTA
	INTO PIECES		CHOPPED FRESH PARSLEY
4	OUNCES CHOPPED TASSO		AND CHOPPED GREEN ONIONS
	(SEE NOTE, PAGE 187)		FOR GARNISH
2	TO 3 TABLESPOONS		
	UNSALTED BUTTER		

Rinse the crawfish and shrimp and drain well. Heat the olive oil in a large skillet. Add the onion and sauté until nearly translucent. Add the garlic and sauté for 5 to 6 minutes. Add some of the wine as needed for cooking liquid. Add the tomato paste and chicken and sauté until the chicken is cooked through. Stir in the tasso, crawfish and shrimp. Remove from the heat. Melt the butter in a saucepan and stir in the flour. Cook over medium heat for 5 minutes, stirring constantly. Add the half-and-half gradually and stir until thickened. Add enough of the remaining wine to reach desired consistency. Add the Parmesan cheese and stir until melted. Combine the sauce with the seafood mixture in a large saucepan. Stir in 2 tablespoons chopped parsley and 2 tablespoons chopped green onions. Cook the pasta according to package directions and drain. Arrange the pasta on serving plates and top with the seafood sauce. Garnish with chopped parsley and chopped green onions.

Recipe provided by House of Windsor

THE PORT OF NEW ORLEANS

THE HISTORY OF THE PORT OF NEW ORLEANS DATES BACK TO HERNANDO DESOTO'S CLAIM OF THE MISSISSIPPI BASIN FOR SPAIN IN 1541. THIS CLAIM HAD LAPSED BY 1682 WHEN RENE ROBERT CAVALIER, SIEUR DE LA SALLE, TOOK POSSESSION OF THIS AREA FOR FRANCE, NAMING THE COLONY "LOUISIANE" IN HONOR OF LOUIS XIV. BY THE LATE 1700S, CARGO WAS TRAVELING DOWN THE MISSISSIPPI FROM THE OHIO RIVER VALLEY TO THE PORT OF NEW ORLEANS. THE LOUISIANA PURCHASE IN 1803 GAVE AMERICA PERMANENT ACCESS TO THE MISSISSIPPI VIA THIS PORT. OVER THE YEARS, THE PORT OF NEW ORLEANS HAS CONTINUED TO DEVELOP AND TO MODERNIZE ITS FACILITIES. TODAY IT IS THE NUMBER ONE U.S. COFFEE PORT AND SITE OF THE WORLD'S LARGEST BULK GREEN COFFEE HANDLING PLANT.

Poultry

Poultry

Thomas Toby House
2340 Prytania Street

Known as Toby's Corner, this lovely house is perhaps the oldest in the Garden District. In 1838 Henry Lockett purchased this lot in the recently subdivided Livaudais Plantation on behalf of Clemence Toby, wife of Thomas Toby. Thomas had relocated to New Orleans from Philadelphia in 1817 and become a successful commission merchant and wheelwright. He was prominent in the affairs of the Republic of Texas. In 1836 he was authorized by that government to raise funds through the sale of Texas lands and to purchase arms for the new republic. Thomas and his brother, Samuel, were subsequently declared sole agents for Texas in the United States. However, loans Thomas made to finance the Texas Revolution were not paid off and, consequently, he had to rely on his wife's funds to build this house in 1838.

❖

Tradition asserts that Toby imported the building materials from Philadelphia on his father's ships. During this time in New Orleans, agricultural products commonly were exported and building materials imported. The sizable importation of building materials to New Orleans is well documented in the lawsuit brought against the Baroness Pontalba by her general contractor, Samuel Stewart, for compensation allegedly owed for the construction of the historic Pontalba Apartments.

❖

The Toby House was built with a *rez-de-chaussée* and a *premier étage*. The *rez-de-chaussée* was a "basement" at grade level and originally was used for utilitarian purposes. The *premier étage*, literally translated as "first floor," was actually the second story and was used for most household functions.

❖

After Toby's death in 1849, his wife continued to live in the house. In October 1855, she entered into a contract with builders Lilly & Woods for the improvements and additions that give the house its Greek Revival appearance. Three years later Mrs. Toby lost the house as the result of a lawsuit filed against her by William Hepp, her agent and superintendent for the 1855 renovation. At a sheriff's sale the house was bought by Thomas Dugan, whose family retains ownership to this day. It became the JLNO Show House IV in 1984, and the present owners are Mr. and Mrs. Thomas D. Westfeldt, II.

Roast Chicken with Herbs

Yield: 4 servings

1	(3- TO 4-POUND) CHICKEN	3/4	TEASPOON SALT
1½	TEASPOONS CHOPPED FRESH ROSEMARY	½	TEASPOON BLACK PEPPER
1½	TEASPOONS CHOPPED FRESH THYME	4½	TEASPOONS OLIVE OIL
1½	TEASPOONS CHOPPED FRESH OREGANO OR MARJORAM	2	GARLIC CLOVES, MINCED

Rinse the chicken inside and out with cold water. Remove the 2 pockets of fat just inside the cavity. Pat dry with a paper towel. Combine the rosemary, thyme, oregano, salt, pepper, olive oil and garlic in a small bowl and mix well to make a paste. Place the chicken on a work surface. Make a slit in the chicken skin and pull back the skin. Rub the paste all over the meat and replace the skin. Set the chicken on a rack in a roasting pan with the breast side up. Roast at 350 degrees for 1¼ hours or until cooked through. Baste the chicken occasionally during roasting. Remove from the oven and cover with foil. Let stand for 20 minutes before carving to seal in the juices.

Chicken aux Courants

YIELD: 4 SERVINGS

1   (4-POUND) CHICKEN, CUT UP
    SALT AND PEPPER TO TASTE
½   CUP RED WINE VINEGAR
½   CUP PACKED BROWN SUGAR
¼   CUP OLIVE OIL
12 SPANISH OLIVES, PITTED
3   GARLIC CLOVES, PRESSED
½   CUP WHITE WINE

½   CUP WATER
2   TABLESPOONS FRESH TARRAGON
    LEAVES
2   HEADS OF GARLIC, SEPARATED
    INTO CLOVES, PEELED
1   TABLESPOON SOY SAUCE
½   CUP DRIED CURRANTS

Season the chicken with salt and pepper and arrange in a glass dish. Combine the vinegar, brown sugar, olive oil, olives and 3 cloves of pressed garlic in a food processor. Process for 30 seconds. Add the wine and water and pour over the chicken. Cover and chill for 2 to 24 hours. Spread the tarragon leaves over the bottom of a large roasting pan. Remove the chicken pieces from the marinade and place in a single layer on top of the tarragon. Reserve ½ cup of the marinade and discard the rest. Arrange the whole garlic cloves around the chicken. Bake, covered, at 425 degrees for 30 minutes. Uncover and bake for 10 minutes or until cooked through. Place under the broiler for 1 to 2 minutes if necessary for browning. Remove the chicken and garlic to a large heatproof serving dish and keep warm. Strain all but a few of the tarragon leaves from the pan juices and pour the juices into a saucepan. Add the reserved marinade, soy sauce and currants. Bring to a boil and boil for 5 minutes. Pour over the chicken and garlic and serve immediately.

RECONSTRUCTION IN NEW ORLEANS

THE CITY SUFFERED GREATLY DURING THE CIVIL WAR AND RECONSTRUCTION, BUT THE HARD TIMES ALSO BROUGHT OUT THE FEISTY NATURE OF ITS PEOPLE. NEW ORLEANIANS WERE OPENLY HOSTILE TO UNION GENERAL BENJAMIN "BEAST" BUTLER, WHO RULED THE CITY DURING OCCUPATION. WELL-BRED NEW ORLEANS LADIES OFTEN SANG SOUTHERN SONGS IN THE PRESENCE OF YANKEE OFFICERS AND REFUSED TO REMAIN IN ANY ROOM THAT A YANKEE ENTERED. AFTER THE WAR, ALMOST EVERY LOCAL BANK FAILED, AND HOMEOWNERS PAID EXORBITANT TAXES. STILL, NEW ORLEANIANS HELD ONTO WHAT THEY HAD. THE RESULT IS THAT MANY OF THE CITY'S ANTEBELLUM STRUCTURES ARE STANDING TODAY.

Poussins Prytania

YIELD: 2 SERVINGS

3	TABLESPOONS UNSALTED BUTTER, SOFTENED	1/4	TEASPOON PEPPER
3	TABLESPOONS CHOPPED FRESH CILANTRO	2	(1-POUND) POUSSINS (YOUNG CHICKENS)
1/2	TEASPOON GRATED LEMON ZEST	1	TABLESPOON UNSALTED BUTTER
1/4	TEASPOON GROUND CUMIN		SALT AND PEPPER TO TASTE
1/4	TEASPOON SALT	1/3	CUP DRY WHITE WINE

Mix 3 tablespoons butter, cilantro, lemon zest, cumin, 1/4 teaspoon salt and
1/4 teaspoon pepper in a small bowl. Trim the necks of the chickens flush with the bodies
if necessary. Rinse the chickens inside and out with cold water. Pat dry. Slide your
fingers between the skin and the meat to loosen the skin, starting at the neck end. Work
carefully so as not to tear the skin. Place 1/4 of the butter mixture under the skin of
each breast half. Spread the butter evenly by pressing on the outside of the skin. Place the
chickens in a roasting pan just large enough to hold them. Melt 1 tablespoon
butter and brush onto the chickens. Season with salt and pepper. Roast in the upper
third of the oven at 425 degrees for 45 minutes or until cooked through. Remove
to a platter and cover with foil to keep warm. Add the wine to the roasting pan
and deglaze over medium heat. Remove from the heat and skim off the fat.
Serve the sauce with the chickens.

Honey Praline Fried Chicken

YIELD: 6 TO 8 SERVINGS

2	(2½- TO 3-POUND) CHICKENS, CUT INTO PIECES	½	TEASPOON GARLIC POWDER
4	CUPS BUTTERMILK	¼	TEASPOON CAYENNE PEPPER
1	CUP SELF-RISING FLOUR	⅛	TEASPOON BLACK PEPPER
¾	TEASPOON SALT		VEGETABLE OIL
		2	CUPS HONEY PRALINE SAUCE

Rinse chicken pieces and pat dry. Pour the buttermilk into a large bowl. Add the chicken and stir to coat. Cover and chill for 1½ hours. Combine the flour, salt, garlic powder, cayenne pepper and black pepper in a shallow dish. Remove the chicken from the buttermilk. Coat with the flour mixture, shaking off any excess. Let the chicken stand at room temperature for 20 minutes. Heat ½ to ¾ inch oil to 375 degrees in a large heavy skillet. Fry the chicken in batches for 7 minutes per side or until golden brown and cooked through. Drain on paper towels. Arrange on a serving platter and pour the Honey Praline Sauce (below) over the chicken. Serve immediately.

Honey Praline Sauce

YIELD: 2 CUPS

1	CUP (2 STICKS) BUTTER	½	CUP COARSELY CHOPPED PECANS
½	CUP HONEY		

Melt the butter in a saucepan. Stir in the honey and bring to a boil. Add the pecans and reduce the heat. Simmer for 15 minutes, stirring occasionally.

Chicken Marigny

Yield: 10 servings

½	CUP CAPERS	6	BAY LEAVES
1	HEAD OF GARLIC, SEPARATED INTO		SALT AND PEPPER TO TASTE
	CLOVES, PEELED, MINCED	4	CHICKENS, QUARTERED
¼	CUP DRIED OREGANO	1	CUP PACKED BROWN SUGAR
½	CUP RED WINE VINEGAR	1	CUP WHITE WINE
½	CUP OLIVE OIL	¼	CUP FINELY CHOPPED ITALIAN
1	CUP PITTED PRUNES		PARSLEY
½	CUP PITTED SPANISH OLIVES		

Drain the capers, reserving ½ teaspoon of the liquid. Mix the garlic, oregano, vinegar, olive oil, prunes, olives, capers, reserved liquid and bay leaves in a large bowl. Season with salt and pepper. Add the chicken and stir to coat. Cover and chill for 8 hours. Remove the chicken from the marinade and arrange in a single layer in 2 large shallow baking pans. Spoon the marinade evenly over the chicken. Sprinkle with the brown sugar and pour the wine around the edges of the chicken. Bake at 350 degrees for 50 to 60 minutes or until cooked through. Baste frequently with the pan juices during cooking. Discard the bay leaves. Remove the chicken, prunes, olives and capers with a slotted spoon to a serving platter. Spoon some of the pan juices over the chicken and sprinkle with parsley. Serve hot or cold.

Roquefort Chicken

YIELD: 4 SERVINGS

3	TABLESPOONS OLIVE OIL	5	GARLIC CLOVES, MINCED
1	(3½-POUND) CHICKEN, CUT INTO 8 PIECES	1	TEASPOON HERBES DE PROVENCE
1	TEASPOON CAYENNE PEPPER	1	CUP CRUMBLED ROQUEFORT CHEESE
1	CUP HEAVY CREAM		BLACK PEPPER TO TASTE
¼	CUP DRY WHITE WINE		CHOPPED FRESH CHIVES FOR GARNISH

Heat the olive oil in a large skillet over medium-high heat. Sprinkle the chicken pieces with the cayenne pepper. Fry the chicken for 8 minutes or until golden brown on all sides. Add the cream, wine, garlic and herbes de Provence. Cover and simmer for 20 minutes or until the chicken is tender and cooked through. Turn the chicken once during cooking. Remove the chicken to a serving platter and keep warm. Boil the cooking liquid for 5 minutes or until it is the consistency of a sauce. Reduce the heat and add the cheese. Whisk until the cheese is melted and the sauce is smooth. Season generously with black pepper. Pour over the chicken. Garnish with chives.

Bourbon Street Bird

YIELD: 12 SERVINGS

1	CUP (2 STICKS) BUTTER OR MARGARINE	½	TEASPOON DRIED THYME
1	CUP DRY WHITE WINE	2	TABLESPOONS CHOPPED PARSLEY
	JUICE OF 1 LEMON	12	CHICKEN BREASTS
¼	CUP WORCESTERSHIRE SAUCE	¾	CUP BREAD CRUMBS
1	TEASPOON SALT	½	CUP FRESHLY GRATED PARMESAN CHEESE
½	TEASPOON CAYENNE PEPPER		

Melt the butter in a saucepan. Add the wine, lemon juice, Worcestershire sauce, salt, cayenne pepper, thyme and parsley. Cook over medium-high heat until the mixture comes to a boil, stirring constantly. Remove from the heat. Rinse the chicken breasts and pat dry. Arrange in a large baking dish. Sprinkle with the bread crumbs and then the Parmesan cheese. Pour the sauce over the top. Bake at 375 degrees for 50 to 60 minutes or until cooked through.

Chicken Brie

1	CUP FLOUR	4	JARS HOT PEPPER JELLY
	SALT AND PEPPER TO TASTE	2	MEDIUM ROUNDS BRIE CHEESE, CUT INTO
10	CHICKEN BREASTS		2-INCH PIECES
3	TABLESPOONS VEGETABLE OIL	1	POUND ALMONDS, TOASTED
1	TABLESPOON BUTTER OR VEGETABLE OIL		CHOPPED FRESH PARSLEY FOR GARNISH
	JUICE OF 2 ORANGES		BELL PEPPER RICE
5	APPLES, CORED, SLICED		

Season the flour with salt and pepper. Coat the chicken with the flour. Heat the oil in a skillet and lightly brown the chicken on both sides. Arrange the chicken on a foil-covered baking sheet. Bake at 350 degrees for 30 to 40 minutes or until cooked through. Arrange the chicken in a single layer in a serving dish and keep warm. Melt the butter in a saucepan. Stir in the orange juice and sliced apples. Sauté until the apples are tender. Add the jelly and cook for 2 minutes or until heated through, stirring constantly. Place a piece of Brie on top of each chicken breast. Top with the hot apple mixture. Sprinkle with the almonds and garnish with parsley.
Serve with the Bell Pepper Rice (below).

Bell Pepper Rice

Yield: 10 servings

4	CUPS UNCOOKED RICE	2	TEASPOONS DRIED THYME, OR
8	CUPS CHICKEN STOCK OR BROTH		4 TEASPOONS CHOPPED FRESH THYME
1	SMALL ONION, CHOPPED	2	GARLIC CLOVES, MINCED
2	RED BELL PEPPERS, CHOPPED		SALT TO TASTE
2	GREEN OR YELLOW BELL PEPPERS, CHOPPED		

Combine the rice, chicken stock, onion, bell peppers, thyme and garlic in a saucepan. Season with salt. Cover and cook according to the package directions for the rice.

Recipe provided by Patti Constantin

Chicken Enchiladas

Yield: 4 to 6 servings

1	TABLESPOON BUTTER	1/8	TEASPOON CAYENNE PEPPER, OR
1	ONION, CHOPPED		TO TASTE
4	CHICKEN BREASTS, COOKED,		SALT TO TASTE
	BONED, SHREDDED	4	TEASPOONS TABASCO SAUCE, OR
8	OUNCES CREAM CHEESE,		TO TASTE
	CUT INTO CUBES, SOFTENED	8	TO 12 FLOUR TORTILLAS
1	CUP SOUR CREAM	12	OUNCES SHREDDED MONTEREY
1	(4-OUNCE) CAN CHOPPED		JACK CHEESE
	GREEN CHILES	1/2	CUP HEAVY CREAM

Melt the butter in a saucepan and add the onion. Sauté until translucent. Combine the sautéed onion, chicken, cream cheese, sour cream, green chiles and cayenne pepper in a bowl. Season with salt and Tabasco sauce and mix well. Warm the tortillas in a greased skillet over low heat. Divide the chicken mixture among the tortillas and roll up. Place the rolls in a 9x13-inch baking pan. Sprinkle with the Monterey Jack cheese. Pour the cream evenly over the top. Bake at 350 degrees for 30 minutes. Serve with Creole Tomato Salsa (below).

Creole Tomato Salsa

Yield: 4 to 6 servings

4	TO 5 MEDIUM CREOLE	1	TEASPOON SEA SALT
	TOMATOES, CHOPPED	1/4	TEASPOON CAYENNE PEPPER
1/3	CUP CHOPPED FRESH CILANTRO	1	TEASPOON WHITE VINEGAR
	JUICE OF 1 LIME		FRESHLY GROUND BLACK
1	TO 2 JALEPEÑO CHILES, SEEDED,		PEPPER TO TASTE
	FINELY CHOPPED		

Combine the tomatoes, cilantro, lime juice, jalepeños, salt, cayenne pepper and vinegar in a bowl and mix well. Season with black pepper. Chill for 3 to 4 hours before serving. Note: Regular tomatoes may be substituted for Creole tomatoes.

CREOLE TOMATOES

CREOLE TOMATOES, LOVED FOR THEIR SWEETNESS, ARE HARVESTED FROM LATE MAY UNTIL MID-JUNE. THEY ARE GROWN IN ST. BERNARD, ST. JOHN, PLAQUEMINES, AND ST. CHARLES PARISHES. THE DELTA SOIL IN THESE AREAS PRODUCES TOMATOES WITH LESS ACIDITY.

Grilled Chicken Kabobs

Yield: 4 servings

12	OUNCES BONELESS SKINLESS CHICKEN BREASTS	¼	TEASPOON GROUND ALLSPICE
3	TABLESPOONS LEMON JUICE	¼	TEASPOON GROUND NUTMEG
¾	TEASPOON SALT	¼	CUP HEAVY CREAM
1	GARLIC CLOVE, MASHED INTO A PASTE	1	RED BELL PEPPER, CUT INTO CUBES
1	TEASPOON FINELY GRATED PEELED FRESH GINGER	2	TABLESPOONS OLIVE OIL

Cut the chicken into 1¼-inch cubes. Combine the chicken, lemon juice and salt in a bowl. Toss to mix. Let stand for 30 minutes. Stir in the garlic, ginger, allspice, nutmeg and cream. Cover and chill for 1 to 3 hours. Preheat the broiler. Thread ¼ of the chicken pieces and ¼ of the bell pepper pieces on an 8- to 10-inch metal skewer. Begin with the bell pepper and alternate 1 piece of bell pepper for every 2 pieces of chicken. Repeat with 3 more skewers. Brush the kabobs with olive oil. Arrange on a rack in a broiler pan. Place the pan 4 inches from the heat source. Broil for 8 to 10 minutes or until cooked through, turning frequently.

Maque Choux Chicken

Yield: 5 servings

¼	CUP RENDERED PORK FAT OR VEGETABLE OIL	¼	TEASPOON SALT
1	LARGE ONION, CHOPPED	¼	TEASPOON PEPPER
1	CUP FRESH CORN KERNELS		SALT AND PEPPER TO TASTE
6	TOMATOES, PEELED, SEEDED, CHOPPED	1	EGG, LIGHTLY BEATEN
½	CUP BOURBON, WARMED	5	WHOLE BONELESS SKINLESS CHICKEN BREASTS (ABOUT 3¼ POUNDS)
½	CUP CHICKEN BROTH	10	SLICES LEAN BACON, BLANCHED, DRAINED
1	CUP VERY THINLY SLICED COLLARD GREENS, RINSED, DRIED	2	TABLESPOONS PEANUT OIL
1	TEASPOON CELERY SEEDS	1	CUP CHICKEN BROTH
1	TEASPOON MUSTARD SEEDS	2	CUPS VERY THINLY SLICED COLLARD GREENS, RINSED, DRIED
1	TEASPOON DRIED THYME, CRUMBLED	1	CUP CHICKEN BROTH
⅛	TEASPOON FRESHLY GRATED NUTMEG		

Heat the pork fat in a skillet over medium heat. Add the onion and corn and sauté for 5 minutes. Add the tomatoes and sauté for 4 minutes. Add the bourbon and ignite. Shake the pan until the flames die out. Stir in ½ cup chicken broth, 1 cup collard greens, celery seeds, mustard seeds, thyme, nutmeg, ¼ teaspoon salt and ¼ teaspoon pepper. Simmer for 30 to 40 minutes or until most of the liquid evaporates. Season with salt and pepper. Remove half the mixture to a small bowl and let cool to room temperature. Add the egg to the bowl and mix well. Place the chicken breasts between layers of plastic wrap and pound to flatten to an even thickness. Spoon the stuffing onto the center of each breast. Roll up lengthwise and wrap each with 2 slices of bacon. Secure the rolls with wooden picks. Heat the peanut oil in a very large ovenproof skillet over high heat. Add the chicken when the oil is hot but not smoking. Brown the chicken on all sides and remove to a plate with a slotted spoon. Pour off the fat in the skillet and return the chicken to the skillet. Add 1 cup chicken broth and bring to a boil. Place the skillet in the oven. Bake at 450 degrees for 12 minutes or until cooked through. Keep warm. Add 2 cups collard greens and 1 cup broth to the remaining tomato mixture. Simmer over medium-low heat for 10 minutes. Purée in a food processor. Strain the purée and return to the saucepan. Season with salt and pepper. Remove the wooden picks from the chicken and place the chicken on a heated serving platter. Spoon the sauce over the chicken. Serve immediately.

Chicken Parmesan with Apricot Sauce

YIELD: 4 SERVINGS

2	TABLESPOONS MARGARINE	¼	CUP ITALIAN BREAD CRUMBS
½	CUP GRATED PARMESAN CHEESE	4	BONELESS SKINLESS CHICKEN BREASTS

Melt the margarine in a saucepan. Mix the Parmesan cheese and bread crumbs in a bowl and remove to a plate. Rinse the chicken breasts and pat dry. Dip the chicken in the melted margarine and then coat in the bread crumb mixture. Place on a baking sheet sprayed with nonstick cooking spray. Bake at 400 degrees for 25 minutes or until cooked through. Serve with the Apricot Sauce (below).
Note: Mango chutney works well in place of the apricot sauce.

Apricot Sauce

YIELD: ABOUT 1 CUP

½	JAR APRICOT PRESERVES	1	TABLESPOON SOY SAUCE
2	TABLESPOONS BALSAMIC VINEGAR		

Combine the preserves, vinegar and soy sauce in a bowl and mix well.

Chicken with Sautéed Pears Marsala

Yield: 4 servings

2	TABLESPOONS VEGETABLE OIL	2	TEASPOONS VEGETABLE OIL
½	CUP CHOPPED ONION	1	BOSC PEAR, CORED, QUARTERED,
3	TO 4 GARLIC CLOVES, MINCED		THINLY SLICED
2	CUPS APPLE JUICE	4	BONELESS SKINLESS CHICKEN BREASTS,
½	CUP RED WINE		HALVED
2	TABLESPOONS BALSAMIC VINEGAR		SALT AND PEPPER TO TASTE
2	TABLESPOONS DRIED ROSEMARY	1	TABLESPOON VEGETABLE OIL
1½	TEASPOONS CHOPPED FRESH THYME	¼	CUP MARSALA
¼	TEASPOON CRUSHED RED PEPPER	1	TEASPOON CHOPPED FRESH PARSLEY
½	CUP HEAVY CREAM		FOR GARNISH

Heat 2 tablespoons oil in a medium heavy saucepan over medium-high heat. Add the onion and garlic and sauté for 5 minutes or until soft. Add the apple juice, red wine, vinegar, rosemary, thyme and red pepper and bring to a boil. Reduce the heat. Simmer for 20 minutes or until reduced to 1½ cups, stirring occasionally. Strain the mixture into a small saucepan. Add the cream and simmer for 15 minutes or until thickened. Set aside. Heat 2 teaspoons oil in a medium skillet over medium heat. Add the pear slices and sauté for 8 minutes or until golden brown. Remove from the heat and cover with foil to keep warm. Season the chicken with salt and pepper. Heat 1 tablespoon oil in a large heavy skillet over medium-high heat. Sauté the chicken for 4 minutes per side or until golden brown and cooked through. Add the marsala and bring to a boil. Stir in the sauce and turn the chicken to coat. Cook for 2 minutes. Divide the chicken among 4 serving plates. Spoon the sauce over the chicken and top with the pear slices. Garnish with parsley.

Chicken with Creamy Paprika Sauce and Green Onion Noodles

Yield: 4 servings

4	BONELESS CHICKEN BREAST HALVES	2	TABLESPOONS PAPRIKA
2	TEASPOONS PAPRIKA	2	LARGE PLUM TOMATOES, SEEDED,
1/8	TEASPOON SALT, OR TO TASTE		CHOPPED
1/8	TEASPOON PEPPER, OR TO TASTE	2	CUPS CANNED LOW-SODIUM
4	TABLESPOONS (1/2 STICK) BUTTER		CHICKEN BROTH
1	CUP CHOPPED ONION	1/2	CUP SOUR CREAM

Cut the chicken into 1/2-inch strips. Sprinkle with 2 teaspoons paprika, salt and pepper.
Melt 3 tablespoons of the butter in a large skillet over medium-high heat.
Sauté the chicken for 4 minutes or until cooked through. Remove to a plate with a
slotted spoon. Add the remaining 1 tablespoon butter to the skillet. Add the
onion and sauté for 3 minutes or until beginning to soften. Add 2 tablespoons paprika
and stir for 10 seconds. Add the tomatoes and sauté for 1 minute or until soft.
Add the broth and increase the heat to high. Boil for 5 minutes or until the mixture
thickens enough to lightly coat a spoon. Add the chicken and any collected
juices. Reduce the heat to low and add the sour cream. Stir until heated through but
do not boil. Serve with Green Onion Noodles (below).

Green Onion Noodles

Yield: 4 servings

8	OUNCES WIDE EGG NOODLES	1 1/4	CUPS CHOPPED GREEN ONIONS
3	TABLESPOONS BUTTER	2	TEASPOONS POPPY SEEDS

Cook the noodles according to package directions. Drain and reserve 1/2 cup of the
cooking liquid. Melt the butter in the pan used to cook the noodles. Stir in the green onions
and reserved cooking liquid. Add the noodles and poppy seeds and toss to coat.

Chicken Pecan Picante

Yield: 4 servings

1	TABLESPOON OLIVE OIL	2	TABLESPOONS DRIED
1/3	CUP CHOPPED PECANS		CRANBERRIES
2	GARLIC CLOVES, MINCED	1	TEASPOON HONEY
4	BONELESS CHICKEN BREASTS,	3/4	TEASPOON GROUND CUMIN
	SLICED	1/2	TEASPOON GROUND CINNAMON
1	CUP SALSA	3	CUPS COOKED RICE
1/4	CUP WATER		

Heat the olive oil in a large skillet over medium-high heat. Add the pecans and cook until lightly toasted, stirring constantly. Remove the pecans and set aside. Add the garlic to the skillet and sauté for 30 seconds. Add the chicken and sauté for 4 to 5 minutes or until golden brown. Set aside. Combine the salsa, water, cranberries, honey, cumin and cinnamon in a medium bowl and mix well. Add to the skillet. Reduce the heat to medium. Cook, covered, for 20 minutes or until the chicken is cooked through, stirring occasionally. Stir in the pecans and serve over the rice.

CITY OF LAFAYETTE

FROM 1833 TO 1852, A CITY OF COMMERCE AND ELEGANCE EXISTED JUST ABOVE NEW ORLEANS. KNOWN AS THE CITY OF LAFAYETTE, IT WAS FORMED FROM SEVERAL COMMUNITIES THAT HAD ENCOMPASSED FIVE LARGE PLANTATIONS: D'HAUTERIVE, BROUTIN, DARBY, CARRIERE, AND LIVAUDAIS. IN ITS HEYDAY, LAFAYETTE BOASTED A BUSY PORT, HANDLING CATTLE, COTTON, AND GRAIN. THE CITY ITSELF HAD ITS OWN GASLIGHT COMPANY AND A THEATER. AT THE TIME IT WAS ANNEXED BY NEW ORLEANS, LAFAYETTE CITY HAD A POPULATION OF MORE THAN 12,000. ITS RESIDENTIAL SECTION, THE GARDEN DISTRICT, IS NOW A "MUST-SEE" FOR TOURISTS IN NEW ORLEANS.

Sage Sautéed Chicken

Yield: 4 servings

4	BONELESS SKINLESS CHICKEN BREAST HALVES	2	TABLESPOONS EXTRA-VIRGIN OLIVE OIL
			SEA SALT TO TASTE
3	TABLESPOONS FRESH LEMON JUICE		FRESHLY GROUND BLACK PEPPER TO
3	TABLESPOONS EXTRA-VIRGIN OLIVE OIL		TASTE
25	WHOLE FRESH SAGE LEAVES	2	LEMONS, HALVED FOR GARNISH
3	TABLESPOONS BUTTER		

Place the chicken in an 8-inch square glass baking dish. Add the lemon juice, 3 tablespoons olive oil and the sage leaves. Turn the chicken to coat. Cover and let stand at room temperature for 30 minutes. Remove the chicken and pat dry. Strain the marinade into a small bowl and reserve the sage leaves separately. Melt the butter and combine with 2 tablespoons olive oil in a large nonreactive skillet over medium-high heat. Add the chicken, breast side down. Cook for 5 minutes or until browned on the bottom. Turn the chicken over and season with sea salt and pepper. Tuck the reserved sage leaves around the chicken. Cook for 5 minutes or until browned on the bottom and cooked through. Remove the chicken to a cutting board and season with sea salt and pepper. Slice on the diagonal into 1/2-inch slices. Arrange on a warmed serving platter and top with the sage leaves. Cover loosely with foil to keep warm. Pour off the fat in the skillet. Heat the skillet over medium-high heat until hot. Add the reserved marinade and stir with a wooden spoon to remove the browned bits from the bottom of the pan. Cook for 1 minute or until reduced to a brown glaze, stirring constantly. Pour over the chicken.
Garnish with lemon halves.

Chicken and Dumplings

Yield: 6 servings

1	CUP SELF-RISING FLOUR	2	TEASPOONS DRIED THYME
1	TEASPOON PEPPER	1	TABLESPOON DRIED ROSEMARY
3	POUNDS CHICKEN THIGHS	2	TEASPOONS GRATED LEMON ZEST
¼	CUP VEGETABLE OIL	2	TABLESPOONS LEMON JUICE
1	MEDIUM ONION, CHOPPED	2	CUPS SELF-RISING FLOUR
2	GARLIC CLOVES, MINCED	1	CUP HEAVY CREAM
1	TABLESPOON SELF-RISING FLOUR	¼	CUP SOUR CREAM (OPTIONAL)
3	(14-OUNCE) CANS CHICKEN BROTH		
2	TABLESPOONS CHOPPED FRESH BASIL, OR		
	2 TEASPOONS DRIED BASIL		

Combine 1 cup flour and pepper. Coat the chicken in the flour. Heat the oil in a large heavy saucepan over medium heat. Add the chicken and fry until golden brown, turning once. Add additional oil if needed. Remove the chicken to a plate. Add the onion and garlic to the pan drippings and sauté for 5 minutes or until soft. Add 1 tablespoon flour and stir for 1 minute. Stir in the broth gradually. Add the basil, thyme, rosemary, lemon zest and lemon juice and bring to a boil. Add the chicken and reduce the heat. Cover and simmer for 30 minutes or until the chicken is cooked through. Remove the chicken and keep warm. Reduce the heat under the broth to very low. Mix 2 cups flour and the cream with a fork in a bowl. The mixture will be dry and crumbly. Pat gently into 2-inch balls. Handle the dough as little as possible. Bring the chicken broth to a rolling boil. Add the dumplings and cover. Reduce the heat and simmer without stirring for 7 to 10 minutes or until the dumplings are firm. Remove the dumplings and stir the sour cream into the broth. Serve the chicken and dumplings with the broth.

Cajun Fried Turkey

Yield: 12 servings

1	(16-POUND) TURKEY, THAWED, DRAINED
16	OUNCES CAJUN INJECTOR MARINADE
⅓	CUP CAJUN SEASONING
	PEANUT OIL (ENOUGH TO SUBMERGE THE TURKEY)

Remove the giblets from the turkey. Rinse inside and out and pat dry. Inject the marinade using the injector that comes with the marinade. Inject through the top of the turkey on both sides of the breast. Move the injector around to be certain the marinade reaches all areas of the breast. Rub the outside of the turkey with Cajun seasoning. Place the turkey in the basket of a crawfish boiling setup. (See sidebar at left.) Heat the peanut oil to 350 degrees in the pot of a crawfish boiling setup. Lower the basket slowly into the hot oil so that the turkey is covered by oil. Deep-fry for 3 minutes per pound or until cooked through. Remove the turkey and drain. Place on a platter and let stand, covered loosely with foil, for 15 to 25 minutes before carving.

SAFETY TIPS

PEANUT OIL HAS A HIGHER BURNING TEMPERATURE THAN OTHER OILS. KEEP CHILDREN AND PETS AWAY WHILE THE OIL IS HOT. FRY OUTSIDE ON A HARD SURFACE, SUCH AS CONCRETE, AND AWAY FROM GRASS. OIL CAN SPLASH AND IGNITE GRASS. IF THE OIL BECOMES TOO HOT AND IGNITES, TURN OFF THE GAS AND COVER WITH THE LID. DO NOT SPRAY BURNING OIL WITH WATER. IT IS SAFER AND EASIER TO REMOVE THE COOKED TURKEY IF TWO PEOPLE WORK TOGETHER, USING SOMETHING WITH A HEAVY HANDLE TO MOVE THE BASKET INTO AND OUT OF THE OIL.

Slow-Roasted N'Awlins Turkey

YIELD: 12 SERVINGS

1	(14- TO 18-POUND) TURKEY	2	TABLESPOONS BLACK PEPPER
1/4	CUP POULTRY SEASONING	1/2	CUP (1 STICK) MARGARINE,
2	TABLESPOONS SALT		SOFTENED

Remove the giblets and rinse the turkey inside and out. Pat dry inside and out with paper towels. Mix the poultry seasoning, salt and pepper in a small bowl. Rub the mixture on the inside and outside of the turkey. Rub the margarine on the inside, outside and under the skin. Coat all surfaces of the turkey with the seasonings and margarine. Place the turkey in a high-sided baking pan large enough to hold it. Wrap foil around the wing tips and ends of the drumsticks. Roast, uncovered, at 500 degrees for 20 minutes or just until the turkey turns a honey brown color. Reduce the temperature to 200 degrees and roast for 40 to 50 minutes per pound or until cooked through. Place on a platter and cover loosely with foil. Let stand for 15 to 20 minutes before carving.

Recipe provided by Frank Davis

TURKEY AND ROASTED PEPPER SANDWICHES

2 TABLESPOONS FAT-FREE CREAM CHEESE
1 TABLESPOON REDUCED-FAT MAYONNAISE
1 TABLESPOON CREOLE MUSTARD
1/8 TEASPOON PEPPER
1/4 CUP CHOPPED ROASTED RED BELL PEPPERS
2 TABLESPOONS SLICED GREEN ONIONS
8 SLICES 7-GRAIN BREAD OR PUMPERNICKEL
3/4 POUND SLICED TURKEY BREAST
1/4 CUP ARUGULA OR MIXED GREENS

Combine the cream cheese, mayonnaise, mustard and pepper in a bowl; mix well. Stir in the bell peppers and green onions. Lay 4 slices of bread on a work surface and spread with the cream cheese mixture. Layer with turkey and arugula. Top with remaining slices of bread. Cut in half and serve. Yield: 4 servings

Basil and Lemon Turkey Scaloppine

YIELD: 8 SERVINGS

4	TURKEY TENDERLOINS, WELL TRIMMED	4	SMALL PLUM TOMATOES, SEEDED, CHOPPED
4½	TABLESPOONS FRESH LEMON JUICE	¼	CUP CHOPPED FRESH BASIL
4	TEASPOONS OLIVE OIL	1	TEASPOON GRATED LEMON ZEST
1	SMALL ONION, CHOPPED	½	TEASPOON SEA SALT
5	GARLIC CLOVES, MINCED	⅛	TEASPOON CAYENNE PEPPER, OR TO TASTE
6	TABLESPOONS DRY WHITE WINE		FRESHLY GROUND BLACK PEPPER TO TASTE
½	CUP CHICKEN BROTH		

Cut the tenderloins into 1-inch pieces. Place each piece between sheets of waxed paper and pound with a mallet to flatten to ¼ inch thick. Place on a large platter and sprinkle with the lemon juice. Cover and chill for 10 minutes. Heat the olive oil in a large heavy skillet over medium-high heat. Fry the tenderloins in batches for 4 minutes or until cooked through. Turn once during frying. Remove to a platter and cover with foil to keep warm. Add the onion and garlic to the skillet and sauté for 4 minutes or until soft. Stir in the wine and simmer for 1 minute or until reduced to a glaze. Stir in the broth, tomatoes, basil, lemon zest, sea salt and cayenne pepper. Cover and simmer for 3 minutes or until slightly thickened. Season with black pepper. Pour over the tenderloins and serve.

Grilled Turkey Satay with Peanut Sauce

YIELD: 4 SERVINGS

1	POUND TURKEY TENDERLOINS	1/2	TEASPOON RED PEPPER FLAKES
3	TABLESPOONS SKIM MILK	1/2	TEASPOON GRATED LEMON ZEST
1	TABLESPOON OLIVE OIL	1/4	TEASPOON GROUND GINGER
1	TEASPOON SOY SAUCE	1/8	TEASPOON COCONUT EXTRACT
1	TABLESPOON MINCED ONION		

Cut the turkey tenderloins in half lengthwise. Place each piece between sheets of waxed paper and pound with a mallet to flatten. Cut into 1-inch wide strips. Combine the milk, olive oil, soy sauce, onion, red pepper flakes, lemon zest, ginger and coconut extract in a sealable plastic freezer bag. Add the turkey strips, seal the bag and turn the bag to coat the strips. Chill for 4 hours or longer. Turn the bag occasionally during marinating. Soak wooden skewers in water for 30 minutes. Lightly coat the grill rack with nonstick cooking spray. Prepare the grill for direct heat grilling. Weave the turkey strips onto the skewers. Discard the marinade. Grill for 2 to 3 minutes per side or until cooked through. Serve with the Peanut Sauce (below).

Peanut Sauce

YIELD: 1/2 CUP

1	SMALL GARLIC CLOVE	1/8	TEASPOON CAYENNE PEPPER
1	TABLESPOON CHOPPED ONION	1/8	TEASPOON COCONUT EXTRACT, OR
1/4	CUP PEANUT BUTTER		TO TASTE
1 1/2	TEASPOONS LEMON JUICE	1/4	CUP SKIM MILK
1/4	TEASPOON SOY SAUCE		

Process the garlic and onion in a food processor for 10 seconds. Add the peanut butter, lemon juice, soy sauce, cayenne pepper and coconut extract and process for 20 seconds. Add the milk in a slow stream, processing constantly until smooth. Pour into a microwave-safe serving bowl and microwave on High for 20 to 30 seconds. Stir and serve.

Turkey Breast Terpsichore

Yield: 6 servings

1	TABLESPOON BUTTER		SALT AND FRESHLY GROUND
3/4	CUP CHOPPED FRESH		PEPPER TO TASTE
	MUSHROOMS	6	SLICES HAM
	BREAST FROM AN 8- TO 9-POUND		CHICKEN BROTH
	TURKEY		FRESHLY GRATED PARMESAN
	FLOUR		CHEESE
10	TABLESPOONS (1¼ STICKS)		CHOPPED FRESH PARSLEY FOR
	BUTTER		GARNISH
7	TABLESPOONS VEGETABLE OIL		

Melt 1 tablespoon butter in a saucepan. Add the mushrooms and sauté just until softened. Set aside and keep warm. Place the turkey breast on a work surface and remove the bones, leaving the fillet whole. Slice into 6 slices, each about ³/₈-inch thick. Place each slice between sheets of waxed paper and pound with a mallet to flatten slightly. Coat with flour. Heat 5 tablespoons of the butter and half the oil in each of 2 large skillets. Add 3 turkey slices to each skillet. Sauté for 10 minutes or until cooked through, turning frequently. Season with salt and pepper. Top each with a slice of ham and 1 tablespoon sautéed mushrooms. Spoon on a little broth and sprinkle with Parmesan cheese. Reduce the heat, cover and simmer for 5 minutes. Remove the turkey slices to serving plates. Spoon the sauce over the turkey. Garnish with parsley.

NINE MUSES STREET

When the American section of New Orleans was surveyed and planned in the early 1800s, Greek Revivalism was in fashion in the United States. There are many examples of Greek Revival architecture to be found in the Garden District and its environs. As further evidence of a fascination with all things Greek, nine streets in the lower Garden District were named for the nine Greek muses: Calliope, Clio, Erato, Euterpe, Melpomene, Polymnia, Terpsichore, Thalia, and Urania. To this day, all are pronounced with a French flair, rather than with classical Greek articulation.

Sautéed Turkey Medallions with Cranberry Orange Glaze

Yield: 4 servings

1	EGG WHITE	1	CUP CRANBERRY JUICE COCKTAIL
3/4	TEASPOON SALT	2½	TABLESPOONS BROWN SUGAR
1	CUP FINE DRY BREAD CRUMBS	2	TABLESPOONS CIDER VINEGAR
	PEPPER TO TASTE	½	TEASPOON GRATED ORANGE ZEST
4	(⅓-INCH-THICK) TURKEY CUTLETS		VEGETABLE OIL

Whisk the egg white and salt in a bowl until foamy. Place the bread crumbs in a shallow dish and season with pepper. Place each turkey cutlet between sheets of waxed paper and pound with a mallet to flatten to ¼ inch thick. Dip the cutlets into the egg white and then coat in the bread crumbs. Press into the bread crumbs to coat well. Place the cutlets on a rack on a baking sheet. Chill, uncovered, for 15 minutes. Boil the cranberry juice cocktail in a small saucepan until reduced to ½ cup. Stir in the brown sugar and vinegar and boil until the mixture is syrupy and reduced to about 3 tablespoons. Remove from the heat and stir in the orange zest. Keep warm. Pour ¼ inch of oil into a large heavy skillet. Heat over high heat until hot but not smoking. Fry the cutlets in 2 batches for 45 seconds per side or until cooked through. Remove to paper towels to drain. Place the cutlets on serving plates and drizzle with the glaze.

Turkey and Red Wine Lasagna

Yield: 8 servings

2	TABLESPOONS OLIVE OIL	1/8	TEASPOON GROUND ALLSPICE
2	LARGE ONIONS, CHOPPED		SALT AND PEPPER TO TASTE
5	LARGE GARLIC CLOVES, MINCED	15	OUNCES RICOTTA CHEESE
1½	POUNDS GROUND TURKEY		(ABOUT 2 CUPS)
2	CARROTS, FINELY CHOPPED	1	EGG, LIGHTLY BEATEN
1	LARGE RED BELL PEPPER, FINELY CHOPPED	2	GREEN ONIONS, CHOPPED
1	(28-OUNCE) CAN WHOLE TOMATOES	12	NO-BOIL LASAGNA NOODLES
1½	CUPS RED WINE	12	OUNCES SHREDDED PART-SKIM
1	TEASPOON DRIED BASIL, CRUMBLED		MOZZARELLA CHEESE
1	TEASPOON DRIED THYME, CRUMBLED	1/4	CUP FRESHLY GRATED PARMESAN
1/4	TO ½ TEASPOON RED PEPPER FLAKES		CHEESE

Heat the olive oil in a large saucepan over medium-low heat. Add the onions and garlic. Cook until soft, stirring occasionally. Add the turkey, carrots and bell pepper. Cook until the carrots are tender-crisp, stirring to break up the turkey. Stir in the tomatoes, wine, basil, thyme, red pepper flakes and allspice. Season with salt and pepper. Break up the tomatoes with a spoon. Simmer, uncovered, for 30 minutes. Combine the ricotta cheese, egg and green onions in a bowl. Season with salt and pepper. Mix well. Pour 1 cup tomato sauce into a 9x13-inch baking dish. Arrange 3 lasagna noodles on the sauce, making certain the noodles do not touch. Spread 2 cups of the tomato sauce on the noodles. Top with 1/3 of the ricotta mixture by spoonfuls and spread. Sprinkle with 1/4 of the mozzarella cheese. Repeat the layers 2 more times, beginning with the noodles and ending with the mozzarella cheese. Sprinkle with the Parmesan cheese. Cover with foil, tenting so that the foil does not touch the cheese. Bake at 375 degrees for 30 minutes. Remove the foil and bake for 10 minutes longer to brown the cheese.

Corn Bread-Crusted Turkey Potpie

YIELD: 8 SERVINGS

1	LARGE ONION, CUT INTO PIECES	1	(19-OUNCE) CAN BLACK BEANS, RINSED
5	GARLIC CLOVES, COARSELY CHOPPED		AND DRAINED
1	LARGE RED BELL PEPPER, CUT INTO PIECES	1/3	CUP FINELY CHOPPED CILANTRO
1	LARGE GREEN BELL PEPPER, CUT INTO	1	CUP FLOUR
	PIECES	1	CUP YELLOW CORNMEAL
1/4	CUP VEGETABLE OIL	1	TABLESPOON SUGAR
1/4	CUP PURE HOT CHILE POWDER	2	TEASPOONS BAKING POWDER
1	(35-OUNCE) CAN WHOLE TOMATOES,	1	TEASPOON SALT
	UNDRAINED, COARSELY CHOPPED	1	CUP MILK
2	TEASPOONS SALT	2	EGGS
1 1/4	POUNDS COOKED TURKEY, CUT INTO	3	TABLESPOONS VEGETABLE OIL
	3/4-INCH PIECES		

Process the onion and garlic in a food processor until finely chopped. Remove to a bowl. Process the bell peppers until finely chopped. Heat 1/4 cup oil in a large heavy skillet over high heat. Add the onion, garlic and chile powder and sauté for 5 minutes or until the onion is soft. Add the bell peppers and sauté for 5 minutes or until the bell peppers are barely soft. Stir in the undrained tomatoes and 2 teaspoons salt. Cook for 10 minutes, stirring frequently. Add the turkey, beans and cilantro and mix well. Spread the mixture in a buttered 9x13-inch baking dish. Sift the flour, cornmeal, sugar, baking powder and 1 teaspoon salt into a bowl. Whisk the milk, eggs and 3 tablespoons oil in another bowl. Stir the egg mixture into the dry ingredients. Spoon on top of the turkey mixture. The topping will spread as it bakes so do not try to evenly spread the topping. Place on a baking sheet. Bake at 400 degrees for 35 minutes or until the crust is golden brown. Let stand for 10 minutes before serving.

Tortilla Turkey Wraps

Yield: 4 servings

3/4 POUND BONELESS TURKEY THIGHS,
CUT INTO STRIPS

1/4 TEASPOON GROUND RED PEPPER

1/4 TEASPOON SALT

2 SMALL RIPE AVOCADOS, PEELED,
PITTED, MASHED

3/4 CUP SOUR CREAM

2 TABLESPOONS OLIVE OIL

1 CUP THINLY SLICED RED ONION

1 CUP THINLY SLICED RED BELL PEPPER

4 LARGE FLOUR TORTILLAS

1 1/2 CUPS SHREDDED MONTEREY JACK
CHEESE

1 TABLESPOON OLIVE OIL

Combine the turkey, cayenne pepper and salt in a bowl; mix well. Cover and chill. Mix the avocados and sour cream in a separate bowl. Set aside. Heat 2 tablespoons olive oil in a medium skillet. Add the onion and bell pepper. Sauté for 3 to 4 minutes or until tender. Remove to a bowl. Add the turkey strips to the skillet. Sauté for 5 minutes or until cooked through. Remove from the heat. Place the tortillas on a work surface. Spread each with the avocado mixture. Top with the sautéed vegetables and sprinkle with the cheese. Arrange the turkey strips in a single layer near the edge of the tortillas. Fold the edge over the turkey and then fold in the sides. Roll up the tortillas. Heat 1 tablespoon olive oil in a medium skillet. Add the wraps, seam side down. Cook for 1 to 2 minutes or until all sides are browned. Serve with salsa.

Camelback Cornish Hens

Yield: 4 servings

4	Cornish game hens		½	cup port
	Salt and pepper to taste		2	tablespoons flour
	Corn Bread Stuffing		½	cup beef stock or broth
4	slices bacon		1	tablespoon port
½	cup beef stock or broth			

Rinse the hens; pat dry. Season with salt and pepper. Stuff the hens with the Corn Bread Stuffing (below). Place the hens in a nonstick 9x13-inch baking pan. Cut the bacon slices in half; place 2 halves over each breast. Add ½ cup beef stock and ½ cup port to the pan. Roast at 400 degrees for 1 hour or until cooked through, basting occasionally. Brown under the broiler for 3 to 4 minutes if desired. Remove the hens to a 9x13-inch serving dish; keep warm. Reserve the pan drippings. Bring 6 tablespoons of pan drippings to a boil in a heavy saucepan. Stir in the flour and cook until the mixture is a brown color. Strain the remaining drippings and add to the saucepan. Stir in ½ cup beef stock and 1 tablespoon port. Simmer for 5 minutes or until thickened. Strain into a bowl; skim the fat. Pour into a gravy boat.

Corn Bread Stuffing

Yield: 4 servings

1	POUND BULK PORK SAUSAGE		1	APPLE, PEELED, CORED, CHOPPED
2	TABLESPOONS BUTTER		½	CUP RAISINS
1	ONION, CHOPPED		1	(7-OUNCE) PACKAGE CORN BREAD
1	RIB CELERY, CHOPPED			STUFFING MIX, PREPARED
1	TABLESPOON MINCED GARLIC			SALT AND PEPPER TO TASTE

Brown the sausage in a large skillet. Remove with a slotted spoon; drain on paper towels. Add the butter to the drippings in the skillet and melt. Add the onion, celery and garlic; sauté until tender. Stir in the apple and raisins. Cook for 2 to 3 minutes over medium-low heat. Add the sausage and stuffing and mix well. Season with salt and pepper.

ORAL TRADITIONS: SHOTGUNS/ CAMELBACKS AND ARMOIRES/ROOMS

ORAL TRADITION STATES THAT "SHOTGUN" COTTAGES ARE SO-NAMED BECAUSE THEIR ROOMS ARE IN A STRAIGHT LINE, THROUGH WHICH A BULLET COULD PASS FROM ONE END OF THE HOUSE TO THE OTHER. THE STYLE MAY BE AKIN TO THE "BOXCAR" OF PENNSYLVANIA. "CAMELBACK" HOUSES, SO THE STORY GOES, EVOLVED FROM A TAX BASED ON THE HEIGHT OF A HOUSE AT THE FRONT PROPERTY LINE. IN ORDER TO REDUCE THE HOMEOWNER'S TAX, HE BUILT HIS SECOND FLOOR ONLY ON THE REAR OF THE HOUSE. HOMEOWNERS ALSO WERE TAXED ACCORDING TO THE NUMBER OF ROOMS IN A HOUSE. HEARSAY HAS IT THAT BECAUSE CLOSETS WERE CONSIDERED AN ADDITIONAL ROOM, ARMOIRES (FREE-STANDING WARDROBES) WERE USED INSTEAD OF CLOSETS. FEW ORIGINAL HOMES IN NEW ORLEANS' OLDEST DISTRICTS WERE EQUIPPED WITH CLOSETS.

Cornish Hens au Champagne

Yield: 4 servings

4	YELLOW ONIONS, CUT INTO LARGE PIECES	4	CORNISH GAME HENS
1	BUNCH GREEN ONIONS, CUT INTO LARGE PIECES	½	BOTTLE CHAMPAGNE
			SALT, PEPPER AND MINCED GARLIC TO TASTE

*P*lace half the chopped yellow onions in the hen cavities. Place the other half in a large baking dish. Add the chopped green onions to the baking dish. Arrange the hens on the onions and season with salt, pepper and garlic. Pour the Champagne over the hens. Cover and bake at 350 degrees for 3 hours or until cooked through. Drink the rest of the Champagne and enjoy!

Cornish Hens Framboise

Yield: 4 servings

¼	TEASPOON PEPPER	2	CUPS COOKED LONG GRAIN AND WILD RICE MIX
¼	TEASPOON SALT		
¼	TEASPOON GARLIC POWDER	6	TABLESPOONS BUTTER
2	(1½-POUND) CORNISH GAME HENS	¼	CUP HONEY
		¼	TEASPOON SALT
			RASPBERRY SAUCE (AT LEFT)

*M*ix the pepper, ¼ teaspoon salt and garlic powder in a bowl. Rinse the hens; pat dry inside and out. Season the cavities with half the pepper mixture. Stuff with the rice. Close the cavities with skewers; tuck the wing tips under the hens. Place the hens in a roasting pan. Combine the butter, honey and ¼ teaspoon salt in a saucepan. Heat until the butter melts, stirring constantly. Brush the hens liberally with the honey butter. Sprinkle with the remaining pepper mixture. Roast at 450 degrees for 40 to 45 minutes or until cooked through. Baste frequently during roasting with honey butter. Remove the hens to a cutting board. Cut each in half and place 1 half on each of 4 serving plates. Spoon the Raspberry Sauce over the hens.

RASPBERRY SAUCE

1 (10-OUNCE) PACKAGE FROZEN WHOLE UNSWEETENED RASPBERRIES, THAWED
¼ CUP WATER
2½ TABLESPOONS SUGAR
1 TABLESPOON GRATED LEMON ZEST

COMBINE THE RASPBERRIES, WATER, SUGAR AND LEMON ZEST IN A MEDIUM HEAVY SAUCEPAN. COOK OVER MEDIUM-HIGH HEAT FOR 10 MINUTES OR UNTIL THE SAUCE THICKENS, STIRRING FREQUENTLY. SERVE WITH CORNISH HENS FRAMBOISE.
YIELD: 4 SERVINGS

Cornish Hens with Mushroom Barley

3	(1½-pound) Cornish game hens	2½	cups chicken broth
⅓	cup soy sauce	1½	cups chopped fresh mushrooms
2	tablespoons honey	¾	cup chopped water chestnuts
2	tablespoons dry sherry	4	green onions, chopped
1	teaspoon garlic powder		Salt and pepper to taste
1	cup uncooked barley		Chopped green onions for garnish

Place the hens in a large heavy-duty sealable plastic bag. Mix the soy sauce, honey, sherry and garlic powder in a bowl. Pour into the cavities and over the hens in the bag. Seal the bag. Chill for 3 to 4 hours, turning frequently. Combine the barley and broth in a saucepan. Bring to a boil. Reduce the heat, cover and simmer for 15 minutes or until the liquid is absorbed. Remove from the heat and stir in the mushrooms, water chestnuts and 4 chopped green onions. Season with salt and pepper. Remove the hens from the bag and place on a work surface. Pour the reserved marinade into a saucepan and bring to a boil. Boil for 5 minutes. Stuff the hen cavities with the barley mixture, reserving any extra. Place the hens breast side up on a rack in a shallow roasting pan. Season with salt and pepper. Roast the hens at 375 degrees for 1½ hours or until cooked through. Baste occasionally during roasting with the heated marinade. Serve the hens with any extra heated barley mixture.

Cornish Hens Parisienne

½	cup whole-grain mustard	½	cup olive oil
¼	cup Dijon mustard		Salt and pepper to taste
6	to 8 large garlic cloves, pressed	4	(1¼-pound) Cornish game hens
3	tablespoons chopped fresh rosemary		Fresh rosemary sprigs

Mix the whole-grain mustard, Dijon mustard, garlic and chopped rosemary in a bowl. Whisk in the olive oil gradually. Season with salt and pepper. Rub the cavities and outside of the hens with the mustard mixture. Season with salt and pepper. Place a few sprigs of rosemary inside the cavities. Arrange the hens in a roasting pan. Roast at 375 degrees for 1¼ hours or until cooked through. Cover the hens with foil if becoming too brown.

Meat & Game

Meat & Game

William Adler House
6153 St. Charles Avenue

The *Daily Picayune* reported on September 1, 1903, that "Emile Weil is in charge of the plans of the new two-story stone residence of William Adler at Palmer Avenue and St. Charles, which will have fifteen rooms and a basement, perhaps the first basement in a residence in the city. The basement is constructed with concrete and will be perfectly dry."

✦

The addition of the basement was remarkable because New Orleans historically has battled against rain flooding and the rising waters of the Mississippi with its consequent floods. New Orleans is, on average, six feet below sea level and has an annual average rainfall of more than fifty-eight inches. Despite being equipped with one of the world's largest drainage systems, the city floods frequently. Although basements exist in houses constructed before this one, they are extremely rare in New Orleans.

✦

This imposing Renaissance Revival house was built for William Adler, president of the State National Bank and vice-president of Schwartz Foundry Company, at a cost of $20,000, a huge sum in 1903. While there was a minor Renaissance Revival prior to the Civil War, one such local example being the James Robb mansion (demolished) in the Garden District, the movement became more popular following the 1893 Chicago World Columbian Exposition. It was favored by the very wealthy in America during the late nineteenth and early twentieth centuries. Renaissance details on this house include the symmetrical facade and classically detailed front porch.

✦

Jacob Wilzin purchased the house in 1910 for $39,000 and sold it in 1954 to Mario Bermudez. The house was sold by Mr. Bermudez in 1973 to Drs. Jay and Geraldine Seastrunk. It became the JLNO Show House II in 1976, and the present owners are Mr. and Mrs. Gothard J. Reck.

Dixie Brisket

YIELD: 12 SERVINGS

1	(6-POUND) BRISKET, TRIMMED		1	(12-OUNCE) BOTTLE DIXIE BEER
1	(12-OUNCE) JAR CHILI SAUCE			SALT AND PEPPER TO TASTE

Place the brisket in a large covered skillet. Pour the chili sauce and beer over the meat and season with salt and pepper. Bring to a boil and boil for 3 minutes. Reduce the heat, cover and simmer for 3 hours or until tender.

Asian Flank Steak

YIELD: 4 SERVINGS

1½	POUNDS FLANK STEAK		2	TABLESPOONS MINCED JALAPEÑO
⅓	CUP FRESH LIME JUICE			CHILES
¼	CUP MINCED FRESH MINT		3	GARLIC CLOVES, MINCED
¼	CUP LOW-SODIUM SOY SAUCE			
2	TABLESPOONS MINCED FRESH GINGER			

Combine the steak, lime juice, mint, soy sauce, ginger, jalapeños and garlic in a sealable plastic bag. Seal the bag and turn to coat. Chill for 8 to 12 hours, turning the bag occasionally during marinating. Remove the steak and discard the marinade. Prepare the grill or preheat the broiler. Lightly coat the grill rack or broiler pan with nonstick cooking spray. Grill or broil for 8 minutes per side. Remove the steak to a cutting board and cover loosely with foil. Let stand for 10 minutes before slicing.

Magazine Street Mignons

Yield: 4 servings

4	(6- TO 8-OUNCE) FILETS MIGNONS	1	CUP BEEF BROTH
8	TEASPOONS GREEN PEPPERCORNS	1/3	CUP BRANDY OR COGNAC
1	TABLESPOON BUTTER	2	TABLESPOONS TOMATO PASTE
1	TABLESPOON VEGETABLE OIL	4	TO 5 TABLESPOONS BUTTER
1	TABLESPOON BUTTER		
1	BUNCH SCALLIONS, FINELY CHOPPED		

Trim any fat from the steaks. Pat the steaks thoroughly dry with paper towels and place on a plate. Press 1 teaspoon of green peppercorns into each side of each steak. Heat 1 tablespoon butter and the oil in a large skillet over medium-high heat. Add the steaks and sear for 2 to 3 minutes per side for medium-rare. Remove to an au gratin dish. Pour any pan drippings from the skillet over the steaks. Place in the oven at a very low temperature to keep warm. Add 1 tablespoon butter to the skillet. Melt over medium-high heat and add the scallions. Sauté the scallions while scraping any browned bits from the bottom of the skillet. Add the broth when the scallions are soft. Cook until simmering while scraping the bottom of the skillet. Stir in the brandy and increase the heat to high. Boil for 1 minute. Stir in the tomato paste. Remove from the heat. Stir in 4 to 5 tablespoons butter, 1 tablespoon at a time, melting before adding more butter. Place the steaks on serving plates. Spoon some of the sauce over the steaks. Serve the remaining sauce on the side.

THE GRAND MANSIONS THEY BUILT WERE SMALLER AND MORE MANAGEABLE THAN THEIR COUNTERPARTS ELSEWHERE IN THE COUNTRY, SO THEIR CHARACTER HAS BEEN RETAINED. THE 1890S SAW THE ESTABLISHMENT OF HOLY NAME OF JESUS CHURCH, LOYOLA UNIVERSITY, AND TULANE UNIVERSITY UPTOWN ON ST. CHARLES AVENUE. AUDUBON PARK LIES ACROSS THE AVENUE FROM THE CHURCH AND UNIVERSITIES, AND A MASSIVE RENOVATION OF THE AUDUBON ZOOLOGICAL GARDENS IN THE 1970S HAS CONSISTENTLY PLACED IT ON THE TOP TEN LIST OF ZOOS THROUGHOUT THE COUNTRY.

Tenderloin Tchoupitoulas

Yield: 4 servings

4   (8-ounce) beef tenderloin steaks   Salt and pepper to taste
      Olive oil   Marsala Mushroom Sauce

Prepare the grill at medium-high heat or preheat the broiler. Brush the steaks with olive oil. Season with salt and pepper. Grill or broil for 4 minutes per side for medium-rare. Remove to serving plates and top with Marsala Mushroom Sauce (below).

Marsala Mushroom Sauce

Yield: 4 servings

2   tablespoons butter   2/3   cup dry marsala
1   cup chopped leek, white and pale   2/3   cup beef stock or broth
     part only   2   tablespoons butter
4   teaspoons minced garlic   Salt and pepper to taste
4   cups sliced mixed wild mushrooms
     (such as oyster, stemmed portobello
     or stemmed shiitake)

Melt 2 tablespoons butter in a large heavy skillet over medium-low heat. Add the leek and garlic and sauté for 5 minutes or until almost tender. Increase the heat to medium-high and add the mushrooms. Sauté for 6 minutes or until golden brown. Add the marsala and stock and boil for 4 minutes or until the liquid is reduced by half. Strain the sauce and reserve the mushrooms. Pour the sauce back into the skillet and bring to a simmer. Remove from the heat and whisk in 2 tablespoons butter gradually. Add the reserved mushrooms. Cook over low heat until hot, stirring constantly. Season with salt and pepper. Serve over tenderloin steaks. Note: This sauce can be made 1 day ahead through the point of straining. Cover the sauce and mushrooms and chill separately.

Beef Wellington for Two

YIELD: 2 SERVINGS

½	TEASPOON PEPPER		1	TABLESPOON BUTTER
½	TEASPOON SALT		¼	CUP MUSHROOM DUXELLES (BELOW)
¼	TEASPOON DRIED THYME		1	SHEET FROZEN PUFF PASTRY, THAWED
2	(6-OUNCE) TOURNEDOS OF BEEF		1	EGG
1	TEASPOON DIJON MUSTARD		1	TEASPOON MILK

Mix the pepper, salt and thyme in a small bowl. Rub the tournedos with the mustard. Sprinkle all sides with the pepper mixture. Melt the butter in a skillet over medium-high heat. Add the tournedos; sear on all sides. Remove to a plate; let cool to room temperature. Place the tournedos on a baking sheet. Spread half the Mushroom Duxelles over each tournedos. Cut two 4-inch circles out of the puff pastry. Drape each tournedos with 1 circle; pinch the edges to seal. Brush the pastry with mixture of the egg and milk. Top with decorative pieces of scrap pastry if desired. Bake at 425 degrees for 15 minutes for medium-rare. Serve immediately.

Mushroom Duxelles

YIELD: 4 SERVINGS

2	TABLESPOONS BUTTER		2	TEASPOONS CHOPPED FRESH THYME
⅓	CUP MINCED SHALLOTS		3	TABLESPOONS BUTTER
⅓	CUP MINCED LEEKS, WHITE AND PALE PART ONLY		10	OUNCES SHIITAKE MUSHROOMS, STEMS REMOVED, FINELY CHOPPED
2	GARLIC CLOVES, MINCED		1	TABLESPOON CHOPPED FRESH CHIVES
8	OUNCES BUTTON MUSHROOMS, FINELY CHOPPED		½	TEASPOON SALT
				PEPPER TO TASTE

Melt 2 tablespoons butter in a 10-inch skillet over low heat. Add the shallots, leeks and garlic. Cook until translucent, stirring occasionally. Add the button mushrooms and thyme. Cook until the liquid has evaporated and the mixture is barely moist, stirring occasionally. Remove to a bowl. Add 3 tablespoons butter to the skillet. Add the shiitake mushrooms and sauté until the mushrooms begin to stick to the skillet. Remove from the heat. Drain the button mushroom mixture. Add the shiitake mushrooms and mix well.
Stir in the chives and salt and season with pepper.

French Market Meat Loaf

Yield: 8 servings

2	TABLESPOONS OLIVE OIL	½	TEASPOON DRIED THYME
8	OUNCES ANDOUILLE SAUSAGE,	½	TEASPOON DRIED OREGANO
	FINELY CHOPPED	½	CUP TOMATO SAUCE
1	CUP CHOPPED ONION	½	CUP BEEF BROTH
1	RED BELL PEPPER, FINELY CHOPPED	¼	CUP FRESH BREAD CRUMBS
1	CAYENNE OR OTHER HOT RED	2	POUNDS GROUND BEEF
	PEPPER, SEEDED, MINCED	1	TEASPOON SALT
2	GARLIC CLOVES, MINCED		PEPPER TO TASTE

Heat the olive oil in a large skillet over low heat. Add the sausage, onion, bell pepper, hot pepper, garlic, thyme and oregano and mix well. Cover and cook for 15 minutes. Remove to a bowl and let cool to room temperature. Add the tomato sauce, broth and bread crumbs to the sausage mixture. Crumble the ground beef into the bowl. Add the salt and season with pepper. Mix gently until combined. Pack into a 5x9-inch loaf pan. Bake at 350 degrees for 45 minutes or until cooked through. Pour off the drippings from the pan. Cover the pan loosely with foil and let stand for 10 minutes. Slice and serve.

THE FRENCH MARKET

THE FRENCH MARKET WAS ORIGINALLY AN INDIAN TRADING POST WHERE EVEN INTO THE EARLY 1900S CHOCTAW INDIANS SOLD THEIR *FILÉ* POWDER, GROUND FROM THE TENDER YOUNG LEAVES OF THE SASSAFRAS. FILÉ IS AN ESSENTIAL INGREDIENT OF CREOLE GUMBO. THE FIRST FRENCH MARKET STRUCTURE WAS BUILT IN 1791 AND REFERRED TO AS *LES HALLES DES BOUCHERIES*, MEANING "THE MEAT SHOPS." THE ARCADED COLONNADE SEEN TODAY WAS DESIGNED LATER BY THE SPANISH. IMAGINE THE OLD FRENCH MARKET AT DAWN ON A SUNDAY IN THE MID-NINETEENTH CENTURY:

(CONTINUED ON NEXT PAGE)

Bangkok Beef Stew

Yield: 6 servings

4	CUPS WATER	1/3	CUP FINELY CHOPPED LEMON GRASS
2	(1/2-OUNCE) LARGE BEEF BOUILLON CUBES	1	TABLESPOON CURRY POWDER
1	TABLESPOON OLIVE OIL	2	BAY LEAVES
2 1/4	POUNDS TRIMMED BONELESS BEEF CHUCK, CUT INTO 1 1/2-INCH CUBES	2	LARGE CARROTS, PEELED, CUT INTO 1/2-INCH PIECES
1	TABLESPOON OLIVE OIL	2	SMALL POTATOES, PEELED, CUT INTO 1/2-INCH PIECES
2	CUPS COARSELY CHOPPED ONIONS	8	OUNCES BUTTON MUSHROOMS, STEMS TRIMMED
3	GARLIC CLOVES, MINCED		SALT AND PEPPER TO TASTE
1	(14-OUNCE) CAN DICED TOMATOES IN JUICE		CHOPPED FRESH PARSLEY FOR GARNISH

Bring the water to a boil in a large saucepan. Add the bouillon cubes and stir to dissolve. Set aside. Heat 1 tablespoon olive oil in a large saucepan over high heat. Sauté the beef in batches, for 6 minutes or until browned. Remove the beef with a slotted spoon to a bowl. Add 1 tablespoon olive oil, onions and garlic to the saucepan. Sauté for 5 minutes or until the onions are soft. Add the bouillon, tomatoes, lemon grass, curry powder, bay leaves and browned beef with any juices. Bring to a boil. Reduce the heat to medium-low and cover. Simmer for 1 hour or until the beef is tender, stirring occasionally. Add the carrots, potatoes and mushrooms. Simmer, covered, for 20 minutes or until the vegetables are just tender. Uncover and simmer for 10 minutes or until the potatoes are very tender and the stew has thickened slightly. Season with salt and pepper. Remove the bay leaves. Spoon into a serving bowl and garnish with parsley. Note: Lemon grass is available at Asian markets.

TEMPTING AROMAS OF STRONG COFFEE INTERMINGLE WITH THE PUNGENT SMELLS OF FRUITS, VEGETABLES, MEATS, FISH, AND, PRIOR TO MODERN SANITATION, REFUSE; INDIAN SQUAWS PEDDLE COLORFUL HANDMADE BASKETS AND EXOTIC SPICES; THE TONGUES OF MANY NATIONALITIES BLEND IN CONTINUOUS CONVERSATION; MONKEYS AND PARROTS FOR SALE ADD THEIR NOISY SOUNDS TO A CARNIVAL ATMOSPHERE. BY EIGHT OR NINE O'CLOCK IN THE MORNING, EVERYTHING IS SOLD, DUE TO LACK OF REFRIGERATION.

Veal Sweetbreads in Port Wine Sauce

Yield: 6 servings

2	POUNDS SWEETBREADS	¼	CUP OLIVE OIL
1	CUP VINEGAR	¼	CUP (½ STICK) BUTTER
3	CUPS FLOUR	½	CUP MINCED SHALLOTS
½	TEASPOON SALT	3	TABLESPOONS FLOUR
1	TABLESPOON PEPPER	1	CUP PORT

Wash the sweetbreads in cold water and place in a bowl. Soak in cold water for 2 hours, changing the water several times. Place the sweetbreads in a large saucepan and cover with water. Add the vinegar and simmer for 30 minutes. Drain and place in a bowl of cold water for 5 minutes. Drain and arrange in a single layer on a plate. Cover with another plate and add weight to press down on the sweetbreads. Chill, weighted, for 8 to 12 hours. Remove the sweetbreads to a work surface and remove the membranes gently, being careful not to break the medallion shape. Combine 3 cups flour, salt and pepper in a large flat dish. Coat the sweetbreads in the flour and shake off any excess. Heat the olive oil and butter in a large heavy skillet. Sauté the sweetbreads in batches until browned. Remove to an ovenproof dish and keep warm in a 200-degree oven. Add the shallots to the skillet and sauté for 5 minutes or until soft but not browned. Stir in 3 tablespoons flour and cook for 5 minutes. Add the port and cook while scraping up any browned bits. Cook until slightly thickened. Place the sweetbreads on serving plates and top with the sauce.

THE REVEILLON

The *Reveillon*, a festive New Year's Eve party, was celebrated by the Creoles, who viewed Christmas as a solemn and holy occasion. Family and good friends enjoyed the Reveillon together, often toasting with eggnog and other more spirited drinks late into the night. On New Year's Day, the children received their nicest presents, and visits were made to other relatives and friends. Tables set with the finest china and linen served as backdrops to fancy cakes and sweets, cordials, wines, and liqueurs. A veritable feast of dishes ranging from sweetbreads to coconut custard pie was served at home for dinner. Some local restaurants now offer special Reveillon menus during the holidays.

Veal Vieux Carré

YIELD: 4 SERVINGS

6	TABLESPOONS CHOPPED FRESH ITALIAN PARSLEY	1¼	POUNDS VEAL SCALLOPS
1	TEASPOON MINCED GARLIC	2	TABLESPOONS BUTTER
3	TEASPOONS GRATED LEMON ZEST	5	TEASPOONS MINCED GARLIC
	SALT AND PEPPER TO TASTE	2	TABLESPOONS BUTTER
		3	TABLESPOONS FRESH LEMON JUICE

Mix the parsley, 1 teaspoon garlic, lemon zest, salt and pepper in a bowl. Season the veal with salt and pepper. Melt 2 tablespoons butter in a large heavy nonstick skillet over medium-high heat. Add the veal. Sauté for 2 minutes per side or until cooked through; remove and keep warm. Add 5 teaspoons garlic and 2 tablespoons butter to the skillet. Sauté for 30 seconds. Add the lemon juice. Bring to a boil, scraping up any browned bits. Spoon the sauce over the veal and sprinkle with the parsley mixture.

Mint Julep Lamb Chops

YIELD: 4 SERVINGS

1	CUP FRESH MINT	8	(4-OUNCE) LAMB CHOPS
½	CUP SUGAR		SALT AND PEPPER TO TASTE
¼	CUP WHITE WINE VINEGAR	3	TABLESPOONS BUTTER
2	TABLESPOONS BOURBON	3	TABLESPOONS VEGETABLE OIL

Place the mint in a food processor. Pulse until finely chopped. Add the sugar, vinegar and bourbon; process until mixed. Pour into a sealable freezer bag and add the chops. Seal and chill for 8 to 12 hours, turning occasionally. Remove the chops from the marinade and pat dry. Reserve the marinade. Season the chops with salt and pepper. Heat half the butter with half the oil in each of 2 large heavy skillets over high heat. Add 4 chops to each skillet. Sauté for 4 minutes per side for medium-rare. Remove chops and keep warm. Boil the reserved marinade in a saucepan for 5 to 6 minutes. Spoon the sauce over the chops.

VIEUX CARRÉ

THE VIEUX CARRÉ IS THE ORIGINAL CITY OF NEW ORLEANS, FOUNDED IN 1718 BY JEAN BAPTISTE LE MOYNE, SIEUR DE BIENVILLE. VIEUX CARRÉ MEANS "OLD SQUARE," ALTHOUGH IT IS ACTUALLY A RECTANGLE. IT IS MOST OFTEN REFERRED TO AS THE FRENCH QUARTER. IT IS BOUNDED BY CANAL STREET, ESPLANADE AVENUE, RAMPART STREET, AND THE MISSISSIPPI RIVER. THE ONLY AUTHENTIC FRENCH COLONIAL STRUCTURE WITHIN ITS BORDERS IS THE URSULINE CONVENT. THE PRESENT ARCHITECTURE IS SPANISH IN ORIGIN, DUE TO THE TWO GREAT FIRES OF 1788 AND 1794. THE FIRST FIRE DESTROYED 856 BUILDINGS; THE SECOND, THE REMAINING FRENCH BUILDINGS—EXCEPT FOR THE URSULINE CONVENT. IN 1762 NEW ORLEANS WAS CEDED TO SPAIN FROM FRANCE. THE FIRES STRUCK WHILE THE CITY WAS UNDER SPANISH RULE, AND THE ARCHITECTURE REFLECTS THE SPANISH INFLUENCE ON THE AREA. HOWEVER, THE FRENCH INFLUENCE AND CULTURE STILL PREVAIL IN KEEPING THE VIEUX CARRÉ THE UNIQUE PLACE THAT IT IS TODAY.

Crown Roast of Pork with Apple Stuffing

Yield: 10 servings

1	(8-POUND) CROWN ROAST OF PORK (12 RIBS)		APPLE STUFFING (PAGE 139)
2	TABLESPOONS VEGETABLE OIL	4	TEASPOONS CORNSTARCH
1	TEASPOON SALT	¼	CUP BRANDY
1	TEASPOON SUGAR	1	CUP CANNED BEEF BROTH
1	TEASPOON DRIED THYME	½	CUP CANNED BEEF BROTH
½	TEASPOON DRIED SAGE	1	CUP APPLE CIDER
½	TEASPOON PEPPER		SALT AND PEPPER TO TASTE

Place the roast on a 9- to 10-inch diameter tart pan bottom. Set on a deep-sided baking sheet. Brush the roast with the oil. Combine 1 teaspoon salt, sugar, thyme, sage and ½ teaspoon pepper in a small bowl. Rub the spice mixture over the pork. Cover with plastic wrap and chill overnight. Fill the cavity of the roast with enough Apple Stuffing to mound in the center. Cover the bone tips with foil. Roast the pork in the bottom third of the oven at 450 degrees for 20 minutes. Reduce the temperature to 325 degrees and roast for 1 hour and 50 minutes or until a meat thermometer inserted near the center of the pork registers 150 degrees. Remove the foil from the bones and continue roasting for 15 minutes or until a meat thermometer registers 155 degrees. Remove the roast carefully to a platter and cover loosely with foil to keep warm. Dissolve the cornstarch in the brandy in a small bowl. Add 1 cup broth to the baking sheet used to roast the pork. Scrape up any browned bits. Pour into a small saucepan and place in the freezer for 15 minutes. Skim off the fat. Add ½ cup broth and the apple cider to the saucepan. Bring to a boil and whisk the cornstarch mixture into the saucepan. Boil for 3 minutes or until slightly thickened. Season with salt and pepper. Pour into a gravy boat. Carve the roast between the bones to separate the chops. Serve with the remaining Apple Stuffing and the gravy.

Apple Stuffing

2	TABLESPOONS VEGETABLE OIL		3	EGGS, LIGHTLY BEATEN
1¼	CUPS CHOPPED CELERY		⅓	CUP CHOPPED FRESH PARSLEY
⅓	CUP CHOPPED SHALLOTS		2	TEASPOONS DRIED SAGE, CRUMBLED
1	TABLESPOON MINCED GARLIC		2	TEASPOONS SALT
2	POUNDS GROUND PORK		¾	TEASPOON PEPPER
1	CUP BREAD CRUMBS		¼	TEASPOON GROUND ALLSPICE
4	OUNCES DRIED APPLES, CHOPPED		1	CUP (ABOUT) CANNED BEEF BROTH

*H*eat the oil in a medium skillet over medium heat. Add the celery and sauté for 3 minutes or until tender. Add the shallots and garlic and sauté for 2 minutes or until the shallots are tender. Remove the mixture to a large bowl. Add the pork, bread crumbs, apples, eggs, parsley, sage, salt, pepper and allspice. Mix well. Stir in enough of the broth to moisten the stuffing. Set aside enough stuffing in a bowl to fill the cavity of the crown roast of pork. Place the remaining stuffing in an 5x9-inch loaf pan. Cover with foil. Bake the stuffing at 375 degrees for 1 hour. Invert the stuffing onto a platter. Slice the stuffing and serve with the Crown Roast of Pork (page 138).

Pork Tenderloin with
Red Chile Mustard Marinade

Yield: 6 to 8 servings

2	CUPS DIJON MUSTARD		SALT AND FRESHLY GROUND PEPPER
3	TABLESPOONS ANCHO CHILE POWDER		TO TASTE
1	TABLESPOON HONEY	1	(3- TO 4-POUND) PORK TENDERLOIN
1½	TABLESPOONS WATER		

Mix the mustard, chile powder, honey and water in a bowl. Season with salt and pepper. Place the pork in a deep dish and pour the marinade over the top. Cover and chill for 8 to 12 hours. Turn the pork several times during marinating. Prepare the grill at medium-high heat or preheat the broiler. Remove the pork and discard the marinade. Grill or broil the pork for 15 to 20 minutes or until cooked through, turning occasionally. Remove the pork to a cutting board and slice into medallions. Serve immediately.

Marinated Pork Chops

Yield: 4 to 6 servings

⅓	CUP TERIYAKI SAUCE	¼	TEASPOON GRATED LEMON ZEST
2	TABLESPOONS PLUM JAM	4	TO 6 PORK CHOPS
1	TABLESPOON BROWN SUGAR		

Mix the teriyaki sauce, jam, brown sugar and lemon zest in a shallow dish. Add the pork chops and turn to coat. Cover and chill for 4 to 12 hours. Remove the chops to a plate. Heat the marinade in a small saucepan and boil for 5 to 6 minutes. Grill, broil or bake the chops until cooked through, basting with the heated marinade.

Rack of Venison with Hunter Whiskey Sauce

YIELD: 4 SERVINGS

2	CUPS VEAL DEMI-GLACE		SALT AND PEPPER TO TASTE	
1	CUP DRY RED WINE		2	TABLESPOONS BUTTER
1	BAY LEAF		2	TABLESPOONS VEGETABLE OIL
½	TEASPOON DRIED THYME, CRUMBLED		½	CUP SOUR MASH WHISKEY
½	TEASPOON DRIED SAVORY, CRUMBLED		6	TABLESPOONS (¾ STICK) BUTTER,
1	(2½-POUND) RACK OF VENISON			SOFTENED, CUT INTO TABLESPOONS
2	GARLIC CLOVES, MINCED			

Combine the demi-glace, wine, bay leaf, thyme and savory in a saucepan and mix well. Bring to a simmer and cook for 30 minutes, stirring occasionally. Set aside. Place the venison on a platter and pat dry. Rub lightly with the garlic and season with salt and pepper. Heat 2 tablespoons butter and the oil in a large heavy ovenproof skillet over medium-high heat. Add the venison and brown on both sides. Place the skillet in the oven and roast at 350 degrees for 40 minutes for medium-rare. Remove the venison to a platter and keep warm. Add the whiskey to the hot skillet and scrape up any browned bits. Strain the whiskey and pan drippings into the demi-glace mixture. Warm over low heat until hot. Remove from the heat and whisk in 6 tablespoons butter, 1 tablespoon at a time. Place 2 venison ribs on each of 4 serving plates. Top with the sauce.

Note: Demi-glace is available at specialty food stores.

Southern-Fried Venison with Cream Gravy

Yield: 2 servings

1	POUND VENISON ROUND STEAK	½	CUP VEGETABLE OIL
1	CUP FLOUR	½	CUP (OR MORE) WHOLE MILK
2	TEASPOONS SALT		SALT AND PEPPER TO TASTE
1	TEASPOON PEPPER		

Place the venison on a cutting board and cut into 2 pieces. Pound with a mallet to tenderize. Combine the flour, 2 teaspoons salt and 1 teaspoon pepper in a large flat dish. Coat the venison with flour. Set aside the remaining flour. Heat the oil in a skillet. Add the venison and brown on both sides. Remove the venison to an ovenproof plate lined with a paper towel. Keep warm in a 200-degree oven. Pour off all but 3 tablespoons of the pan drippings. Whisk the remaining flour into the milk in a bowl. Add to the drippings in the skillet. Cook over low heat until thickened, stirring constantly. Stir in additional milk 1 tablespoon at a time if the sauce is too thick. Season with salt and pepper. Place the venison on serving plates. Top with the gravy.

Deep Woods Jambalaya

Yield: 12 servings

1	POUND ANDOUILLE SAUSAGE	3	RIBS CELERY, CHOPPED
2	POUNDS BONELESS PORK BUTT	2	CANS TOMATOES WITH GREEN CHILES, CHOPPED
2	Cornish game hens		
1	(4- TO 5-POUND) RABBIT	3	CANS CHICKEN BROTH
5	TABLESPOONS BACON DRIPPINGS OR VEGETABLE OIL	3	(8-OUNCE) BOXES JAMBALAYA MIX
			SALT AND CAYENNE PEPPER TO TASTE
1	LARGE ONION, CHOPPED	1	PINT CHERRY TOMATOES
1	LARGE BELL PEPPER, CHOPPED		

Cut the sausage, pork butt, Cornish game hens and rabbit into serving pieces on a cutting board. Heat the bacon drippings in a very large heavy saucepan. Brown the meat in batches and remove with tongs to a platter. Add the onion, bell pepper and celery. Sauté until tender. Stir in all the browned meat, canned tomatoes, broth and jambalaya mixes. Bring to a boil. Reduce the heat to low, cover and simmer for 30 minutes or until all the meat is cooked through. Season with salt and cayenne pepper. Press the cherry tomatoes evenly into the mixture. Cover and cook for 2 minutes. Serve immediately.

Tally-Ho Alligator Stew

Yield: 10 servings

5	BAY LEAVES	8	OUNCES SPINACH LEAVES, FINELY CHOPPED
2	TEASPOONS SALT		
2	TEASPOONS WHITE PEPPER	2	CUPS MINCED ONIONS
1¾	TEASPOONS GARLIC POWDER	1	CUP MINCED CELERY
1	TEASPOON CAYENNE PEPPER	3½	CUPS TOMATO SAUCE
1	TEASPOON ONION POWDER	⅔	CUP FLOUR
1	TEASPOON DRIED THYME	1	TEASPOON MINCED GARLIC
1	TEASPOON DRY MUSTARD	11	CUPS BEEF STOCK OR BROTH
1	TEASPOON BLACK PEPPER	⅓	CUP DRY SHERRY
1	TEASPOON DRIED BASIL	1	CUP CHOPPED FRESH PARSLEY
½	TEASPOON CUMIN	¼	LEMON, SEEDED
¼	CUP (½ STICK) UNSALTED BUTTER	6	HARD-COOKED EGGS, QUARTERED
¼	CUP (½ STICK) MARGARINE		
3	POUNDS FRESH ALLIGATOR MEAT, CUT INTO 2-INCH CUBES		

Mix the bay leaves, salt, white pepper, garlic powder, cayenne pepper, onion powder, thyme, dry mustard, black pepper, basil and cumin in a small bowl. Melt the butter and margarine in a large saucepan over high heat. Add the alligator meat and sauté for 6 to 8 minutes or until browned. Stir in the seasoning mixture, spinach, onions and celery and sauté for 15 minutes. Stir in the tomato sauce and cook for 10 minutes, stirring frequently near the end of the cooking time. Stir in the flour and garlic. Cook for 5 minutes, stirring constantly and scraping the bottom of the pan. Add 2 cups of the stock and stir to remove any browned bits on the bottom of the pan. Stir in 7 more cups of stock and continue to scrape the bottom of the pan. Bring the mixture to a boil, stirring occasionally. Boil for 5 minutes. Reduce the heat and simmer for 45 minutes. Add the remaining 2 cups of stock and the sherry. Cook for 20 minutes, stirring frequently. Remove the bay leaves. Mince the parsley and lemon in a food processor. Add the eggs and process for a few seconds or until the eggs are coarsely chopped. Spoon the stew into bowls and top with the egg mixture.

Sportsman's Paradise

Many of the first residents of New Orleans were professional trappers who found a variety of small animals with valuable pelts in the bayous and swamps. Other settlers, by necessity, were hunters and fishermen. The abundance of seafood and waterfowl in early New Orleans helped Louisiana build a reputation as a "Sportsman's Paradise." The first organized hunting and fishing club in America, the Tally-Ho, was formed in New Orleans in 1815 and is still active today.

Panéed Rabbit for Two

Yield: 2 servings

	Flour	3/4	cup sliced shiitake mushrooms
	Salt and pepper to taste	1	garlic clove, minced
1	egg	1/4	teaspoon fresh thyme, or to taste
2	teaspoons water	1/2	cup white wine
1	rabbit, boned	1/2	cup rabbit stock or chicken broth
	Bread crumbs	1/2	cup (1 stick) butter
	Olive oil	2	cups fresh spinach leaves

Mix the flour, salt and pepper in a dish. Mix the egg and water in a dish. Dredge the rabbit in the flour, then in the egg mixture. Coat with the bread crumbs. Brown rabbit on all sides in oil in a skillet; reduce heat and fry until cooked through. Remove and keep warm. Pour off all but 2 tablespoons of the pan drippings. Add the mushrooms and garlic. Sauté for 1 minute. Stir in the thyme, wine and stock. Cook until reduced by 3/4. Whisk in the butter 2 tablespoons at a time. Stir in the spinach and cook just until wilted. Cut the rabbit in half. Place on serving plates and top with the spinach.

Recipe provided by Kevin Vizard

Rabbit with Dark Raisin Gravy

Yield: 4 to 6 servings

2	whole rabbits, quartered	1/2	teaspoon ground allspice
1/2	cup vinegar		(optional)
2	teaspoons salt	1/2	cup dark raisins
1	small onion, chopped	1/4	cup packed brown sugar
4	whole cloves	1/4	cup cornstarch
2	bay leaves	1/4	cup cold water

Combine the rabbit pieces with cool water to cover in a deep stockpot. Add half the vinegar. Boil for 5 minutes; drain. Cover again with cool water. Add the remaining vinegar, salt, onion, cloves, bay leaves and allspice. Bring to a boil; reduce the heat. Cook until the rabbit is tender. Add the raisins and brown sugar. Simmer until the rabbit is cooked through; remove and keep warm. Stir a mixture of the cornstarch and water into the cooking liquid. Cook until thickened. Serve the rabbit topped with the thickened gravy.

Slow-Roasted Duck with Orange Sherry Sauce

YIELD: 4 SERVINGS

2	MEDIUM RED BELL PEPPERS		4	LARGE SPRIGS OF FRESH ROSEMARY
2	MEDIUM CARROTS, JULIENNED		2	CUPS FRESH ORANGE JUICE
2¼	POUNDS YELLOW ONIONS, COARSELY CHOPPED		1	CUP DRY SHERRY
½	CUP (1 STICK) UNSALTED BUTTER, MELTED		½	CUP SOY SAUCE
			2	TABLESPOONS UNSALTED BUTTER
2	(5-POUND) DUCKS		4	OUNCES SMALL OYSTER MUSHROOMS, STEMS TRIMMED
	SALT AND FRESHLY GROUND PEPPER TO TASTE		4	CHIVES, CUT INTO 1-INCH PIECES, FOR GARNISH

Roast the bell peppers directly over a gas flame or under the broiler until evenly charred. Wrap in a paper bag and let stand for 10 minutes. Peel, seed and cut into strips. Place in a bowl. Blanch the carrots in boiling water for 1 minute. Drain and add to the peppers. Set aside. Toss the onions with the melted butter in a large bowl. Rinse the ducks and pat dry. Season inside and out with salt and pepper. Place 2 rosemary sprigs in each cavity. Pack each cavity tightly with the onion mixture and place the ducks in a large roasting pan. Roast at 500 degrees for 10 minutes. Reduce the temperature to 300 degrees and cover the pan loosely with foil. Roast for 4½ hours, draining the fat from the pan every hour during roasting. Remove from the oven and drain the fat from the pan. Add the orange juice, sherry and soy sauce to the ducks in the roasting pan. Return to the oven, uncovered, and roast at 300 degrees for 30 minutes or until the ducks are cooked through. Remove the ducks to a platter and allow to cool slightly. Cut the ducks in half on a cutting board. Discard the onions, rosemary and all bones except the leg bone, keeping it attached to the breast. Place the ducks on an ovenproof platter and keep warm in a 200-degree oven. Pour the juices from the roasting pan into a saucepan, discarding any duck skin. Skim off the fat. Bring the juices to a boil over medium-high heat. Cook until reduced to 1½ cups. Strain and return to the saucepan. Melt 2 tablespoons butter in a skillet. Add the mushrooms and sauté until tender. Stir in the bell peppers, carrots and orange sauce. Season with salt and pepper. Cook just until heated through. Spoon the sauce onto 4 serving plates. Top each with half a duck and garnish with the chives.

Recipe provided by Greg Sonnier, Gabrielle Restaurant

Cabernet Canard

YIELD: 2 SERVINGS

2	(1-POUND) DUCK BREAST HALVES, BONED, WITH THE SKIN ON	1	TEASPOON MINCED FRESH ROSEMARY
3/4	CUP CABERNET SAUVIGNON OR OTHER DRY RED WINE	1/4	TEASPOON SALT
1	TABLESPOON EXTRA-VIRGIN OLIVE OIL	1/8	TEASPOON FRESHLY GROUND PEPPER
4	GARLIC CLOVES, PRESSED	1 1/2	TEASPOONS HONEY

Score the skin of each breast with a sharp knife. Combine the wine, olive oil, garlic, rosemary, salt and pepper in a large ceramic dish and mix well. Add the duck breasts and turn to coat. Let marinate at room temperature for 30 minutes or in the refrigerator for up to 2 hours. Remove the breasts from the marinade and pat dry on paper towels. Reserve the marinade. Heat a large cast-iron skillet over medium-high heat. Add the breasts skin side down and cook for 7 minutes or until the skin is crisp and dark golden brown. Reduce the heat slightly if the fat starts to smoke. Turn the breasts over and cook for 3 minutes or until cooked through. Remove to a warmed platter. Drain the fat from the skillet. Add the reserved marinade and the honey. Cook over medium heat for 1 minute, scraping up any browned bits. Pour over the duck breasts and serve.

BONING GAME BIRDS

BONE GOOSE OR DUCK YOURSELF OR GET IT FROM YOUR BUTCHER, BUT LEAVE THE SKIN ON. A STUFFING MAY BE USED IN A BIRD WITHOUT BONING, BUT THE PRESENTATION IS MORE IMPRESSIVE IF BONED AND THE BIRD IS EASIER TO SLICE.

Duck Confit

Yield: 4 servings

4	DOMESTIC DUCK LEG PORTIONS WITH THIGHS ATTACHED (ABOUT 2 POUNDS), OR 8 WILD DUCK LEG-THIGH PORTIONS	½	TEASPOON CAYENNE PEPPER
1	TABLESPOON KOSHER SALT	4	LARGE OR 8 SMALL GARLIC CLOVES, PEELED, MASHED
½	TEASPOON FRESHLY GROUND BLACK PEPPER	4	BAY LEAVES
		4	CUPS OLIVE OIL, SHORTENING AND/OR RENDERED DUCK FAT

Trim excess fat from the duck legs and set aside. Place the duck legs skin side down on a platter. Sprinkle with the kosher salt, black pepper and cayenne pepper. Place half the garlic cloves and bay leaves on each of 2 leg portions. Place 1 of the remaining legs on top of each of the seasoned legs, meaty side to meaty side. To render the duck fat, combine the reserved fat with water to cover in a large stockpot. Cook, covered, over medium heat for 20 to 25 minutes or until any skin pieces are light golden brown; the fat must remain clear yellow.

Do not boil; the temperature should not exceed 325 degrees. Remove and discard the skin pieces. Let the rendered fat stand until cool. Cover and store in the refrigerator until needed. Wipe excess salt from the duck with paper towels. Melt the rendered fat in a large ovenproof stockpot. Add the duck, making sure that the duck is completely covered with liquid. Place in a 200-degree oven.

Cook until the duck is tender and cooked through. Discard the garlic and bay leaves before serving. To preserve the duck, remove the duck from the rendered fat. Place the duck in a crock or earthenware bowl fitted with a rack. Bring the rendered fat to a simmer and cook for 5 minutes. Line a strainer with several thicknesses of cheesecloth.

Pour the liquid fat through the strainer over the duck.

Shake the crock gently to distribute evenly. Once the duck is completely covered, let stand until the fat has congealed. Cover with plastic wrap and store in the refrigerator. Duck will keep for 3 to 4 months at 37 degrees. To remove the duck pieces, set the crock in a bowl of hot water to soften the fat. Remove desired number of pieces. Cover the remaining pieces with fat and store as directed above.

GAME BIRDS

GAME BIRDS INCLUDE PARTRIDGE, GROUSE, PHEASANT, DOVE, PIGEON, SQUAB, WILD GOOSE, WILD DUCK, WOODCOCK, QUAIL, SNIPE, AND PLOVER. WITH THE EXCEPTION OF PARTRIDGE AND QUAIL, THE FLESH OF GAME BIRDS IS DARKER IN COLOR. ALSO, WITH THE EXCEPTION OF SOME WILD DUCKS AND GEESE, GAME BIRDS CONTAIN LESS FAT THAN DOMESTIC POULTRY.

Pistachio Stuffing

1 TABLESPOON BUTTER
1 TABLESPOON OLIVE OIL
1 SMALL ONION, CHOPPED
¾ POUND GROUND
PORK OR VEAL
1 CUP BREAD CRUMBS
1 TEASPOON CHOPPED PARSLEY
1 TEASPOON DRIED SAGE
¼ CUP DRY SHERRY
3 THIN SLICES BOILED
HAM, CHOPPED
8 PISTACHIO NUTS, CHOPPED
1 EGG, LIGHTLY BEATEN
1 TEASPOON SALT
1 TEASPOON PEPPER

HEAT THE BUTTER AND
OLIVE OIL IN A LARGE SKILLET.
ADD THE ONION AND SAUTÉ
UNTIL TENDER. COMBINE THE
GROUND PORK, BREAD CRUMBS,
PARSLEY, SAGE, SHERRY, HAM,
PISTACHIOS, EGG, SALT AND
PEPPER IN A BOWL. ADD THE
SAUTÉED ONION AND MIX
WELL. USE TO STUFF GOOSE
OR OTHER GAME BIRDS.
YIELD: 8 SERVINGS

Ballontine of Goose
YIELD: 8 SERVINGS

2	TABLESPOONS OLIVE OIL	½	CUP CHICKEN STOCK OR BROTH
1	TABLESPOON FINELY CHOPPED CARROT	1	(3 TO 4-POUND) GOOSE (OR DUCK) PISTACHIO STUFFING (AT LEFT)
1	TABLESPOON MINCED ONION	2	TABLESPOONS OLIVE OIL
1	TABLESPOON MINCED CELERY	¼	CUP DRY SHERRY
1	TABLESPOON FLOUR	2	TABLESPOONS BUTTER
1	CUP CHICKEN STOCK OR BROTH	1	PINT MUSHROOMS, SLICED
4	MUSHROOMS	¼	CUP CHICKEN STOCK OR BROTH
1	TABLESPOON TOMATO PASTE	1	TABLESPOON FLOUR
	BOUQUET GARNI (SEE NOTE)		

Heat 2 tablespoons olive oil in a skillet. Add the carrot, onion and celery and sauté until soft but not browned. Add 1 tablespoon flour and cook slowly until the mixture is a rich brown color, stirring constantly. Add 1 cup stock, 4 mushrooms, tomato paste and bouquet garni. Bring to a boil. Reduce the heat and simmer, partially covered, for 25 minutes. Add ½ cup chicken stock and simmer for 5 minutes. Strain into a saucepan and set aside. Place the goose on a work surface and stuff with Pistachio Stuffing (at left). Close the cavity with skewers. Set the stuffed goose on a rack in a roasting pan. Brush with 2 tablespoons olive oil. Roast at 400 degrees for 1 to 1½ hours or until cooked through, basting every 20 minutes. Turn the goose halfway during roasting. Remove the goose and keep warm. Drain the fat from the roasting pan. Add the sherry and scrape up any browned bits in the pan. Strain and add to the vegetable mixture in the saucepan. Melt the butter in a skillet and add 1 pint sliced mushrooms. Sauté until tender. Add to the saucepan. Mix ¼ cup stock and 1 tablespoon flour. Add to the saucepan. Cook until the sauce has thickened, stirring constantly. Serve the goose whole or sliced with some of the sauce poured over it. Serve the remaining sauce in a gravy boat. Note: For bouquet garni, place 1 tablespoon parsley, 3 peppercorns, 1 bay leaf and ½ teaspoon thyme on a piece of cheesecloth and tie securely.

Pheasant Normandy

Yield: 4 servings

¼	CUP (½ STICK) BUTTER		2	TEASPOONS SALT
2	PHEASANTS, CLEANED		½	TEASPOON PEPPER
2	CUPS CHOPPED TART APPLES		1	TABLESPOON CORNSTARCH
½	CUP Calvados		1	TABLESPOON COLD WATER
2	CUPS HEAVY CREAM			HOT COOKED WILD RICE
¼	CUP FRESH LEMON JUICE			

Melt the butter in a heavy skillet. Add the pheasants and sauté until lightly browned on all sides. Remove to a platter and keep warm. Add the apples to the skillet and sauté for 3 minutes. Remove the apples with a slotted spoon and spread evenly in the bottom of a covered baking dish large enough to hold the birds. Arrange the birds on top of the apples. Drain the fat from the skillet. Add the Calvados to the skillet. Cook over high heat for 2 minutes, scraping up any browned bits. Pour over the birds. Bake, covered, at 350 degrees for 45 minutes. Combine the cream, lemon juice, salt and pepper in a bowl. Pour over the birds. Bake, uncovered, at 350 degrees for 30 minutes or until cooked through. Remove the birds to a serving platter and keep warm. Pour the cooking liquid and apples from the casserole into a saucepan. Mix the cornstarch and water in a bowl and add to the saucepan. Cook over medium heat for 2 minutes or until the sauce is the consistency of gravy, stirring constantly. Pour into a gravy boat. Serve the birds on a bed of wild rice and pass the sauce separately.

PHEASANT NORMANDY

THE RECIPE AT LEFT DEPICTS THE WAY PHEASANT IS PREPARED IN NORMANDY, WHERE CALVADOS ORIGINATES. CALVADOS IS AN APPLE BRANDY AND CAN BE FOUND IN MOST LIQUOR STORES.

Quail Amandine

8	QUAIL, BONED	1½	CUPS ORANGE JUICE
¼	TEASPOON SALT	½	CUP SLIVERED BLANCHED
¼	CUP (½ STICK) BUTTER		ALMONDS
2	TABLESPOONS FLOUR	1	CUP RAISINS
¼	TEASPOON SALT	1	CUP PEELED SEEDED ORANGE
⅛	TEASPOON GROUND CINNAMON		SECTIONS
⅛	TEASPOON GROUND GINGER, OR	4	CUPS COOKED RICE, PREFERABLY
	TO TASTE		WILD

*R*inse the quail pieces in cold water and pat dry. Sprinkle with ¼ teaspoon salt. Heat the butter in a large skillet over medium heat. Add the quail and sauté until lightly browned. Remove to a plate. Mix the flour, salt, cinnamon and ginger in a bowl. Stir into the pan drippings in the skillet to make a smooth paste. Add the orange juice and cook until the sauce bubbles and thickens, stirring constantly. Stir in the browned quail, almonds and raisins and reduce the heat to low. Cover and simmer for 30 minutes or until the quail is cooked through. Stir in the orange sections and cook until heated through. Serve the quail on a bed of rice and top with the sauce.

PORT WINE SAUCE

1 TEASPOON OLIVE OIL
¼ CUP MINCED SHALLOTS
1 TABLESPOON MINCED GARLIC
1 TEASPOON SALT
⅛ TEASPOON PEPPER, OR
TO TASTE
1 TEASPOON SUGAR
1 CUP PORT
3 CUPS CHICKEN STOCK
OR BROTH

HEAT THE OLIVE OIL IN A LARGE SAUCEPAN OVER HIGH HEAT. ADD THE SHALLOTS, GARLIC, SALT AND PEPPER AND SAUTÉ FOR 1 MINUTE. STIR IN THE SUGAR AND PORT AND BRING TO A BOIL. COOK FOR 3 MINUTES. ADD THE CHICKEN STOCK AND COOK OVER HIGH HEAT FOR 20 MINUTES, STIRRING FREQUENTLY. SERVE WITH FRENCH QUARTER QUAIL (PAGE 151)
YIELD: 1⅓ CUPS

French Quarter Quail

Yield: 4 servings

8	QUAIL	8	SLICES BACON
4	TEASPOONS OLIVE OIL	1⅓	CUPS PORT WINE SAUCE
4	TEASPOONS CREOLE SEASONING		(SEE SIDEBAR, PAGE 150)
2	CUPS MUSHROOM AND ANDOUILLE STUFFING		

Bone the quail, except for the leg bones. Rinse the quail in cold water and pat dry. Place on a work surface. Brush each bird with ½ teaspoon of the olive oil, dividing the oil between the inside and outside of the bird. Sprinkle each bird with ½ teaspoon Creole seasoning, dividing the seasoning between the inside and outside of the bird. Stuff each bird with ¼ cup Mushroom and Andouille Stuffing (below). Wrap 1 slice of bacon around each bird and place on a baking sheet lined with parchment paper. Roast at 400 degrees for 15 to 20 minutes or until the skin is golden brown and crisp and the birds are cooked through. Arrange 2 quail on each of 4 serving plates. Pour the Port Wine Sauce over the birds and serve immediately.

Mushroom and Andouille Stuffing

Yield: about 2 cups

3	CUPS CHOPPED ASSORTED WILD MUSHROOMS	1	TABLESPOON OLIVE OIL
4	OUNCES ANDOUILLE SAUSAGE, CHOPPED (ABOUT ½ CUP)	1	TEASPOON CREOLE SEASONING
		1	TEASPOON SALT
¼	CUP CHOPPED ONION	1	TEASPOON PEPPER
1	TABLESPOON MINCED GARLIC	½	CUP PORT
		¾	CUP BREAD CRUMBS

Combine the mushrooms, sausage, onion and garlic in a food processor. Process until the mixture forms a coarse paste. Heat the olive oil in a medium skillet over high heat. Add the mushroom mixture, Creole seasoning, salt and pepper. Sauté for 4 minutes. Stir in the port and cook for 1 minute. Reduce the heat and add the bread crumbs. Cook for 2 minutes, stirring constantly. Remove from the heat and allow to cool to room temperature.

Side Dishes & Sauces

Side Dishes & Sauces

James Robb House
1237 Washington Avenue

A banker, railroad tycoon, commission merchant, and proprietor of the New Orleans Gas Company, James Robb was one of the wealthiest residents of the Garden District in the mid-1800s. The Garden District acquired its name from the fact that suburban villas generally were placed on one corner of a large square lot, leaving space on the side of the house for a flanking garden. Robb's elaborate residence was centered on an entire municipal square. He wrote: "I have been engaged in almost every branch of business, and made money until I did not know what to do with it. I have sat at the table with royalty, seen every phase of life, traveled the whole civilized globe and seen all its art treasures."

⚜

Robb commissioned the architectural firm of Gallier, Turpin & Co. to build this house and its twin at 1136 Washington for $25,000 in 1856 as rental property. The original plan is atypical for the Garden District, lacking the obligatory double parlors and employing instead three small rooms on the ground floor and four bedrooms upstairs. When first built, the house also lacked its present cast-iron veranda, rendering a rather austere facade with not even a projecting balcony.

⚜

The house was rented from 1856 to 1860 to Emile Marqueze, a boot and shoe merchant, for $1,300 per year. A financial crisis caused Robb to liquidate his Garden District real estate in 1858, including this house, which was sold in 1860 to Edmund Wailes for $12,000. From the mid-1860s forward, the house was sold to various owners. It became the JLNO Show House VI in 1990.

Marinated Asparagus Bundles

2½	POUNDS ASPARAGUS		1	TEASPOON DRIED OREGANO
10	GREEN ONIONS, GREEN PART ONLY		1	TEASPOON DRIED TARRAGON
2	RED BELL PEPPERS, CUT INTO 20 STRIPS		1	TEASPOON DRY MUSTARD
1	CUP FINELY CHOPPED ONION		1	TEASPOON WORCESTERSHIRE SAUCE
1	CUP RED WINE VINEGAR		½	TEASPOON SALT
½	CUP WATER		¼	TEASPOON PEPPER
2	TEASPOONS SUGAR			

Snap off the tough-ends of the asparagus. Cook, covered, in a small amount of boiling water in a saucepan for 5 minutes or until tender-crisp. Drain and rinse under cold running water. Drain well. Place the green onion tops in a bowl. Cover with boiling water. Drain immediately and rinse under cold running water. Drain well. Arrange the asparagus into 10 bundles. Add 2 bell pepper strips to each bundle. Tie each bundle with a green onion strip. Arrange the bundles in a 9x13-inch baking dish. Combine the chopped onion, vinegar, water, sugar, oregano, tarragon, mustard, Worcestershire sauce, salt and pepper in a bowl and mix well. Pour over the asparagus bundles. Cover and chill for 2 to 8 hours. Remove the asparagus bundles and discard the marinade. Arrange the bundles on a serving platter and serve.

Asparagus with Rosemary Aïoli

Yield: 6 servings

¼	CUP EXTRA-VIRGIN OLIVE OIL
4	GARLIC CLOVES, UNPEELED
3	FRESH ROSEMARY SPRIGS
1	TABLESPOON BALSAMIC VINEGAR
2	CUPS MAYONNAISE

ZEST AND JUICE OF ½ ORANGE
ZEST AND JUICE OF 1 LEMON
FRESHLY GROUND PEPPER TO TASTE
2 POUNDS ASPARAGUS, TRIMMED

Combine the olive oil, garlic, rosemary and vinegar in a food processor. Process for 30 seconds. Let stand for 5 minutes. Place a strainer over a bowl and strain the rosemary mixture. Press with the back of a spoon to extract all the liquids. Discard the solids. Add the mayonnaise, orange zest, orange juice, lemon zest and lemon juice. Season with pepper. Stir well to mix. Cover and chill. Cook the asparagus, covered, in a large pot of boiling water for 3 minutes or until tender-crisp. Immediately plunge into cold water to cool. Drain well. Divide the asparagus among 6 serving plates. Spoon 3 tablespoons of the rosemary aïoli over the asparagus and serve.
Note: The rosemary aïoli can be made up to 1 week ahead.

LAFAYETTE CEMETERY

LAFAYETTE CEMETERY IS JUST ONE OF MORE THAN FORTY ABOVEGROUND CEMETERIES IN NEW ORLEANS. THE CEMETERIES ARE REFERRED TO AS OUTDOOR MUSEUMS AND AS CITIES OF THE DEAD. THE DEAD ARE BURIED IN ABOVEGROUND TOMBS BECAUSE THE CITY IS SIX TO EIGHT FEET BELOW SEA LEVEL. MANY OF THE TOMBS RESEMBLE HOUSES AND OTHER BUILDINGS. LAFAYETTE CEMETERY NO. 1 IS LOCATED IN THE GARDEN DISTRICT IN A SQUARE BOUNDED BY WASHINGTON AVENUE, PRYTANIA, COLISEUM, AND SIXTH STREETS. THE CEMETERY IS THE BURIAL SITE OF NUMEROUS VICTIMS OF YELLOW FEVER EPIDEMICS. IT SITS ON WHAT WAS ONCE PART OF THE LIVAUDAIS PLANTATION. ESTABLISHED IN 1833, IT WAS THE CITY'S FIRST PLANNED CEMETERY AND HAS BEEN IN CONTINUOUS USE EVER SINCE. THE INTERSECTING AVENUES OF THE CEMETERY WERE DESIGNED TO ALLOW FUNERAL PROCESSIONS TO TRAVEL THROUGH THE SITE TO THE APPROPRIATE TOMB.

Hot Sesame Broccoli

Yield: 6 servings

1½	TEASPOONS DARK SESAME OIL	1	TABLESPOON SUGAR
1½	TEASPOONS VEGETABLE OIL	1	TABLESPOON LEMON JUICE
½	TEASPOON RED PEPPER FLAKES	1	TABLESPOON WATER
2	GARLIC CLOVES, MINCED	1½	POUNDS BROCCOLI
¼	CUP SOY SAUCE		

Heat the sesame oil and vegetable oil in a saucepan until hot but not smoking. Remove from the heat and add the red pepper flakes. Let stand for 10 minutes. Return to the heat and add the garlic, soy sauce, sugar, lemon juice and water. Cook until heated through. Reduce the heat to very low. Trim the broccoli and separate into spears. Steam until tender-crisp. Place in a bowl and add the soy mixture. Toss well to coat and serve immediately.

Haricots Verts with Bleu Cheese and Pecans

Yield: 6 servings

1	POUND HARICOTS VERTS, TRIMMED	1½	CUPS CHOPPED PECANS
3	SLICES BACON, CUT INTO ¼-INCH PIECES		PEPPER TO TASTE
4	OUNCES BLEU CHEESE, CRUMBLED		

Cook the green beans in a small amount of boiling water in a saucepan for 3 to 4 minutes or until tender-crisp. Drain. Fry the bacon in a skillet until crisp. Remove with a slotted spoon to paper towels to drain. Add the beans to the bacon drippings and cook over medium heat for 2 minutes. Add the bleu cheese and heat until the cheese melts. Stir in the bacon and pecans and season with pepper.

Red Beans and Rice

Yield: 10 servings

1	POUND DRIED KIDNEY BEANS	1	TABLESPOON WORCESTERSHIRE SAUCE
2	QUARTS WATER		
3	CUPS CHOPPED ONIONS	½	CUP TOMATO SAUCE
1	CUP CHOPPED FRESH PARSLEY	¼	TEASPOON DRIED OREGANO
1	CUP CHOPPED GREEN ONIONS	¼	TEASPOON DRIED THYME
2	GARLIC CLOVES, CHOPPED	1	POUND HOT SAUSAGE, SLICED
¼	TEASPOON CAYENNE PEPPER	1	POUND HAM STEAK, DICED
½	TEASPOON BLACK PEPPER		HOT COOKED RICE
¼	TEASPOON TABASCO SAUCE, OR TO TASTE		

Combine the kidney beans and water in a large heavy saucepan. Bring to a boil. Reduce the heat and simmer for 45 minutes. Stir in the onions, parsley, green onions, garlic, cayenne pepper, black pepper, Tabasco sauce, Worcestershire sauce, tomato sauce, oregano and thyme. Cook over medium heat for 1 hour. Add the sausage and ham and cook over medium heat for 45 minutes. Remove from the heat and allow to cool completely. Return to the heat and bring to a boil. Reduce the heat and simmer for 30 to 40 minutes, stirring frequently. If the beans appear dry, stir in a small amount of water. Serve over hot cooked rice.

RED BEANS AND RICE

BECAUSE IT CAN BE LEFT TO SIMMER IN AN UNWATCHED POT, RED BEANS AND RICE BECAME A DISH TO MAKE ON MONDAY, THE TRADITIONAL LAUNDRY DAY IN NEW ORLEANS. RED BEANS AND RICE ON MONDAYS ALSO BECAME A POPULAR DISH IN RESTAURANTS. IT TASTES DELICIOUS AND, BETTER YET, IS ECONOMICAL. A CHILDREN'S POEM DEMONSTRATES THE DISH'S POPULARITY AT THE TURN OF THE TWENTIETH CENTURY: "A QUARTEE BEANS, A QUARTEE RICE AND A LITTLE LAGNIAPPE TO MAKE IT NICE." BECAUSE QUARTEE MEANT A QUARTER AND LAGNIAPPE MEANT "A LITTLE EXTRA," THE ENTIRE NOURISHING MEAL COST ONLY 50 CENTS.

Corn and Crab Pudding

YIELD: 8 SERVINGS

2	TABLESPOONS BUTTER	1½	TEASPOONS SALT
½	CUP MINCED SHALLOTS	1	TEASPOON SUGAR
¼	CUP MINCED FRESH POBLANO CHILE	¼	TEASPOON GROUND NUTMEG
12	OUNCES FROZEN CORN KERNELS, THAWED (ABOUT 3 CUPS)	¼	TEASPOON WHITE PEPPER
		1½	CUPS PACKED FRESH CRAB MEAT, FLAKED
1¾	CUPS HALF-AND-HALF	¼	CUP FRESHLY GRATED PARMESAN CHEESE
6	EGGS		
3	TABLESPOONS FLOUR		

Melt the butter in a small heavy skillet over medium heat. Add the shallots and chile and sauté for 3 minutes or until the chile is tender. Remove from the heat. Purée the corn in a food processor. Add the half-and-half, eggs, flour, salt, sugar, nutmeg and pepper. Pulse until the mixture is smooth. Pour into a large bowl. Add the crab meat and chile mixture and stir to mix. Divide the mixture among 8 buttered ¾-cup custard cups or soufflé dishes. Sprinkle with the Parmesan cheese. Place the cups in a large roasting pan. Pour hot water into the pan to come halfway up the sides of the cups. Bake at 350 degrees for 50 minutes or until the custards are set in the center and a knife inserted near the center comes out clean. Note: The custard can be made up to 8 hours before baking. Store, covered, in the refrigerator until baking time.

Seafood-Stuffed Eggplant

Yield: 12 servings

3	EGGPLANT, PEELED, CUBED	1	POUND UNCOOKED MEDIUM SHRIMP, PEELED, DEVEINED
1/4	CUP OLIVE OIL		
4	OUNCES CUBED HAM	1 1/3	CUPS BREAD CRUMBS
1	ONION, CHOPPED	2	EGGS, LIGHTLY BEATEN
1	RIB CELERY, CHOPPED	1/8	TEASPOON CAYENNE PEPPER
3	GARLIC CLOVES, MINCED	1/8	TEASPOON WHITE PEPPER
2 1/4	TEASPOONS CHICKEN BASE	8	OUNCES CLAW CRAB MEAT, FLAKED
1	TABLESPOON SEAFOOD BASE		
1/2	TEASPOON DRIED THYME	8	OUNCES JUMBO LUMP CRAB MEAT, FLAKED
1/2	TEASPOON DRIED OREGANO		
3/4	CUP CHOPPED GREEN ONIONS	1/3	CUP GRATED ROMANO CHEESE

Boil the eggplant in enough water to cover in a saucepan until tender. Drain and set aside. Heat the olive oil in a large saucepan over medium heat. Add the ham and sauté until browned. Add the onion, celery and garlic and sauté until the onion is caramelized. Add the chicken base, seafood base, thyme, oregano, green onions and shrimp. Sauté for 10 minutes. Add the eggplant, bread crumbs, eggs, cayenne pepper and white pepper. Cook for 5 minutes, stirring constantly. Remove from the heat and fold in the claw crab meat and lump crab meat. Spoon into a large baking dish and sprinkle with the Romano cheese. Bake at 350 degrees for 30 minutes or until golden brown.

Recipe provided by Mark Defelice, Pascal's Manale Restaurant

CREOLE: A MUCH DISPUTED TERM APPLIED TO A PERSON OR THING WITH FRENCH AND SPANISH ROOTS. FROM THE SPANISH *CRIOLLO*, MEANING "NATIVE."

MAKING GROCERIES: TO BUY GROCERIES. THIS IS A LITERAL TRANSLATION OF THE FRENCH VERB *FAIRE*, MEANING "TO DO OR MAKE."

FAUBOURG: A NEIGHBORHOOD. FROM THE FRENCH WORD MEANING "SUBURB."

RIVERSIDE AND LAKESIDE: THE DIRECTIONS USUALLY REPLACE "NORTH" AND "SOUTH" IN NEW ORLEANS. THE LAKE IS GENERALLY NORTH AND THE RIVER IS GENERALLY SOUTH, BUT WATCH OUT! THE RIVER CAN BE EAST OR WEST BECAUSE IT WRAPS AROUND THE CITY IN A CRESCENT SHAPE.

Mushroom Melange

Yield: 8 servings

½	CUP HOT WATER	1	TABLESPOON BUTTER
1	OUNCE DRIED PORCINI MUSHROOMS	1	CUP CHOPPED FRESH PARSLEY
			SALT AND PEPPER TO TASTE
5	OUNCES FRESH SHIITAKE MUSHROOMS	1	TABLESPOON BUTTER
2	TABLESPOONS BUTTER	1½	CUPS HEAVY CREAM
½	CUP THINLY SLICED SHALLOTS	4	EGGS
12	OUNCES BUTTON MUSHROOMS, CHOPPED	2	EGG YOLKS
		¼	TEASPOON GROUND NUTMEG
3	TABLESPOONS DRY WHITE WINE	⅔	CUP CREAMY BUTTER SAUCE

*P*our the hot water over the porcini mushrooms in a bowl. Let soak for 20 minutes or until the mushrooms are soft. Drain and chop the mushrooms. Chop half the shiitake mushrooms and slice the other half. Melt 2 tablespoons butter in a large heavy skillet over medium-high heat. Add the shallots and sauté for 3 minutes. Add the button mushrooms. Cook for 15 minutes or until the mushrooms are browned and dry, stirring occasionally. Add the wine and boil for 1 minute. Pour the mixture into a medium bowl. Melt 1 tablespoon butter in the skillet over medium-low heat. Add the porcini mushrooms and the chopped shiitake mushrooms. Cover and cook for 10 minutes or until tender, stirring occasionally. Add to the button mushrooms and stir in the parsley. Season with salt and pepper. Melt 1 tablespoon butter in the skillet over medium heat. Add the sliced shiitake mushrooms and sauté for 5 minutes. Set aside for the garnish. Combine the cream, eggs, egg yolks and nutmeg in a large bowl. Season with salt and pepper. Spoon ⅓ cup of the mushroom mixture into each of 8 buttered ¾-cup ramekins. Top each with ⅓ cup of the cream mixture. Place the ramekins in a large roasting pan. Pour hot water into the pan to come halfway up the sides of the ramekins. Bake at 350 degrees for 40 minutes or until the custards are set in the center. Run a small sharp knife around the edge of the ramekins to loosen the custards. Invert onto serving plates. Reheat the sliced shiitake mushrooms in a heavy skillet over medium heat. Spoon the Creamy Butter Sauce (at left) over the custards and top with the sliced shiitake mushrooms.

CREAMY BUTTER SAUCE

1 CUP CANNED LOW-SODIUM CHICKEN BROTH
¼ CUP HEAVY CREAM
6 TABLESPOONS (¾ STICK) BUTTER
1 TABLESPOON MINCED FRESH PARSLEY
SALT AND PEPPER TO TASTE

COMBINE THE BROTH AND CREAM IN A SMALL HEAVY SAUCEPAN. BOIL FOR 15 MINUTES OR UNTIL REDUCED TO ⅓ CUP. WHISK IN THE BUTTER GRADUALLY AND STIR IN THE PARSLEY. SEASON WITH SALT AND PEPPER.
YIELD: ⅔ CUP

Spinach-Stuffed Portobello Mushrooms

Yield: 6 servings

½	cup Red Wine Vinaigrette
6	portobello mushroom caps
	Olive oil
1	onion, finely chopped
1	teaspoon minced garlic
¼	teaspoon lemon juice
2	cups fresh spinach leaves

8	sun-dried tomatoes in oil, drained, chopped
	Tabasco sauce to taste
	Salt and pepper to taste
¼	cup freshly grated Parmesan cheese

Combine the Red Wine Vinaigrette (below) and the mushrooms in a bowl. Stir to coat. Let marinate for 4 to 6 hours. Remove the mushrooms and discard the marinade. Grill or broil the mushrooms for 6 to 8 minutes per side. Remove to a plate and set aside. Heat a small amount of olive oil in a large skillet. Add the onion and garlic and sauté for 3 to 5 minutes or until tender. Add the lemon juice, spinach and tomatoes and sauté for 3 to 4 minutes or until the spinach wilts. Season with Tabasco sauce, salt and pepper. Arrange the cooled mushroom caps on a baking sheet. Sprinkle the insides with half the Parmesan cheese. Mound the spinach mixture into each cap. Sprinkle with the remaining Parmesan cheese. Broil for 5 minutes or until hot and the cheese is golden brown. Remove to a serving platter and serve immediately.

Red Wine Vinaigrette

Yield: ½ cup

1	tablespoon red wine vinegar
¼	cup olive oil
1½	teaspoons Dijon mustard
¼	teaspoon sugar

¼	teaspoon salt
¼	teaspoon pepper
¼	teaspoon chopped chives

Combine the vinegar, olive oil, mustard, sugar, salt, pepper and chives in a bowl. Whisk until well mixed.

SINFUL SPINACH

2 (10-ounce) packages frozen chopped spinach
1 cup water
8 ounces Barefoot Boursin (page 32)

Combine the spinach and water in a saucepan. Cook over medium heat until hot. Drain well and return to the saucepan. Stir in the boursin. Cook over low heat until heated through, stirring until well mixed. Note: You can substitute 3 cups chopped cooked spinach for the frozen spinach.
Yield: 6 servings

Green Onion Pancakes

YIELD: 24 PANCAKES

1	CUP CORNMEAL		2	EGGS, LIGHTLY BEATEN
½	CUP FLOUR		1¼	CUPS BUTTERMILK
1	TEASPOON SUGAR		2	TABLESPOONS UNSALTED BUTTER,
2	TEASPOONS BAKING POWDER			MELTED, COOLED
½	TEASPOON BAKING SODA		⅔	CUP FINELY CHOPPED GREEN ONIONS
½	TEASPOON SALT			BACON DRIPPINGS OR VEGETABLE OIL

Sift the cornmeal, flour, sugar, baking powder, baking soda and salt into a large bowl. Beat the eggs, buttermilk and melted butter in a bowl. Add the egg mixture to the dry ingredients and stir until smooth. Let stand for 10 minutes. Stir the green onions into the batter. Heat ⅛ inch of bacon drippings in a heavy skillet over medium-high heat until hot but not smoking. Working in batches, drop the batter by tablespoonfuls into the skillet. Fry for 1 minute or until the bottoms are golden brown. Turn the pancakes and fry the other side for 1 minute or until the bottoms are golden brown. Remove the pancakes to a heated platter as they are cooked. Add more drippings or oil to the skillet as needed for frying.

Peas Primavera

Yield: 4 servings

1	TABLESPOON UNSALTED BUTTER	½	CUP JULIENNED FRESH BASIL
1	TABLESPOON MINCED SHALLOTS		LEAVES
2	CUPS HEAVY CREAM	⅛	TEASPOON Tabasco SAUCE
½	CUP GRATED Parmesan CHEESE	2	CUPS COOKED PEAS

Melt the butter in a small skillet over medium-low heat. Add the shallots and sauté for 2 to 3 minutes or until translucent. Bring the cream to a boil in a saucepan. Reduce the heat and simmer for 2 to 4 minutes or until slightly reduced. Add the shallots and Parmesan cheese to the cream and cook for 2 to 3 minutes or until slightly thickened. Stir in the basil, Tabasco sauce and peas. Cook for 2 minutes or until heated through. Serve immediately. Delicious tossed with pasta.

Potatoes Pontalba

Yield: 6 servings

2	POUNDS SMALL NEW POTATOES, QUARTERED	2	OUNCES CRUMBLED BLEU CHEESE
1	TABLESPOON BUTTER OR MARGARINE, SOFTENED	¼	TEASPOON SALT
		¼	TEASPOON PEPPER
1	CUP CHOPPED GREEN ONIONS	6	SLICES BACON, COOKED, CRUMBLED
¾	CUP HEAVY CREAM	2	TEASPOONS CHOPPED FRESH PARSLEY
1	TABLESPOON FLOUR		

Cook the potatoes in boiling salted water in a saucepan for 15 minutes or until tender. Drain and place in a bowl. Add the butter and green onions and toss to coat. Whisk the cream and flour in a saucepan. Stir in the bleu cheese. Cook over medium heat for 3 minutes or until thickened, stirring constantly. Stir in the salt and pepper. Add to the potato mixture and toss to mix. Sprinkle with the bacon and parsley. Serve immediately.

HEAT AND HUMIDITY

THE HEAT AND HUMIDITY OF NEW ORLEANS' TROPICAL CLIMATE DIRECTLY INFLUENCED FOOD PRESERVATION IN DAYS PRECEDING REFRIGERATION. CISTERNS WERE OFTEN ELEVATED ON BRICK BASES EQUIPPED WITH SHELVES WHERE FOOD COULD BE KEPT COOL. ANOTHER SYSTEM OF PRESERVING FOODS WAS CAVES: A TRICKLE OF WATER WAS RUN THROUGH A CAVE, OR SHALLOW TROUGH, ONE OR TWO BRICKS DEEP, AND JARS OF BUTTER AND MILK WERE PLACED IN THE STREAM TO KEEP THEM COOL. PRIOR TO AIR CONDITIONING, LOCAL ARCHITECTURE ALSO DEVELOPED FEATURES TO COMBAT THE CLIMATE. HIGH CEILINGS AND TRANSOMS ABOVE DOORS WERE EMPLOYED TO CIRCULATE THE RISING HOT AIR, WHILE OUTDOOR GALLERIES PROVIDED SHELTER FROM SUN AND RAIN.

Shrimp Succotash

YIELD: 4 SERVINGS

½ CUP DRIED BABY LIMA BEANS	1 SLICE BACON
5 CUPS (OR MORE) WATER	1 SMALL ONION, CHOPPED
1 (1-INCH-THICK) ONION SLICE	2 CUPS FRESH CORN KERNELS OR THAWED
1 STALK CELERY WITH LEAVES	FROZEN CORN KERNELS
2 GARLIC CLOVES, PRESSED	SALT AND PEPPER TO TASTE
1 BAY LEAF	2 TABLESPOONS CHOPPED CHIVES OR
8 OUNCES UNCOOKED LARGE SHRIMP	GREEN ONIONS

Place the beans in a bowl and cover with cold water by 3 inches. Let stand overnight. Drain. Combine 5 cups water, onion slice, celery stalk, garlic and bay leaf in a medium saucepan. Bring to a boil and boil for 5 minutes. Add the shrimp and simmer for 3 minutes or until the shrimp are pink. Remove the shrimp with tongs to a bowl. Reserve the cooking liquid. Peel, devein and cut the shrimp into ½-inch pieces. Set aside. Add the drained beans to the cooking liquid. Cover and simmer for 40 minutes or until the beans are tender and the liquid is reduced to ½ cup. Add more water during cooking if necessary. Remove the bay leaf, onion slice and celery stalk and discard. Cook the bacon in a large skillet over medium heat for 5 minutes or until crisp. Remove to paper towels to drain. Crumble the bacon and set aside. Pour off all but 1 teaspoon of the bacon drippings. Add the chopped onion to the skillet and sauté over medium-low heat for 10 minutes or until golden brown. Stir in the corn and the beans with their cooking liquid. Cook for 8 minutes or until the corn is tender. Stir in the shrimp and bacon and cook for 3 minutes or until heated through. Season with salt and pepper and sprinkle with the chives.

Note: The shrimp and beans can be made 1 day ahead. Cover separately and chill.

Easy Squash Soufflé

Yield: 6 to 8 servings

8	TO 10 YELLOW SQUASH, COARSELY CHOPPED	6	EGGS
4	TO 5 GARLIC CLOVES	2	CUPS ITALIAN BREAD CRUMBS
1	CUP FRESH PARSLEY	2	CUPS HEAVY CREAM
½	CUP (1 STICK) BUTTER, MELTED		SALT AND CAYENNE PEPPER TO TASTE
			GRATED PARMESAN CHEESE

*P*lace the squash in a microwave-safe dish and microwave until tender. Process the squash, garlic, parsley, butter, eggs, bread crumbs and cream in 2 batches in a food processor until well mixed. Season with salt and cayenne pepper. Spoon the mixture into a baking dish that has been coated with nonstick cooking spray. Sprinkle the Parmesan cheese on top. Bake at 350 degrees for 35 to 40 minutes or until a knife inserted near the center comes out clean.

Recipe provided by Susan Ridgeway, Best of Susan Catering

Sweet Potato Casserole with Praline Topping

Yield: 8 servings

1	CUP FLOUR	4	MEDIUM SWEET POTATOES, PEELED, HALVED (ABOUT 2½ POUNDS)
⅔	CUP PACKED BROWN SUGAR	½	CUP SUGAR
¼	CUP CHOPPED TOASTED PECANS	1½	TEASPOONS VANILLA EXTRACT
¼	CUP (½ STICK) MARGARINE, MELTED	1	EGG WHITE
½	TEASPOON GROUND CINNAMON	1	(5-OUNCE) CAN FAT-FREE EVAPORATED MILK

*M*ix the flour, brown sugar, pecans, melted margarine and cinnamon in a bowl until crumbly. Place the sweet potatoes in a large heavy saucepan and cover with water. Bring to a boil. Cover, reduce the heat and simmer for 30 minutes or until very tender. Drain well and mash in a bowl. Stir in 1 cup of the flour mixture, sugar, vanilla, egg white and evaporated milk. Spoon into a 2-quart baking dish that has been coated with nonstick cooking spray. Top with the remaining flour mixture. Bake at 350 degrees for 45 minutes.

Roast Tomatoes Provençal

YIELD: 8 SERVINGS

12	FIRM TOMATOES	¼	CUP CHOPPED FRESH MIXED HERBS
¼	CUP EXTRA-VIRGIN OLIVE OIL		(SUCH AS PARSLEY, TARRAGON, BASIL
	SALT TO TASTE		AND ROSEMARY)
¼	CUP BALSAMIC VINEGAR		

Core the tomatoes and cut in half lengthwise. Heat the olive oil in a large skillet over medium-high heat. Place as many tomato halves as will fit comfortably into the skillet, cut side down. Sear the tomatoes for 3 to 4 minutes or until dark brown on the bottom and almost caramelized. Do not stir or move the tomatoes in the skillet until searing is completed. Place the tomatoes cut side up in a large baking dish. Sear remaining tomato halves and place in the baking dish. Overlap the tomatoes slightly in the baking dish if necessary. Season lightly with salt. Add the vinegar to the skillet. Cook over high heat while scraping up any browned bits. Pour over the tomatoes in the baking dish. Sprinkle with the herbs. Bake at 400 degrees for 30 minutes or until soft. Serve hot or at room temperature. Note: Herbes de Provence can be used in place of the mixed fresh herbs.

Fresh Tomato Tart

Yield: 8 to 10 servings

1¼ CUPS FLOUR	4 TO 5 RIPE ROMA TOMATOES,
1 TABLESPOON SUGAR	CUT INTO ¼-INCH SLICES
¼ TEASPOON SALT	½ TEASPOON SALT
½ CUP (1 STICK) CHILLED UNSALTED	¼ TEASPOON PEPPER
BUTTER, CUT INTO 8 PIECES	¼ CUP EXTRA-VIRGIN OLIVE OIL
2 TABLESPOONS COLD WATER	CHOPPED FRESH BASIL LEAVES FOR
8 OUNCES SHREDDED MOZZARELLA CHEESE	GARNISH
2 TABLESPOONS CHOPPED FRESH	
BASIL LEAVES	

Combine the flour, sugar and ¼ teaspoon salt in a food processor. Add the butter. Pulse until the mixture resembles dry oats. Add 1 tablespoon of the water and process for a few seconds. Add the remaining 1 tablespoon water and pulse 3 or 4 times. Place the dough in a bowl and form into a ball. Cover and chill for 30 minutes. Place the dough on a floured surface. Roll the dough into an 11-inch circle. Fit the dough into a 10-inch tart pan. Arrange the cheese over the dough and sprinkle with 2 tablespoons basil. Arrange the tomato slices on top. Sprinkle with ½ teaspoon salt and pepper and drizzle with the olive oil. Bake at 400 degrees for 30 to 40 minutes or until the crust is golden brown. Garnish with basil. Serve hot or at room temperature.

Note: A pre-made pie shell may be used in place of the dough.

Gris Gris Grits

YIELD: 6 TO 8 SERVINGS

1	POUND FRESH MIXED GREENS (SUCH AS COLLARD, MUSTARD OR SWISS CHARD)	¼	TO ½ CUP MILK
		¼	CUP (½ STICK) BUTTER OR MARGARINE
1	CUP CHICKEN BROTH	1	TO 1½ CUPS FRESHLY GRATED PARMESAN CHEESE
1	CUP HEAVY CREAM		
3	CUPS CHICKEN BROTH	¼	TO ½ TEASPOON FRESHLY GROUND PEPPER
1	CUP GRITS (NOT INSTANT)		

Remove and discard the stems and any discolored spots from the greens. Rinse the greens thoroughly and drain. Chop into ½-inch strips. Combine the greens and 1 cup chicken broth in a large skillet. Bring to a boil, reduce the heat and simmer for 5 minutes or until tender. Drain and plunge into ice water until cooled. Remove to paper towels to drain. Combine the cream and 3 cups chicken broth in a large saucepan. Bring to a boil and gradually stir in the grits. Cook over medium heat until the mixture returns to a boil. Reduce the heat and cover. Simmer for 25 to 30 minutes, stirring frequently. Stir in the milk gradually to reach the desired consistency. Add the butter, Parmesan cheese and pepper and mix well. Cook until the butter and cheese melt, stirring constantly. Add the cooked greens. Cook until heated through, stirring constantly.

Jambalaya Lo Mein

Yield: 4 servings

2	TEASPOONS VEGETABLE OIL	1	TABLESPOON VEGETABLE OIL
1	TABLESPOON MINCED GARLIC	2	CUPS BITE-SIZE MIXED FRESH VEGETABLES
1	TABLESPOON MINCED PEELED GINGER		(SUCH AS BROCCOLI, BELL PEPPERS, SNOW
1	TEASPOON SAMBAL OLEK OR HOT SAUCE		PEAS AND CARROTS)
¼	CUP HOISIN SAUCE	4	OUNCES ANDOUILLE SAUSAGE, SLICED
¼	CUP SOY SAUCE	6	OUNCES CRAWFISH TAILS
2	TABLESPOONS SUGAR	4	OUNCES COOKED CHICKEN, CHOPPED
½	CUP CHICKEN STOCK OR	16	OUNCES COOKED ASIAN EGG NOODLES
	BROTH		OR LINGUINE
¼	CUP CORNSTARCH		FRESH BEAN SPROUTS AND CHOPPED
3	TABLESPOONS COLD WATER		GREEN ONIONS FOR GARNISH

Heat 2 teaspoons oil in a saucepan. Add the garlic and ginger and sauté for
2 minutes. Add the sambal olek, hoisin sauce, soy sauce, sugar and stock and bring
to a boil. Dissolve the cornstarch in the water in a small bowl. Add to the saucepan.
Cook for 2 minutes or until thickened, stirring constantly. Set aside. Heat 1 tablespoon
oil in a wok until hot but not smoking. Add the vegetables and sausage. Stir-fry
for 2 minutes. Add the crawfish, chicken and noodles. Cook until heated through.
Add the sauce mixture and cook until very hot, stirring constantly. Remove to
a serving platter and garnish with bean sprouts and green onions.

Recipe provided by Adolfo Garcia, Lucky Cheng's

Fettuccini with Sweet Pepper and Cayenne Sauce

Yield: 8 side dish or 4 main course servings

3	TABLESPOONS BUTTER	½	CUP GRATED PARMESAN CHEESE
2	LARGE RED BELL PEPPERS, CUT INTO ¼-INCH STRIPS	12	OUNCES FETTUCCINI
3	GARLIC CLOVES, MINCED	1	CUP FROZEN GREEN PEAS
¾	TEASPOON CAYENNE PEPPER	½	CUP CHOPPED FRESH BASIL LEAVES
1	CUP HEAVY CREAM	½	CUP CHOPPED TASSO (SEE NOTE, PAGE 187)
¾	CUP CANNED LOW-SODIUM CHICKEN BROTH		SALT AND PEPPER TO TASTE
		¼	CUP GRATED PARMESAN CHEESE

Melt the butter in a large heavy skillet over medium heat. Add the bell peppers, garlic and cayenne pepper and stir to mix. Cover the skillet and cook for 7 minutes or until the peppers are tender, stirring occasionally. Add the cream and broth and simmer, uncovered, for 5 minutes or until slightly thickened. Stir in ½ cup Parmesan cheese and remove from the heat. Cook the fettuccini in a large stockpot of boiling salted water until just tender. Add the peas and remove from the heat. Drain the pasta and peas and return to the stockpot. Add the bell pepper mixture, basil and tasso. Toss to mix. Season with salt and pepper. Sprinkle with ¼ cup Parmesan cheese.

Vermicelli Sauce Verde

Yield: 8 servings

8	OUNCES CREAM CHEESE, SOFTENED	¼	CUP OLIVE OIL
½	CUP (OR MORE) CHOPPED FRESH BASIL LEAVES	½	TEASPOON FRESHLY GROUND PEPPER
½	CUP GRATED PARMESAN CHEESE	½	TEASPOON SALT
¼	CUP CHOPPED FRESH PARSLEY	⅔	CUP BOILING WATER
¼	CUP (½ STICK) BUTTER, SOFTENED	16	OUNCES VERMICELLI, COOKED, DRAINED
1	GARLIC CLOVE		

Combine the cream cheese, basil, Parmesan cheese, parsley, butter, garlic, olive oil and pepper in a food processor. Process until puréed. Add the salt and boiling water and process until mixed. Pour over the hot vermicelli and serve.

Coconut and Peanut Rice

Yield: 4 to 6 servings

½	CUP PEANUT OIL	2	CINNAMON STICKS, BROKEN INTO
2	CUPS UNCOOKED RICE		1-INCH PIECES
4	CUPS (ABOUT) BOILING WATER	1	TABLESPOON PEANUT OIL
	SALT TO TASTE	½	CUP RAISINS
6	BAY LEAVES	½	CUP FLAKED COCONUT
1	TABLESPOON WHOLE CLOVES	1	CUP UNSALTED PEANUTS
¼	TEASPOON GROUND CARDAMOM	1	ONION, CUT INTO THIN SLIVERS

Heat ½ cup peanut oil in a saucepan. Add the rice and sauté until lightly browned. Add 4 cups boiling water or enough to cover the rice by 1 inch. Season with salt. Stir in the bay leaves, cloves, cardamom and cinnamon sticks. Bring to a boil. Reduce the heat and cover. Simmer for 45 minutes or until rice is tender and the liquid is absorbed. Discard the bay leaves, cinnamon sticks and cloves. Heat 1 tablespoon peanut oil in a skillet. Add the raisins, coconut, peanuts and onion. Sauté until lightly browned. Remove to paper towels to drain. Serve the rice topped with the peanut mixture.

Lemon Rice Pilaf

Yield: 8 servings

5	TABLESPOONS OLIVE OIL	½	CUP FRESH LEMON JUICE
1½	CUPS MINCED ONIONS	1½	TABLESPOONS GRATED LEMON ZEST
3	CUPS UNCOOKED LONG GRAIN	¾	TEASPOON PEPPER
	WHITE RICE		SALT TO TASTE
3	(14-OUNCE) CANS CHICKEN BROTH		

Heat the olive oil in a large heavy saucepan over medium heat. Add the onions and sauté for 10 minutes or until tender. Add the rice and sauté for 2 minutes. Stir in the broth, lemon juice, lemon zest and pepper. Bring to a boil, stirring occasionally. Reduce the heat to low and cover. Simmer for 20 minutes or until the rice is tender and the liquid is absorbed. Remove from the heat and let stand for 5 minutes. Season with salt.

Forest Mushroom and Roasted Garlic Risotto

Yield: 6 servings

2	LARGE HEADS OF GARLIC, CLOVES SEPARATED, UNPEELED	2	TABLESPOONS CHOPPED FRESH THYME, OR 2 TEASPOONS DRIED THYME
2	TABLESPOONS OLIVE OIL	1½	CUPS UNCOOKED ARBORIO RICE OR MEDIUM GRAIN WHITE RICE
¾	OUNCE DRIED PORCINI MUSHROOMS	½	CUP DRY WHITE WINE
¾	POUND SLICED MIXED FRESH WILD MUSHROOMS (SUCH AS CRIMINI AND SHIITAKE)	3½	TO 4 CUPS CANNED LOW-SODIUM CHICKEN BROTH
1	TABLESPOON OLIVE OIL SALT AND PEPPER TO TASTE	2	CUPS THINLY SLICED FRESH SPINACH LEAVES
1	TABLESPOON OLIVE OIL	⅓	CUP FRESHLY GRATED PARMESAN CHEESE
1	CUP CHOPPED SHALLOTS		

Combine the garlic cloves and 2 tablespoons olive oil in a small baking dish. Bake at 400 degrees for 50 minutes or until the garlic is golden brown and tender. Let cool slightly and peel. Chop the garlic and measure ¼ cup. Set aside. Cover and chill any remaining garlic for another use. Place the porcini mushrooms in a small bowl. Pour enough boiling water over to cover. Let stand for 30 minutes or until softened. Drain the mushrooms and squeeze dry. Chop coarsely. Trim the stems from the shiitake mushrooms if using shiitakes. Heat 1 tablespoon olive oil in a large nonstick skillet over medium-high heat. Add the fresh mushrooms and sauté for 7 minutes or until the mushrooms are golden brown and the juices have evaporated. Add the porcini and sauté for 1 minute. Season with salt and pepper and set aside. Heat 1 tablespoon olive oil in a medium heavy saucepan over medium-high heat. Add the shallots and thyme and sauté for 4 minutes or until the shallots are tender. Add the rice and stir to coat. Stir in the wine and cook until almost evaporated. Stir in the chopped garlic and 3½ cups broth. Reduce the heat to medium. Cook for 20 minutes or until the rice is tender and the mixture is creamy, stirring occasionally. Add more broth during cooking if necessary. Add the mushroom mixture and the spinach. Cook until the spinach wilts, stirring constantly. Stir in the Parmesan cheese and season with salt and pepper.

Onion, Corn and Bacon Risotto

Yield: 6 servings

8	CUPS (ABOUT) CHICKEN BROTH	1	MEDIUM ONION, COARSELY CHOPPED
3	TABLESPOONS VEGETABLE OIL	1	SMALL CARROT, PEELED, COARSELY
	KERNELS OF 3 EARS FRESH CORN		CHOPPED
	SALT AND PEPPER TO TASTE	1	SMALL RIB CELERY, COARSELY CHOPPED
3	TABLESPOONS BUTTER	2	CUPS UNCOOKED ARBORIO RICE
3	LARGE SWEET ONIONS, THINLY SLICED	1	CUP DRY WHITE WINE
4	OUNCES BACON, CUT INTO 2x¼-INCH	¼	CUP BUTTER
	STRIPS	¼	CUP FRESHLY GRATED PARMESAN CHEESE

Bring the chicken broth to a boil in a saucepan. Remove from the heat and cover to keep warm. Heat the oil in a cast-iron skillet over medium-high heat. Add the corn and sauté for 15 minutes or until cooked. Season with salt and pepper and remove to a bowl. Melt 3 tablespoons butter in a saucepan over high heat. Add the sliced onions and sauté for 25 minutes or until the onions are caramelized. Add the onions to the corn. Add the bacon to the saucepan and sauté over high heat for 3 minutes or until brown and crisp. Remove to paper towels to drain. Pour off all but 2 tablespoons of the bacon drippings. Process the chopped onion, carrot and celery in a food processor until finely chopped. Add to the bacon drippings and sauté over medium-high heat for 3 minutes or until tender. Add the rice and stir to coat. Stir in the wine and cook for 2 minutes or until almost evaporated, stirring constantly. Stir in the corn, sliced onions and bacon. Add 1 cup chicken broth and cook until the broth is absorbed, stirring constantly. Continue adding broth ½ cup at a time. Cook until the broth is absorbed before adding more, stirring constantly. Cook for a total time of about 25 minutes or until the rice is tender and the mixture is creamy. Stir in ¼ cup butter and the Parmesan cheese. Season with salt and pepper.

Shrimp and Andouille Corn Bread Dressing

Yield: 8 servings

1	TABLESPOON UNSALTED BUTTER	½	TEASPOON CHOPPED FRESH THYME
1	POUND ANDOUILLE SAUSAGE, SLICED,	2	CUPS CHICKEN BROTH
	QUARTERED	1	POUND UNCOOKED MEDIUM SHRIMP,
1	ONION, SLICED		PEELED, DEVEINED
½	RIB CELERY, CHOPPED	1	BUNCH GREEN ONIONS, FINELY CHOPPED
1	BELL PEPPER, CHOPPED	1	SKILLET CORN BREAD, MADE THE DAY
1	TABLESPOON MINCED GARLIC		BEFORE
2	BAY LEAVES		SALT AND PEPPER TO TASTE

Melt the butter in a heavy stockpot over medium-high heat. Add the sausage and sauté until brown. Add the next 4 ingredients. Sauté until the onion is translucent. Stir in the bay leaves, thyme and broth. Simmer for 10 minutes. Add the shrimp. Cook for 2 minutes. Add the green onions. Crumble the corn bread into the mixture. Remove the bay leaves. Season with salt and pepper; mix well. The dressing should be fairly moist. Spoon into a greased 8x10-inch baking dish. Bake at 350 degrees for 45 to 60 minutes or until golden brown.

Oyster Dressing

Yield: 8 servings

¼	CUP (½ STICK) BUTTER	1	QUART SHUCKED OYSTERS, WITH THEIR
2	TABLESPOONS SHORTENING		LIQUOR
4	LARGE ONIONS, CHOPPED	2	LOAVES DRY FRENCH BREAD
3	RIBS CELERY, CHOPPED		GARLIC SALT, PEPPER AND FRESH OR
1	BUNCH GREEN ONIONS, CHOPPED		DRIED THYME TO TASTE
1	BUNCH PARSLEY, CHOPPED	1	EGG

Heat the butter and shortening in a large saucepan. Add the next 4 ingredients. Sauté until the onions are translucent. Chop the oysters into ½-inch pieces. Break up the bread; add to the oyster liquor. Squeeze the bread until the bread is moistened. Add the bread, any oyster liquor and oysters to the sautéed vegetables. Sauté over medium heat for 10 minutes or until the oysters are cooked through. Season with garlic salt, pepper and thyme. Remove from the heat. Stir in the egg. Spoon into a 9x13-inch baking dish. Bake at 400 degrees until heated through.

Roasted Garlic and Goat Cheese Bread Pudding

Yield: 4 to 6 servings

4	EGGS, BEATEN	3/4	TEASPOON SALT
4	OUNCES SOFT GOAT CHEESE	1/4	TEASPOON BLACK PEPPER
	(CHÈVRE)	1/2	TEASPOON Tabasco SAUCE
1/2	CUP ROASTED GARLIC	1/4	CUP COARSELY CHOPPED
1	CUP HEAVY CREAM		FRESH SAGE
2	CUPS MILK	4	CUPS DRY BREAD CUBES
1/2	TEASPOON WHITE PEPPER	1/2	CUP MINCED GREEN ONIONS

Mix the eggs, cheese and roasted garlic in a bowl. Add the cream, milk, white pepper, salt, black pepper, Tabasco sauce, sage, bread and green onions; mix well. Spoon into a greased 2-quart baking dish. Cover with greased foil. Place in a roasting pan. Add enough hot water to the pan to come 1/4 of the way up the side of baking dish. Bake at 375 degrees for 45 minutes. Serve warm.

Recipe provided by Ann Dunbar, Anna Banana

Mango Barbecue Sauce

Yield: 5 cups

1	VERY RIPE MANGO, PEELED, PITTED, CUT INTO SMALL CUBES	1	(28-OUNCE) CAN CRUSHED PEELED PLUM TOMATOES
1	CUP PREPARED MANGO CHUTNEY	1	TABLESPOON MOLASSES
1	CUP FINELY CHOPPED ONION	1	TEASPOON Tabasco SAUCE
1	TABLESPOON MINCED GARLIC	1	TEASPOON SALT
2	TABLESPOONS CIDER VINEGAR		

Mix the mango, chutney, onion, garlic, vinegar, undrained tomatoes, molasses, Tabasco sauce and salt in a heavy saucepan. Simmer over low heat for 30 to 40 minutes or until thickened. Let cool slightly. Purée in a blender until smooth.

BLENDER HOLLANDAISE SAUCE

4 EGG YOLKS
3 TABLESPOONS LEMON JUICE
1 CUP (2 STICKS) BUTTER

COMBINE THE EGG YOLKS AND LEMON JUICE IN A BLENDER AND PROCESS UNTIL WELL MIXED. MELT THE BUTTER IN A SAUCEPAN. ADD THE HOT BUTTER TO THE BLENDER IN A SLOW STREAM, PROCESSING CONSTANTLY. BLEND UNTIL SLIGHTLY THICKENED. SERVE IMMEDIATELY.
YIELD: 1 1/2 CUPS

Homemade Mayonnaise

1 EGG
½ TEASPOON SALT
¼ TEASPOON DRY MUSTARD
2 TABLESPOONS TARRAGON
VINEGAR
1 CUP VEGETABLE OIL

COMBINE THE EGG, SALT,
MUSTARD, VINEGAR AND
¼ CUP OF THE OIL IN A
BLENDER. TURN ON TO THE
LOWEST SPEED. ADD THE
REMAINING ¾ CUP OIL TO THE
BLENDER IN A SLOW STREAM,
PROCESSING CONSTANTLY.
BLEND UNTIL EMULSIFIED.
COVER AND CHILL.
YIELD: 1¼ CUPS

Cranberry Kumquat Chutney

YIELD: 2 CUPS

1½ CUPS PACKED BROWN SUGAR	1 TEASPOON MINCED GARLIC
1 (12-OUNCE) BAG CRANBERRIES	1 TEASPOON MUSTARD SEEDS
8 OUNCES KUMQUATS, SEEDED, CUT INTO ¼-INCH SLICES	1 CINNAMON STICK
⅓ CUP FINELY CHOPPED ONION	¼ TEASPOON SALT
2 TABLESPOONS MINCED PEELED GINGER	¼ TEASPOON RED PEPPER FLAKES

Combine the brown sugar, cranberries, kumquats, onion, ginger, garlic, mustard seeds, cinnamon stick, salt and red pepper flakes in a medium heavy saucepan. Bring to a boil over high heat, stirring frequently. Reduce the heat to medium. Cook for 20 minutes or until the mixture is thickened and the kumquats are translucent, stirring frequently. Let cool to room temperature. Remove and discard the cinnamon stick. Cover and chill. Note: This chutney can be made up to 5 days ahead.

Ginger Cream Sauce

YIELD: 8 SERVINGS

¾ CUP FRESH ORANGE JUICE	¼ CUP CREAM
¼ CUP MINCED PEELED GINGER	½ CUP (1 STICK) CHILLED BUTTER, CUT INTO TABLESPOONS
1 GARLIC CLOVE, MINCED	SALT AND PEPPER TO TASTE
¼ CUP SOY SAUCE	
¼ CUP CHICKEN BROTH	

Combine the orange juice, ginger and garlic in a medium saucepan. Bring to a boil and cook until reduced by ½. Stir in the soy sauce and chicken broth and cook until reduced by ½ again. Add the cream and reduce the heat. Whisk in the butter 1 tablespoon at a time. Season with salt and pepper. Strain the sauce and keep warm until serving time.

Cool Horseradish Cream Sauce

YIELD: 2 CUPS

½	CUP MAYONNAISE	¾ CUP WHIPPING CREAM
½	CUP DRAINED PREPARED HORSERADISH	⅛ TEASPOON SUGAR, OR TO TASTE
2	TABLESPOONS DIJON MUSTARD	SALT AND PEPPER TO TASTE

Mix the mayonnaise, horseradish and mustard in a bowl. Whip the cream in another bowl until soft peaks form. Fold the whipped cream into the horseradish mixture with a rubber spatula. Stir in the sugar and season with salt and pepper. Spoon into a serving bowl. Serve with corned beef, trout or fillet of beef.

Red Wine and Portobello Mushroom Sauce

YIELD: 3 CUPS

½	CUP (1 STICK) BUTTER	3 CUPS BEEF STOCK OR BROTH
1	CUP CHOPPED ONION	2 CUPS SLICED SCALLIONS
4	OUNCES TOMATO PASTE	1 TABLESPOON WORCESTERSHIRE SAUCE
4	CUPS SLICED PORTOBELLO MUSHROOMS	¾ CUP RED WINE
1½	TABLESPOONS PAPRIKA	1 TABLESPOON MINCED GARLIC
¼	CUP FLOUR	SALT AND PEPPER TO TASTE

Melt the butter in a large saucepan. Add the onion and sauté for several minutes or until soft. Stir in the tomato paste, mushrooms and paprika. Cook until the mushrooms are soft. Add the flour and cook for 2 minutes, stirring constantly. Whisk in the stock and cook until smooth and slightly thickened. Stir in the scallions, Worcestershire sauce, wine and garlic. Season with salt and pepper. Reduce the heat and simmer for 25 minutes. Serve warm.

Brunch & Breads

Brunch & Breads

Pierre Poutz House
1025 St. Louis Street

Within the 40 million pages of notarial acts housed in the New Orleans Notarial Archive is the building contract for this fine Greek Revival house. Notary Amedee Ducatel, on February 6, 1847, recorded a building contract between builders Clairain and Roy and owner Pierre Poutz for this house, which was to cost $13,500. Attached to the act are detailed specifications for the construction of the house, calling for two salons measuring 18 x 21 feet, a smaller one measuring 12 x 18 feet facing the yard, and an 8-foot corridor on the ground floor featuring plaster cornices and black, Italian marble mantels. The original wrought iron balcony was later replaced with cast iron, which became fashionable after the Baroness Pontalba used cast iron verandas on the Pontalba Buildings in 1849. The oak leaf pattern was one of the most popular castings carried by the New Orleans distributors of northeast foundries.

❖

Poutz, a commission merchant, purchased the site in 1847 for $6,000 from Louise Sindos, a free woman of color, and in 1860 sold his house to Caroline Visinier, another free woman of color. Because marriages between whites and people of color were illegal in Louisiana at the time, the daughter of Caroline Visinier and José Caballero, a wealthy Spaniard, was considered illegitimate. In an effort to legitimize their daughter, Maria Dolorosa, at about age sixteen, Caroline and José took her with them to Cuba where they were married, both declaring to be white Cubans. They then traveled to José's home of Cadiz, Spain, for Dolorosa's debut to society.

❖

After Caroline's death, Dolorosa inherited 1025 St. Louis Street in 1861 and sold it to her father that same year. When he died in 1866 following a streetcar accident, multiple wills were found, resulting in a seven-year court battle that revealed Dolorosa's race to her Spanish relatives. They fought her inheritance, but ultimately Dolorosa received the house. In 1875 she sold it for $14,250 to Ernest Gueringer, who likely added the cast iron veranda and made other renovations to the home. After a succession of eight owners, the house was eventually rescued from proposed demolition and restored. It became the JLNO Show House VII in 1993.

Jackson Square Juleps

YIELD: 1 SERVING

3	TABLESPOONS BOURBON	½	CUP CRACKED ICE
3	TO 4 FRESH MINT SPRIGS		FRESH MINT SPRIGS
2	TEASPOONS SIMPLE SYRUP		FOR GARNISH

Combine the bourbon, 3 to 4 mint sprigs, syrup and ice in a tall highball glass. Stir vigorously with a cocktail spoon until the outside of the glass becomes frosted. Garnish with mint sprigs. Note: Simple syrup is prepared by cooking a mixture of sugar and water over low heat until clear and then boiling for about 1 minute. It can be thin (3 parts water, 1 part sugar), medium (2 parts water, 1 part sugar), or thick (equal parts water and sugar).

Milk Punch

YIELD: 1 SERVING

3	TABLESPOONS BOURBON	1	DROP OF VANILLA EXTRACT
¼	CUP WHOLE MILK	¼	CUP CRACKED ICE
¼	CUP HEAVY CREAM		GROUND NUTMEG
¾	TEASPOON CONFECTIONERS' SUGAR		FOR GARNISH

Combine the bourbon, milk, cream, confectioners' sugar, vanilla and ice in a cocktail shaker. Cover and shake for 20 to 30 seconds. Strain into a highball glass. Garnish with nutmeg.

Ramos Gin Fizz

3	TABLESPOONS GIN	½	TEASPOON LEMON JUICE
2	DROPS OF ORANGE FLOWER	¼	CUP HALF-AND-HALF
	WATER	1	DROP OF VANILLA EXTRACT
2	EGG WHITES	½	CUP CRACKED ICE
5	TEASPOONS CONFECTIONERS'		
	SUGAR		

Combine the gin, orange water, egg whites, confectioners' sugar, lemon juice, half-and-half, vanilla and ice in a blender. Blend on high speed for 90 seconds or until thick and fluffy. Pour into a tall highboy glass or double old-fashioned glass.

Minted Iced Tea

YIELD: 1 GALLON

2	QUARTS WATER	1	(6-OUNCE) CAN FROZEN
4	FAMILY-SIZE TEA BAGS		LEMONADE
10	MINT LEAVES		COLD WATER
1½	CUPS SUGAR		FRESH MINT SPRIGS FOR GARNISH

Bring 2 quarts water to boil in a saucepan. Remove from the heat and add the tea bags. Let steep for 15 minutes. Remove the tea bags and discard. Stir in the mint leaves, sugar and lemonade. Pour into a 1-gallon container and add enough cold water to make 1 gallon. Serve over ice and garnish with mint.

ICE

ANYONE WHO HAS SURVIVED A NEW ORLEANS SUMMER KNOWS WHAT A DELIGHT IT IS TO COOL DOWN, EVEN FOR A FEW MOMENTS. SO IT IS NOT SURPRISING THAT ICE WAS A PRIZED COMMODITY IN THE DAYS BEFORE ELECTRIC REFRIGERATION. NEW ORLEANIANS IMPORTED ICE FROM THE NORTH IN THE HOLDS OF SHIPS COMING DOWN THE MISSISSIPPI. UNTIL IT MELTED, THE ICE HELPED TO MAKE THE HEAT SOMEWHAT BEARABLE BY COOLING DRINKS AND PRESERVING FOOD. WITH THE ARRIVAL OF REFRIGERATORS AT THE START OF THE TWENTIETH CENTURY, THE CITY THAT PRIZED ICE BEGAN TO INVENT NEW USES FOR IT. THE ORLANDO SNOWIZARD AND THE EISENMANN FLUFFY ICE MACHINES WERE DEVELOPED IN NEW ORLEANS TO PREPARE A BELOVED SUMMERTIME TREAT: SNOWBALLS.

Grapefruit Grillé

Yield: 2 servings

1	GRAPEFRUIT, PREFERABLY RUBY RED, CUT INTO HALVES	1	TABLESPOON BROWN SUGAR
1	TABLESPOON PURE MAPLE SYRUP	½	TEASPOON GROUND CARDAMOM
		1	TEASPOON UNSALTED BUTTER

Section the grapefruit with a small serrated knife and remove the seeds. Place cut side up on a broiler pan. Drizzle with the maple syrup. Combine the brown sugar and cardamom in a small bowl. Sprinkle on the grapefruit. Dot with the butter. Place under a preheated broiler, 3 inches from the heat source. Broil for 4 to 5 minutes or until bubbly and slightly browned. Serve immediately.

Creole Eggs en Croustade

Yield: 4 to 6 servings

12	SLICES WHITE BREAD, CRUSTS TRIMMED	¼	CUP MILK
	VEGETABLE OIL	3	TABLESPOONS BUTTER
8	EGGS		SALT AND PEPPER TO TASTE
¼	CUP MINCED FRESH TARRAGON		FRESH TARRAGON SPRIGS FOR GARNISH
½	CUP MINCED GREEN ONIONS		

Place the bread on a work surface and roll each slice flat with a rolling pin. Brush each side with oil. Fit each slice into a ½-cup muffin tin. Bake at 350 degrees for 20 minutes. Whisk the eggs, tarragon, green onions and milk in a bowl. Season with salt and pepper. Melt the butter in a skillet. Add the egg mixture and cook for 3 to 5 minutes or just until set. Divide the egg mixture between the croustades and garnish with tarragon. Serve immediately. Note: The croustades can be prepared and baked 1 day ahead. Reheat before adding the egg mixture.

Evangeline Eggs

Yield: 8 servings

1¼	CUPS MILK			VEGETABLE OIL
4	TROUT FILLETS, EACH CUT IN HALF		16	EGGS, POACHED
1½	CUPS FLOUR			TASSO CRAWFISH HOLLANDAISE
1	TEASPOON SALT			CHOPPED GREEN ONIONS FOR GARNISH
¼	TEASPOON PEPPER			

*P*our the milk into a bowl and add the trout. Let soak for 5 minutes. Combine the flour, salt and pepper in a shallow dish. Remove the trout from the milk and roll in the flour mixture to coat. Heat the oil in a skillet or deep fryer to 375 degrees. Fry the trout for 5 minutes or until crisp and golden brown. Remove to paper towels to drain. Place 1 piece of trout on each of 8 heated serving plates. Top each with 2 poached eggs and cover with the Tasso Crawfish Hollandaise (below). Garnish with green onions and serve immediately.

Tasso Crawfish Hollandaise

Yield: 8 servings

1	OUNCE TASSO, CUT INTO STRIPS (SEE NOTE)		1	TABLESPOON WATER
			2	CUPS (4 STICKS) BUTTER, MELTED
4	OUNCES COOKED CRAWFISH TAILS		¼	TO ½ TEASPOON SALT
2	TABLESPOONS CHOPPED GREEN ONIONS		⅛	TEASPOON TABASCO SAUCE
6	EGG YOLKS		2	TABLESPOONS FRESH LEMON JUICE

*C*ook the tasso in a small heavy skillet over medium heat until browned. Remove from the heat and stir in the crawfish and green onions. Let cool for 15 minutes. Whisk the egg yolks and water in a double boiler over simmering water for 5 minutes or until thick and foamy. Remove from over the water. Whisk in the butter gradually. Add the salt and Tabasco sauce. Stir in the lemon juice. Fold the tasso mixture gently into the hollandaise sauce. Use immediately. Note: Tasso is a highly seasoned lean cured pork.

Rockefeller Roulade

YIELD: 6 SERVINGS

6	EGG YOLKS	1/8	TEASPOON CREAM OF TARTAR
1/2	CUP (1 STICK) UNSALTED BUTTER, MELTED, COOLED	1/8	TEASPOON SALT, OR TO TASTE
2	TABLESPOONS FRESH LEMON JUICE		SPINACH PERNOD FILLING (PAGE 189)
3	TABLESPOONS MINCED FRESH PARSLEY		OYSTER SAUCE (PAGE 189)
1/2	TEASPOON SALT	3	TABLESPOONS GRATED PARMESAN CHEESE
1/4	TEASPOON WHITE PEPPER		CHOPPED FRESH PARSLEY FOR GARNISH
6	EGG WHITES, AT ROOM TEMPERATURE		

Beat the egg yolks in a bowl with an electric mixer until thick and pale yellow. Add melted butter, lemon juice, 3 tablespoons parsley, 1/2 teaspoon salt and pepper. Beat until well mixed. Wash and dry the beaters. Beat the egg whites, cream of tartar and 1/8 teaspoon salt in another bowl until soft peaks form. Fold the egg whites into the yolk mixture. Line a buttered 10 1/2x15 1/2-inch baking sheet with sides with waxed paper. Butter and flour the waxed paper. Spoon the egg mixture into the prepared pan and spread evenly. Bake at 350 degrees for 15 to 20 minutes or until puffed and golden brown. Invert the pan onto a baking sheet that has been covered with waxed paper. Peel the waxed paper off the top. Spread the Spinach Pernod Filling evenly over the top, leaving a 1-inch border on all sides. Roll up like a jelly roll, starting with the long side, peeling off the waxed paper as you roll. Trim off the ends and place the roll seam side down on a baking sheet. Place in a warm oven until heated through. Cut the heated roulade into 1-inch slices and place on serving plates. Ladle the Oyster Sauce on top, allowing 6 oysters per serving. Sprinkle with the Parmesan cheese and garnish with chopped parsley. Serve immediately. Note: The roulade can be made 1 day ahead. Wrap tightly and chill. Reheat before serving.

Spinach Pernod Filling

2	TABLESPOONS UNSALTED BUTTER	1	TABLESPOON FRESH LEMON JUICE
1	MEDIUM ONION, MINCED	½	CUP SOUR CREAM
1	GARLIC CLOVE, MINCED	1	TEASPOON DIJON MUSTARD
1	(10-OUNCE) PACKAGE FROZEN CHOPPED	⅓	CUP MINCED FRESH PARSLEY
	SPINACH, THAWED, SQUEEZED DRY	1	TEASPOON PERNOD
2	OUNCES CREAM CHEESE, CUT INTO PIECES		SALT AND PEPPER TO TASTE

Melt the butter in a saucepan over low heat. Add the onion and garlic and sauté until the onion is soft. Add the spinach. Cook for 4 to 5 minutes or until any liquid has evaporated, stirring occasionally. Add the cream cheese and cook until the cheese melts, stirring constantly. Stir in the lemon juice, sour cream, mustard, parsley and Pernod. Season with salt and pepper. Transfer the mixture to a food processor or blender and process until puréed.

Oyster Sauce

36	SHUCKED OYSTERS WITH THEIR LIQUOR	3	TABLESPOONS HEAVY CREAM
1	TABLESPOON FLOUR	2	TABLESPOONS UNSALTED BUTTER
¾	CUP DRY WHITE WINE	¼	CUP MINCED FRESH PARSLEY
⅔	CUP MINCED SHALLOTS		SALT AND PEPPER TO TASTE
¼	TEASPOON DRIED TARRAGON		

Strain the oyster liquor into a bowl. Reserve ⅔ cup and discard the rest. Whisk the reserved oyster liquor and flour in a small bowl until smooth. Combine the wine, shallots and tarragon in a large saucepan. Simmer until the mixture is reduced to ½ cup. Strain into a saucepan. Whisk in the flour mixture. Add the cream and simmer for 2 minutes, whisking constantly. Add the oysters and butter and simmer until the edges of the oysters curl. Stir in the parsley and season with salt and pepper.

Eggs Windsor Court

YIELD: 2 SERVINGS

1	TABLESPOON MINCED SHALLOTS	2	EGGS, POACHED
2	OUNCES CHOPPED FRESH MUSHROOMS	¼	CUP CHORON SAUCE (BÉARNAISE SAUCE WITH A SMALL AMOUNT OF TOMATO SAUCE ADDED)
1	TABLESPOON BUTTER		
2	BRIOCHE MUFFINS	½	OUNCE CAVIAR
2	SLICES SMOKED SALMON		FRESH DILL SPRIGS FOR GARNISH

Sauté the shallots and mushrooms in the butter in a skillet until tender. Cut the top off each brioche and cut a hole in the center of each muffin. Fill the holes tightly with the mushroom mixture. Place on a baking sheet and heat in a warm oven. Remove from the oven. Add 1 slice smoked salmon on top of the mushroom mixture. Top with a poached egg. Spoon the choron sauce over the top and sprinkle with the caviar. Garnish with dill.

Recipe provided by René Bajeux, Windsor Court Hotel

Shirred Eggs in Tomato Tulips

YIELD: 4 SERVINGS

4	FIRM RIPE MEDIUM TOMATOES	4	EGGS
	SALT AND PEPPER TO TASTE	2	TABLESPOONS FRESHLY GRATED PARMESAN CHEESE
4	TEASPOONS MINCED FRESH BASIL		
4	TEASPOONS BUTTER	4	LARGE TOAST ROUNDS, BUTTERED

Remove the tops of the tomatoes in a jagged tulip pattern with a small serrated knife. Remove the center of the tomatoes, leaving a shell. Place the tomato tulips in a baking dish and season the insides with salt and pepper. Sprinkle 1 teaspoon basil inside each tulip. Place 1 teaspoon butter inside each tulip. Crack 1 egg into each tulip. Sprinkle ½ tablespoon Parmesan cheese over each egg. Bake at 350 degrees for 30 minutes or until the eggs are set. Place 1 toast round on each of 4 serving plates and top with a tulip.

Streetcar Strata

YIELD: 12 SERVINGS

1	CUP MILK	1	POUND THINLY SLICED BASIL
½	CUP DRY WHITE WINE		TORTA CHEESE, HAVARTI OR
1	DAY-OLD LOAF FRENCH		FONTINA CHEESE
	BREAD, CUT INTO	3	RIPE TOMATOES, THINLY SLICED
	½-INCH SLICES	½	CUP BASIL PESTO
8	OUNCES THINLY SLICED	4	EGGS
	PROSCIUTTO OR OTHER HAM		SALT AND FRESHLY GROUND
2	CUPS ARUGULA OR SPINACH		PEPPER TO TASTE
	LEAVES	½	CUP HEAVY CREAM OR
3	TABLESPOONS OLIVE OIL		HALF-AND-HALF

Combine the milk and wine in a shallow bowl. Dip 2 slices of bread into the mixture and gently squeeze out as much liquid as possible without tearing the bread. Overlap the slices slightly in a 12-inch round or oval au gratin dish. Top with a slice of prosciutto, several arugula leaves dipped in the olive oil, a few cheese slices and a few tomato slices. Drizzle sparingly with some of the pesto. Repeat the process until all the ingredients are used. Beat the eggs in a bowl. Season with salt and pepper. Pour the eggs over the layers. Cover with plastic wrap and refrigerate overnight. Let the strata warm to room temperature. Drizzle the cream over the top of the strata. Bake at 350 degrees for 45 to 60 minutes or until puffy and golden brown.

Pecan-Crusted Bacon

YIELD: 6 SERVINGS

1	POUND SLICED BACON	1	TEASPOON FLOUR
¼	CUP PACKED DARK BROWN	½	CUP CHOPPED PECANS
	SUGAR		

Arrange the bacon slices close together but not overlapping on a broiler pan. Combine the brown sugar, flour and pecans in a bowl. Sprinkle over the bacon. Bake at 350 degrees for 30 minutes or until crisp and browned. Remove to paper towels to drain.

STREETCARS

OUR ST. CHARLES AVENUE STREETCAR LINE HAS THE DISTINCTION OF BEING THE OLDEST CONTINUOUSLY OPERATING STREET RAILWAY IN THE COUNTRY. ITS FIRST RUN WAS IN 1835 AS THE NEW ORLEANS AND CARROLLTON RAILROAD COMPANY. ORIGINALLY HORSE-DRAWN, THE STREETCARS SWITCHED TO MULE POWER IN THE 1850S WITH THE GROWTH OF THE NEW ORLEANS POPULATION. ONE MULE-CAR DRIVER WAS THE YOUNG SIR THOMAS LIPTON, WHOSE NAME IS NOW SYNONYMOUS WITH TEA. FOLLOWING EXHIBITIONS AT THE NEW ORLEANS COTTON CENTENNIAL EXPOSITION IN 1884-1885, THE LINE SWITCHED TO ELECTRICAL POWER. TODAY, THE STREETCARS DESIGNED BY PERLEY A. THOMAS IN 1923-1924 CONTINUE TO CARRY TOURISTS AND NATIVES ALIKE PAST THE GRACIOUS MANSIONS ALONG ST. CHARLES AVENUE.

Ham Glazed with Creole Mustard and Marmalade

Yield: 12 servings

1	(15- to 20-pound) smoked fully cooked bone-in ham	1	cup orange marmalade
36	whole cloves	¼	cup Dijon mustard
1½	cups water	2	tablespoons water
			Orange Tea Sauce

Trim any rind and excess fat from the ham, leaving a ¼-inch layer of fat on the top side. Score the fat in a 1-inch wide diamond pattern. Insert 1 clove into the center of each diamond. Place the ham in a large heavy roasting pan. Bake in the center of the oven at 325 degrees for 3 hours and 45 minutes or until a meat thermometer inserted near the center registers 120 degrees. Remove the ham to a platter. Place the roasting pan on a burner at medium heat. Whisk in 1½ cups water, scraping up any browned bits. Pour the pan juices into a small saucepan and place in the freezer for 15 minutes. Skim off the fat and reserve the remaining pan juices for the Orange Tea Sauce (below). Line the roasting pan with foil and return the ham to the roasting pan. Melt the marmalade over medium heat in a saucepan. Whisk in the mustard and 2 tablespoons water. Boil for 6 minutes or until thickened. Spoon generously over the ham. Bake at 425 degrees for 20 minutes or until the glaze begins to caramelize. Remove from the oven and let stand for 30 minutes. Carve and serve with Orange Tea Sauce.

Orange Tea Sauce

Yield: 12 servings

2	cups water	1	tablespoon Dijon mustard
4	orange-spice herbal tea bags		Reserved pan juices from the ham
2	cups canned chicken broth	1	tablespoon cornstarch
1	cup orange juice	1	tablespoon water
3	tablespoons orange marmalade		Salt and pepper to taste

Bring 2 cups water to a boil in a heavy saucepan. Add the tea bags. Remove from the heat. Cover and steep for 10 minutes. Discard tea bags. Stir in the broth, orange juice and marmalade. Boil for 12 minutes or until reduced to 3 cups. Whisk in the mustard and reserved pan juices. Bring to a boil. Whisk in a mixture of the cornstarch and 1 tablespoon water. Boil for 4 minutes or until slightly thickened. Season with salt and pepper.

Grillades and Grits

YIELD: 8 SERVINGS

8	(3-OUNCE) VEAL SCALLOPS		1½	TEASPOONS ITALIAN SEASONING
	SALT AND PEPPER TO TASTE		4	RIPE TOMATOES, CHOPPED
½	CUP (1 STICK) BUTTER		1	TABLESPOON WORCESTERSHIRE
½	CUP CHOPPED ONION			SAUCE
½	CUP CHOPPED SCALLIONS		2	TABLESPOONS TOMATO PASTE
3	GARLIC CLOVES, MINCED		1	QUART BEEF STOCK (AT RIGHT)
1½	CUPS CHOPPED GREEN BELL PEPPER		2	TABLESPOONS CORNSTARCH
½	CUP CHOPPED CELERY		¼	CUP WATER
½	CUP OLIVE OIL		2	TABLESPOONS CHOPPED
1	BAY LEAF			FRESH PARSLEY

Pound the veal thin. Season with salt and pepper. Sauté the veal in the butter in a skillet for 3 minutes per side or until lightly browned. Remove to a platter; keep warm. Sauté the next 5 ingredients in the olive oil until tender. Stir in the bay leaf, Italian seasoning, tomatoes, Worcestershire sauce and tomato paste. Add the beef stock and cook for 5 minutes, stirring frequently. Stir a mixture of the cornstarch and water with the parsley into the saucepan. Season with salt and pepper. Cook over medium-high heat until the sauce is reduced by ¼. Remove the bay leaf. Spoon some of the sauce onto 8 serving plates. Center a scallop on each plate. Spoon Plantation Grits (below) beside each scallop. Top with additional sauce and serve.

Recipe provided by Brennan's Restaurant

Plantation Grits

YIELD: 8 TO 10 SERVINGS

5	CUPS WATER		1	CUP GRITS
1	TEASPOON SALT		¼	CUP (½ STICK) BUTTER

Bring the water and salt to a boil in a saucepan. Stir in the grits gradually. Simmer for 5 to 10 minutes or until thickened. Stir in butter.

BEEF STOCK

1 POUND BEEF BONES
1 SMALL WHITE ONION, CHOPPED
1 RIB CELERY, CHOPPED
1 CARROT, CHOPPED
1 GARLIC CLOVE, CHOPPED
½ BUNCH SCALLIONS, CHOPPED
4 QUARTS COLD WATER

ARRANGE THE BEEF BONES IN A SINGLE LAYER IN A ROASTING PAN. ROAST AT 450 DEGREES FOR 15 MINUTES OR UNTIL BROWNED, STIRRING OCCASIONALLY. REMOVE THE BONES TO A LARGE HEAVY SAUCEPAN. ADD THE ONION, CELERY, CARROT, GARLIC, SCALLIONS AND WATER. BRING TO A BOIL OVER HIGH HEAT. SKIM OFF THE FOAM AS IT FORMS. REDUCE THE HEAT AND COOK AT A LOW ROLLING BOIL FOR 2 HOURS OR UNTIL REDUCED BY ½. STRAIN AND USE IMMEDIATELY OR FREEZE IN SMALLER PORTIONS FOR FUTURE USE.

YIELD: 2 QUARTS

Southern Rarebit

Yield: 8 servings

4	CUPS WATER	
½	TEASPOON SALT	
1	CUP QUICK-COOKING GRITS	
1	CUP SHREDDED SHARP CHEDDAR CHEESE	
½	TEASPOON TABASCO SAUCE	
¼	TEASPOON WHITE PEPPER	
	SALT TO TASTE	

3	TABLESPOONS UNSALTED BUTTER
4	FIRM RIPE TOMATOES, CUT INTO ¼-INCH SLICES
6	TABLESPOONS SHREDDED SHARP CHEDDAR CHEESE
	WHITE PEPPER TO TASTE

Bring the water and ½ teaspoon salt to a boil in a heavy saucepan. Stir in the grits in a slow stream. Reduce the heat. Simmer, covered, for 8 minutes or until the grits are tender and most of the liquid is absorbed, stirring occasionally. Uncover and cook for 1 minute or until all the liquid is absorbed. Remove from the heat and stir in 1 cup cheese, Tabasco sauce and ¼ teaspoon white pepper. Season with salt. Let stand for 30 minutes or until cool but not set, stirring occasionally. Pour onto a greased baking sheet with sides and spread into a 1-inch thick rectangle. Smooth the grits with a wet spatula. Let stand at room temperature for 1 hour or until firm. Cut into 16 triangles. Melt the butter in a heavy skillet over medium-high heat. Add the tomatoes once the foam subsides. Fry for 30 seconds per side or until the tomatoes are golden brown but still hold their shape. Arrange the tomatoes on top of the triangles and sprinkle with 6 tablespoons cheese. Season with salt and white pepper to taste. Broil the triangles 6 inches from the heat source until the cheese is bubbly. Serve immediately.

Spicy Grit Cakes with Shrimp and Andouille

Yield: 8 servings

4	CUPS WATER	1	POUND ANDOUILLE SAUSAGE, CHOPPED
½	TEASPOON SALT	1	CUP CHICKEN BROTH
1	CUP QUICK-COOKING GRITS	1	CUP HEAVY CREAM
3	TABLESPOONS MINCED JALAPEÑO CHILES	1	CUP FRESHLY GRATED PARMESAN
¼	TEASPOON WHITE PEPPER		CHEESE
2	TABLESPOONS BUTTER		SALT AND PEPPER TO TASTE
2	POUNDS UNCOOKED MEDIUM SHRIMP, PEELED, DEVEINED		CHOPPED SCALLIONS FOR GARNISH

Bring the water and salt to a boil in a medium saucepan. Stir in the grits gradually. Reduce the heat to low. Simmer, covered, for 8 minutes or until the grits are tender and most of the liquid is absorbed, stirring occasionally. Uncover and cook for 1 minute or until all the liquid is absorbed. Remove from the heat and stir in the jalapeños and white pepper. Let stand for 30 minutes or until cool but not set, stirring occasionally. Drop the grits in 16 generous ¼ cupfuls onto a nonstick baking sheet. Pat to form 3-inch rounds. Let stand at room temperature for 1 hour or until firm. Bake the grit cakes at 350 degrees for 15 minutes or until heated through. Remove to a platter and keep warm. Melt the butter in a large skillet over high heat. Add the shrimp and sausage and sauté until the shrimp are opaque. Remove the shrimp and sausage to a plate with a slotted spoon. Add the chicken stock to the skillet and stir, scraping up any browned bits. Stir in the cream and cook for 3 minutes or until slightly thickened. Add the Parmesan cheese. Cook for 2 minutes or until the cheese melts and the sauce is thick, stirring constantly. Add the shrimp and sausage to the skillet. Cook until heated through, stirring constantly. Season with salt and pepper. Remove from the heat. Place 2 grit cakes on each of 8 serving plates. Spoon the sauce over the top. Garnish with scallions.

Louisiana Seafood Crepes with Fresh Dill Sauce

Yield: 8 crepes

FRESH DILL SAUCE

½ cup white wine
¼ cup brandy
1 teaspoon minced shallots
2 teaspoons lemon juice
2 cups heavy cream
1 tablespoon butter
Salt and white pepper
to taste
1 tablespoon chopped
fresh dillweed

Combine the wine, brandy, shallots and lemon juice in a large saucepan. Cook until reduced by ½. Add the cream and bring to a boil. Cook until the cream begins to thicken and large bubbles appear on the surface, whisking frequently. Whisk in the butter and season with salt and pepper. Stir in the dill, remove from the heat and keep warm.
Yield: 8 servings

¾	cup plus 2 tablespoons flour	1	teaspoon minced shallots
¾	teaspoon salt	½	cup sliced fresh mushrooms
1	cup milk	1	tablespoon Dijon mustard
3	eggs, beaten	1	cup Louisiana crawfish tails
2	tablespoons vegetable oil	¼	cup heavy cream
1	cup uncooked 50/60 count shrimp, peeled, deveined		Salt and white pepper to taste
¼	cup water or stock	¾	cup jumbo lump crab meat, flaked
½	cup crab stock		Fresh dill sprigs for garnish
¼	cup sliced green onions		
1	teaspoon minced garlic		

Sift the flour with ¾ teaspoon salt into a bowl. Whisk in the milk. Add the eggs and oil and whisk until well blended. Let rest for 15 minutes. Heat a nonstick skillet over medium heat. Add ¼ cup of the batter to the skillet and tilt to coat the bottom of the skillet. Turn the crepe with a fork when the edge begins to brown. Cook the other side until golden brown. Remove the crepe to a large plate and keep warm. Repeat with remaining batter. Cook the shrimp with the water in a large deep skillet until ¾ done. The water should just be evaporated. Add the crab stock, green onions, garlic, shallots, mushrooms, mustard, crawfish and cream. Bring to a simmer, stirring constantly. Season with salt and pepper to taste. Fold in the crab meat. Simmer until the crab meat is heated through. Divide the filling between the crepes. Roll up the crepes and place on serving plates. Top with Fresh Dill Sauce (at left) and garnish with dill.

Recipe provided by Dennis Hutley, Le Parvenu Restaurant

196

Sweet Potato and Chicken Breakfast Hash

Yield: 4 servings

4	CUPS CHICKEN BROTH	2	TABLESPOONS UNSALTED BUTTER
2	(3/4-POUND) BONELESS SKINLESS CHICKEN	1	TEASPOON PAPRIKA
	BREASTS, HALVED	1/2	TEASPOON CHILI POWDER
1 1/2	POUNDS SWEET POTATOES, CUT INTO	1/2	TEASPOON FRESHLY GROUND PEPPER
	1/2-INCH CUBES	1/2	TEASPOON DRIED THYME
1	LARGE ONION, FINELY CHOPPED	1/2	TEASPOON SALT
1	SMALL GREEN BELL PEPPER,	1/2	CUP CHOPPED GREEN ONIONS
	FINELY CHOPPED	1/4	CUP CHOPPED FRESH PARSLEY
1	SMALL RED BELL PEPPER, FINELY CHOPPED	1	CUP HALF-AND-HALF
3	GARLIC CLOVES, MINCED		POACHED OR FRIED EGGS

Bring the broth to a boil in a deep skillet. Add the chicken. Reduce the heat and poach for 7 minutes or until cooked through, turning frequently; remove and let cool. Cut into 1/2-inch cubes. Add the potatoes to a saucepan of boiling salted water. Cook for 15 minutes or until tender. Drain. Sauté the onion, bell peppers and garlic in the butter in a skillet for 3 minutes or until soft. Stir in the paprika, chili powder, pepper, thyme and salt. Cook for 1 minute. Add the chicken, potatoes, green onions, parsley and half-and-half. Cook until the half-and-half is reduced slightly and the hash is thickened, stirring constantly. Spoon onto serving plates and top with eggs.

Sausage Savories

Yield: 12 to 15 servings

1 1/2	POUNDS BULK BREAKFAST SAUSAGE	1	CUP SOUR CREAM
1	ONION, CHOPPED	1/2	TEASPOON SALT
1 1/2	CUPS BAKING MIX	1	EGG
3/4	CUP MILK	12	OUNCES SHREDDED CHEDDAR CHEESE
1	EGG		PAPRIKA AND POPPY SEEDS TO TASTE

Brown the sausage with the onion in a skillet, stirring until the sausage is crumbly. Drain well. Combine the baking mix, milk and 1 egg in a bowl. Stir until well mixed. Spread in the bottom of a 9x13-inch baking dish. Top with the cooked sausage. Mix the sour cream, salt and 1 egg in a bowl. Spread over the sausage. Top with the cheese. Sprinkle with paprika and poppy seeds. Bake at 350 degrees for 30 minutes.

Overnight Pain Perdu

Yield: 6 servings

¼	CUP (½ STICK) BUTTER, SOFTENED		2	TABLESPOONS MAPLE SYRUP
12	(¾-INCH-THICK) SLICES FRENCH BREAD		1	TEASPOON VANILLA EXTRACT
6	EGGS		½	TEASPOON SALT
1½	CUPS MILK		½	CUP CONFECTIONERS' SUGAR
¼	CUP SUGAR		2	CUPS MAPLE PECAN SYRUP

Spread the butter over the bottom of a large baking pan with 1-inch sides. Arrange the bread slices in the pan. Beat the eggs, milk, sugar, maple syrup, vanilla and salt in a large bowl. Pour over the bread. Turn the slices over to coat. Cover with plastic wrap and chill overnight. Bake the bread slices at 400 degrees for 10 minutes. Turn the slices over and bake for 5 minutes longer or until puffed and golden brown. Remove to serving plates and sprinkle with confectioners' sugar. Serve with Maple Pecan Syrup (below).

Maple Pecan Syrup

Yield: 2 cups

2	CUPS MAPLE SYRUP		1	CUP TOASTED PECAN HALVES OR PIECES

Combine the maple syrup and pecans in a medium saucepan and mix well. Bring to a simmer and serve hot.

Oatmeal Soufflé

YIELD: 4 SERVINGS

1	CUP MILK	½	TEASPOON GROUND NUTMEG
2	TABLESPOONS BUTTER	½	TEASPOON GROUND CINNAMON
¾	CUP QUICK-COOKING OATS	3	EGG YOLKS, LIGHTLY BEATEN
⅓	CUP CREAM CHEESE	½	CUP RAISINS
¼	TEASPOON SALT	½	CUP CHOPPED WALNUTS OR PECANS
½	CUP PACKED BROWN SUGAR	3	EGG WHITES

Butter a 1½-quart soufflé dish or baking dish. Add a small amount of sugar and tilt to coat. Tap out any excess sugar. Combine the milk and 2 tablespoons butter in a saucepan and heat until barely boiling. Stir in the oats gradually. Cook until thick, stirring frequently. Remove from the heat. Add the cream cheese, salt, brown sugar, nutmeg and cinnamon. Cook until the cheese is melted and the mixture is well blended, stirring constantly. Beat in the egg yolks gradually. Stir in the raisins and walnuts. Beat the egg whites in a bowl until stiff but not dry. Fold the egg whites into the oatmeal mixture with a rubber spatula. Spoon the mixture into the prepared soufflé dish. Bake at 325 degrees for 35 to 40 minutes or until set. Serve immediately.

Bananas Foster Pancakes with Butter Rum Syrup

Yield: 4 servings

1	CUP FLOUR		1	TO 1¼ CUPS MILK
1	TEASPOON BAKING POWDER		1	EGG
¼	TEASPOON BAKING SODA		2	TABLESPOONS BUTTER, MELTED
¼	TEASPOON GROUND CINNAMON		½	TEASPOON VANILLA EXTRACT
3	TABLESPOONS BROWN SUGAR			BUTTER OR VEGETABLE OIL
1	BANANA, MASHED			

Combine the flour, baking powder, baking soda, cinnamon and brown sugar in a bowl and mix well. Combine the banana, milk, egg, melted butter and vanilla in a separate bowl and mix well. Pour the banana mixture into the dry ingredients. Stir until well mixed. Heat a griddle or nonstick skillet. Add a small amount of butter and tilt to coat. Ladle the batter onto the griddle. Flip the pancakes when bubbles appear on top. Cook the other side until golden brown. Serve with Butter Rum Syrup (below) or Cinnamon Syrup (at left).

Butter Rum Syrup

Yield: 1⅓ cups

1	CUP MAPLE SYRUP		¼	CUP DARK JAMAICAN RUM
2	TABLESPOONS UNSALTED BUTTER		¼	TEASPOON GROUND CINNAMON

Combine the maple syrup, butter, rum and cinnamon in a saucepan and mix well. Bring to a simmer and cook for 5 minutes, stirring frequently. Serve warm.

CINNAMON SYRUP

1 CINNAMON STICK
DARK BROWN SUGAR TO TASTE

SOAK THE CINNAMON STICK IN A SMALL AMOUNT OF WATER IN A SAUCEPAN. DISCARD THE CINNAMON STICK. ADD BROWN SUGAR TO THE WATER AND HEAT UNTIL DISSOLVED, STIRRING CONSTANTLY. BOIL UNTIL THE SYRUP IS THE DESIRED CONSISTENCY.
YIELD: VARIABLE

Banana Breakfast Cake

YIELD: 12 SERVINGS

2½ CUPS SUGAR

1¼ CUPS MASHED BANANAS

2 TEASPOONS VANILLA EXTRACT

2 EGGS

1 CUP (2 STICKS) BUTTER, MELTED

1 CUP BUTTERMILK

2⅓ CUPS FLOUR

1 CUP CHOPPED PECANS

1 CUP DRIED CRANBERRIES

1 TEASPOON BAKING POWDER

1 TEASPOON BAKING SODA

1 TEASPOON GROUND CINNAMON

¼ TEASPOON SALT

CONFECTIONERS' SUGAR

Combine the sugar, bananas, vanilla and eggs in a bowl and mix well. Stir in the butter and buttermilk. Combine the flour, pecans, cranberries, baking powder, baking soda, cinnamon and salt in a separate bowl and mix well. Add to the banana mixture and stir until evenly moistened. Pour into a greased and floured 10 inch nonstick bundt pan. Bake at 350 degrees for 1 hour or until a wooden pick inserted in the center comes out clean. Cool in the pan on a wire rack for 15 minutes. Invert onto a serving platter and dust with confectioners' sugar.

Cornmeal Waffles with Wild Mushroom Ragout

Yield: 6 servings

2	TABLESPOONS FLOUR	1	EGG, BEATEN
1	TEASPOON SUGAR	1	CUP BUTTERMILK
½	TEASPOON BAKING POWDER	¼	CUP (½ STICK) BUTTER, MELTED
¼	TEASPOON BAKING SODA	3	SCALLIONS, FINELY CHOPPED
¼	HEAPING TEASPOON SALT	6	OUNCES CRUMBLED GOAT CHEESE
¾	CUP WHITE CORNMEAL		

Sift the flour, sugar, baking powder, baking soda and salt into a bowl. Add the cornmeal. Add the egg and buttermilk gradually; mix well. Beat in the butter. Spoon the batter onto a hot lightly greased waffle iron. Cook using manufacturer's directions. Place the waffles on plates. Top with the Wild Mushroom Ragout (below). Sprinkle with the scallions and cheese.

Wild Mushroom Ragout

Yield: 6 servings

2	CUPS DRIED MOREL MUSHROOMS	1	GARLIC CLOVE, MINCED
2½	CUPS BOILING WATER	1	TABLESPOON FLOUR
3	SLICES BACON	1	TABLESPOON UNSALTED BUTTER,
1	TABLESPOON UNSALTED BUTTER		SOFTENED
1	LARGE LEEK, WHITE AND PALE GREEN		SALT AND PEPPER TO TASTE
	PARTS ONLY		

Soak the mushrooms in the boiling water for 25 minutes or until soft; drain well, reserving the liquid. Strain the liquid into a bowl. Cook the bacon in a saucepan for 8 to 10 minutes or until crisp; drain well, reserving 1 teaspoon drippings. Crumble the bacon. Add 1 tablespoon butter to the drippings in the saucepan. Cut the leeks in half lengthwise; thinly slice crosswise. Add the leeks to the saucepan. Sauté over low heat for 8 minutes or until soft but not brown. Add the mushrooms and garlic. Sauté over medium heat for 2 minutes. Add the reserved liquid and bacon. Simmer, covered, over low heat for 10 minutes or until the mushrooms are tender. Blend the flour and 1 tablespoon butter. Stir into the saucepan. Simmer over low heat until heated through, stirring occasionally. Season with salt and pepper.

Asparagus Tart

YIELD: 6 TO 8 SERVINGS

1½ CUPS FLOUR	1 EGG YOLK
⅛ TEASPOON SALT	1 CUP HEAVY CREAM
½ TEASPOON CARAWAY SEEDS	3 EGGS
5 TABLESPOONS CHILLED UNSALTED BUTTER, CUT INTO TABLESPOONS	¾ TEASPOON SALT
2 TABLESPOONS CHILLED SHORTENING, CUT INTO TABLESPOONS	½ TEASPOON WHITE PEPPER
2 TO 3 TABLESPOONS ICE WATER	¼ POUND THINLY SLICED BOILED HAM, CUT INTO ⅛X2-INCH STRIPS
1½ POUNDS ASPARAGUS	⅓ CUP FRESHLY GRATED PARMESAN CHEESE
4 OUNCES CREAM CHEESE, CUT INTO PIECES, SOFTENED	

Combine the flour, ⅛ teaspoon salt and caraway seeds in a food processor. Process for 3 seconds. Add the butter and shortening. Pulse until the mixture resembles dry oats. Add the ice water, processing constantly until a dough is formed. Place the dough on a work surface and pat into a 6-inch disk. Wrap in waxed paper and chill until firm. Peel the asparagus stems. Cut 2½ inches off the tips of each stalk and set aside. Trim away and discard the bottom of the stalks so that 2½ inches of the stalk remains to be used. Place the asparagus tips and stalks in boiling water in a medium saucepan. Cook for 3 minutes or just until tender. Drain and rinse under cold running water. Drain well. Place the caraway dough on a floured work surface. Roll into a 12-inch circle. Fit into a floured 10-inch tart pan with a removable bottom, trimming any excess dough. Prick the dough with a fork. Place in the freezer for 10 minutes. Beat the cream cheese with the egg yolk in a bowl until blended. Stir in the cream gradually. The mixture will be slightly lumpy. Beat in the eggs 1 at a time. Stir in the salt and pepper. Spread the asparagus stalk pieces and the ham in the bottom of the prepared tart pan. Top with half the custard mixture. Place on the lowest oven rack. Bake at 425 degrees for 15 minutes. Pour the remaining custard mixture over the top and arrange the asparagus tips to form a wheel on top. Sprinkle with the Parmesan cheese. Reduce the oven temperature to 375 degrees. Return the tart to the lowest oven rack. Bake for 40 minutes or until a wooden pick inserted in the center comes out clean. Remove the tart to a wire rack to cool for 15 minutes. Loosen from the side of the pan with a sharp knife and remove the side. Place on a serving plate.

Dixie Beer Bread

YIELD: 1 LOAF

4	CUPS SELF-RISING FLOUR	16	OUNCES DIXIE BEER
¼	CUP SUGAR	2	TABLESPOONS BUTTER, MELTED

Mix the flour and sugar in a bowl. Add the beer and mix well. Pour the batter into a greased loaf pan. Bake at 400 degrees for 50 minutes. Remove from the oven and pour the melted butter on top. Bake for 5 minutes longer. Remove to a wire rack to cool.

Cajun Cheddar Biscuits

YIELD: 12 BISCUITS

3½	CUPS FLOUR	1	CUP SHREDDED SHARP CHEDDAR CHEESE
2	TABLESPOONS BAKING POWDER		
1	TABLESPOON SUGAR	⅔	CUP CHILLED SHORTENING, CUT INTO SMALL PIECES
2	TEASPOONS CAYENNE PEPPER		
½	TEASPOON SALT	1¼	CUPS CHILLED BUTTERMILK
¾	CUP GRATED ROMANO CHEESE		

Sift the flour, baking powder, sugar, cayenne pepper and salt twice into a medium bowl. Stir in the Romano cheese and Cheddar cheese. Add the shortening and rub with fingers until the mixture resembles coarse meal. Add the buttermilk and stir until a dough begins to form. Place the dough on a lightly floured surface. Knead gently about 8 times or until smooth. Roll the dough ³/₄ inch thick. Cut with a 2-inch biscuit cutter. Gather the dough scraps and roll them out. Cut with the biscuit cutter. Place the biscuits on a large buttered baking sheet. Bake at 450 degrees for 15 minutes or until puffed and golden brown. Serve warm.

Sweet Potato Biscuits

2	MEDIUM SWEET POTATOES	1/2	TEASPOON SALT
3/4	CUP MILK	1/4	CUP CHILLED SHORTENING,
13/4	CUPS SIFTED FLOUR		CUT INTO PIECES
1	TABLESPOON BAKING POWDER		

Place the sweet potatoes in a baking dish and prick with a fork. Bake in the bottom third of the oven at 400 degrees for 45 minutes or until tender. Remove to a wire rack to cool slightly. Peel and mash the sweet potatoes. Place 1 cup of the mashed sweet potatoes in a bowl. Discard any remaining sweet potato or reserve for another use.

Add the milk to the sweet potatoes and mix well. Sift the flour, baking powder and salt into a large bowl. Cut in the shortening until the mixture resembles coarse meal. Make a well in the dry mixture and spoon the sweet potato mixture into the well. Stir until a dough begins to form. Place the dough on a heavily floured work surface.

Sprinkle the dough and your hands with flour and pat the dough 3/4 inch thick. Cut out biscuits with a floured 2 1/2-inch biscuit cutter. Arrange the biscuits 1 1/2 inches apart on an ungreased baking sheet. Bake at 400 degrees for 30 minutes or until light brown. Remove the biscuits to a wire rack to cool.

Buckwheat Scones with Smoked Salmon

YIELD: 5 TO 6 SERVINGS

1⅓ CUPS ALL-PURPOSE FLOUR

⅔ CUP BUCKWHEAT FLOUR

1½ TEASPOONS DILLSEEDS

1 TEASPOON BAKING POWDER

1 TEASPOON BAKING SODA

¼ TEASPOON SALT

6 TABLESPOONS (¾ STICK) CHILLED UNSALTED BUTTER, CUT INTO PIECES

⅔ CUP MILK

4 OUNCES CREAM CHEESE, SOFTENED

1½ TEASPOONS DRAINED CAPERS

1½ TEASPOONS FRESH LIME JUICE

1 SMALL SHALLOT, MINCED

¼ TEASPOON FRESHLY GROUND PEPPER

¾ POUND THINLY SLICED SMOKED SALMON

FRESH DILL SPRIGS AND DRAINED CAPERS FOR GARNISH

LIME WEDGES

Combine the all-purpose flour, buckwheat flour, dillseeds, baking powder, baking soda and salt in a food processor. Process for 30 seconds or until blended. Add the butter and pulse for 45 seconds or until the mixture resembles coarse meal. Add the milk and process for 30 seconds or just until a dough begins to form. Place the dough on a lightly floured surface. Pat into a 6-inch disk. Roll the dough into a ½-inch-thick circle. Cut out 10 rounds with a 2½-inch biscuit cutter. Gather the dough scraps and roll them out. Cut 1 or 2 more rounds with the biscuit cutter. Place the scones on a greased baking sheet. Bake at 350 degrees for 15 to 20 minutes or until firm and golden brown. Remove the biscuits to a wire rack to cool. Beat the cream cheese in a small bowl until smooth. Add the capers, lime juice, shallot and pepper and beat until well mixed. Trim the tops off the scones to form a level surface. Spread about 1 tablespoon of the cream cheese mixture on top of each scone. Top with a slice of smoked salmon. Garnish with dill sprigs and capers. Serve with lime wedges.

Scallion Scones

Yield: 16 scones

3	CUPS FLOUR	2¹⁄₃	CUPS CHILLED HEAVY CREAM
1¹⁄₂	TABLESPOONS BAKING POWDER	1¹⁄₂	CUPS THINLY SLICED SCALLIONS
1¹⁄₂	TEASPOONS SALT	2	TABLESPOONS BUTTER, MELTED
1	TEASPOON FRESHLY GROUND PEPPER		

Mix the flour, baking powder, salt and pepper in a large bowl. Combine the cream and scallions in a medium bowl and mix well. Add the cream mixture to the dry ingredients. Stir until evenly moistened. Place the dough on a floured surface. Knead about 8 times or just until the dough holds together. Pat out the dough to an 8-inch square. Cut into sixteen 2-inch square scones. Place the scones 1¹⁄₂ inches apart on a large baking sheet. Brush the tops with the melted butter. Bake at 425 degrees for 18 minutes or until golden brown. Serve warm.

Cayenne Corn Bread

Yield: 18 servings

3	CUPS YELLOW CORNMEAL	2	TEASPOONS SALT
4	CUPS UNBLEACHED FLOUR, SIFTED	¹⁄₂	TEASPOON CAYENNE PEPPER
1	CUP SUGAR	8	EGGS
¹⁄₄	CUP BAKING POWDER	4	CUPS MILK

Combine the cornmeal, flour, sugar, baking powder, salt and cayenne pepper in a large bowl. Beat the eggs and milk in a small bowl. Add to the dry ingredients. Stir just until moistened; do not overmix. Divide the batter between 2 buttered 9x13-inch baking dishes. Bake at 350 degrees for 30 minutes or until golden brown and a wooden pick inserted in the center comes out clean. Remove to a wire rack. Cut into squares when cool.

Focaccia di Frutti

½	CUP ROSEMARY OLIVE OIL OR	2½	TEASPOONS DRY YEAST
	EXTRA-VIRGIN OLIVE OIL	2	TABLESPOONS VIRGIN OLIVE OIL
1	CUP GOLDEN RAISINS	1	TABLESPOON SUGAR
1	CUP SEEDLESS GRAPES	8	CUPS FLOUR
½	CUP TOASTED PINE NUTS	1	TABLESPOON COARSE SALT
2	TABLESPOONS CHOPPED FRESH ROSEMARY	1	TABLESPOON SUGAR
½	CUP (110-DEGREE) MILK	1	TABLESPOON COARSE SALT
2	CUPS (110-DEGREE) WATER		

Heat ½ cup olive oil in a skillet over medium heat. Add the raisins, grapes, pine nuts and rosemary. Toss to coat and remove from the heat. Let cool to room temperature. Beat the milk, water, yeast, 2 tablespoons olive oil, 1 tablespoon sugar and ½ cup of the flour in a bowl with an electric mixer. Let stand for 10 to 15 minutes or until foamy. Add half the raisin mixture and 4 cups of the flour. Beat with the dough hook attachment until well mixed. Add 1 tablespoon salt. Add the remaining flour 1 cup at a time with the mixer running. Knead in the mixer for 3 to 5 minutes or until the dough is elastic. Place the dough in an oiled bowl and turn to coat. Cover with a damp cloth and let rise in a warm place for 1 hour or until doubled in bulk. Place the dough on a lightly floured surface. Roll out the dough to fit a baking sheet. Place on an oiled baking sheet with sides and cover with a damp towel. Let rise in a warm place until doubled in bulk. Press fingers on top of the dough to create shallow indentations. Spread the remaining raisin mixture on the dough. Sprinkle with a mixture of 1 tablespoon sugar and 1 tablespoon salt. Bake at 350 degrees for 35 to 45 minutes or until golden brown. Remove to a wire rack to cool.

Ponchatoula Palmiers

Yield: 15 servings

½	CUP SUGAR	1	SHEET FROZEN PUFF PASTRY,
¼	CUP FLOUR		THAWED, UNFOLDED, OR 1 SHEET
¼	TEASPOON SALT		QUICK PUFF PASTRY (AT RIGHT)
2	CUPS HALF-AND-HALF OR	¼	CUP SUGAR
	LIGHT CREAM	½	TEASPOON GROUND CINNAMON
4	EGG YOLKS, BEATEN	2	CUPS SLICED STRAWBERRIES
1½	TEASPOONS VANILLA EXTRACT	15	WHOLE STRAWBERRIES

*F*or the pastry cream, combine ½ cup sugar, flour and salt in a heavy saucepan. Stir in the half-and-half gradually. Cook over medium heat until thick and bubbly, stirring constantly. Cook for 1 minute longer, stirring constantly. Stir 1 cup of the hot mixture into the egg yolks; stir the egg yolks into the hot mixture. Cook for 2 minutes, stirring constantly. Remove from the heat. Stir in the vanilla. Pour into a bowl and press plastic wrap directly onto the surface. Let cool without stirring. For the palmiers, place the puff pastry on a lightly floured surface. Roll into a 10x14-inch rectangle. Sprinkle with a mixture of ¼ cup sugar and cinnamon. Press the mixture lightly into the pastry. Roll up the 2 short sides to meet in the center. Turn over and cut into ¼-inch slices (freeze briefly if the dough is too soft to cut). Place cut side down 2 inches apart on 2 parchment paper-lined baking sheets. Bake at 375 degrees for 15 minutes or until golden brown and crisp. Remove to a wire rack to cool. Spread 2 tablespoons pastry cream on 1 side of half the palmiers. Arrange sliced strawberries on the cream. Top each with 1 palmier. Place on individual plates. Top each serving with a dollop of pastry cream and a whole strawberry.

QUICK PUFF PASTRY

4 CUPS FLOUR
1 TEASPOON SALT
2 CUPS (4 STICKS) COLD BUTTER,
CUT INTO ½-INCH SLICES
1¼ CUPS ICE WATER

MIX THE FLOUR AND SALT IN A LARGE BOWL. CUT IN THE BUTTER GRADUALLY, STIRRING UNTIL THE BUTTER IS COATED AND SEPARATED. ADD THE ICE WATER AND MIX QUICKLY. THE BUTTER WILL REMAIN IN LARGE PIECES; THE FLOUR WILL NOT BE COMPLETELY MOISTENED. PLACE THE DOUGH ON A LIGHTLY FLOURED SURFACE. KNEAD 10 TIMES. GATHER INTO A BALL. SHAPE INTO A RECTANGLE AND FLATTEN SLIGHTLY. ROLL INTO A 15X18-INCH RECTANGLE ON A HEAVILY FLOURED SURFACE. FOLD CROSSWISE INTO THIRDS, FORMING A 6X15-INCH RECTANGLE. TURN ¼ TURN FOLD CROSSWISE INTO THIRDS, MAKING A 5X6-INCH RECTANGLE WITH 9 LAYERS. REPEAT THE ROLLING AND SHAPING PROCESS ONCE. CHILL, WRAPPED WITH PLASTIC WRAP, FOR 20 MINUTES. REPEAT THE ROLLING AND SHAPING PROCESS TWICE. CHILL FOR 20 MINUTES BEFORE USING.
YIELD: 2 SHEETS

Desserts

Desserts

Willis Hogan House
1138 Third Street

This Italianate double-gallery side-hall residence is typical of many homes built in the Garden District just prior to and shortly after the Civil War. It features a dominant, well-proportioned gallery with Ionic columns on the first floor and Corinthian columns connected by a cast-iron railing on the second. The Italianate is one of the most popular architectural styles in the Garden District.

❖

The house was constructed in 1869 for Willis Hogan, a native of Knox County, Kentucky, and a partner in the firm of Hogan & Patton, cotton factors. Factors served as middlemen in the cotton business, buying from planters and selling to the mills. The profession was very important to the New Orleans economy and was perhaps the most prevalent source of wealth for Garden District residents at that time. The well-known painting *A Cotton Office in New Orleans* was painted by Edgar Degas in 1873 and depicts portraits of Degas' relatives.

❖

The Hogan family retained the house until 1882, when it was sold to Louis Bush. A newspaper advertisement for the sale of the house described it as follows: "The dwelling is modern in style, and complete in construction and arrangement of interior for the comfort and convenience of a large family. This property… is sold subject to a lease of $1200 per annum, expiring 1st October 1882."

❖

Bush gave the house to Susan Bush Maginnis but never paid for it, and in 1886 the house was returned to the Hogan family. In 1888 it was sold to Benjamin Eshleman, who had come to New Orleans in 1850 from Pennsylvania and was in the hardware business. The house remained in his family until 1940, when it was sold to Freeman E. Loeb. Loeb sold it three years later to Dr. and Mrs. Arthur Vidrine. In 1954 the Vidrines sold the home to its present owners, Mr. and Mrs. Hjalmar Breit, for $40,000. It became the JLNO Show House IX in 1999.

Brioche Bread Pudding

YIELD: 8 TO 10 SERVINGS

1	(1-POUND) BRIOCHE OR EGG BREAD LOAF	¼	CUP FRANGELICO (HAZELNUT LIQUEUR)
8	EGGS	1	TABLESPOON VANILLA EXTRACT
2	CUPS HEAVY CREAM	½	TEASPOON ALMOND EXTRACT
2	CUPS MILK	1¼	CUPS BOURBON SAUCE
2	CUPS SUGAR		

Trim the crusts from the brioche and reserve. Cut the brioche into cubes and layer in a 9x13-inch baking pan. Whisk the eggs, cream, milk, sugar, Frangelico, vanilla and almond extract in a large bowl. Pour over the bread cubes. Let stand for 30 minutes, occasionally pressing the bread into the cream mixture. Arrange the reserved crusts on a baking sheet. Bake at 350 degrees for 10 minutes or until dry. Remove to a wire rack to cool. Process the cooled crusts in a food processor until fine crumbs form. Sprinkle 1 cup of the crumbs over the pudding. Bake at 350 degrees for 40 minutes or until set in the center. Remove to a wire rack to cool slightly. Spoon the warm bread pudding onto serving plates. Top each serving with Bourbon Sauce (below). Note: The bread and cream mixture can be prepared up to 2 hours ahead. Cover and chill.

Bourbon Sauce

YIELD: 1¼ CUPS

¼	CUP (½ STICK) UNSALTED BUTTER	¼	CUP HEAVY CREAM
⅔	CUP PACKED DARK BROWN SUGAR	¼	CUP BOURBON

Melt the butter in a small heavy saucepan over low heat. Stir in the brown sugar. Cook until dissolved, stirring constantly. Add the cream and bourbon and increase the heat to medium. Simmer for 5 minutes, stirring occasionally. Serve warm.

White Chocolate Bread Pudding

Yield: 12 servings

1	(24-INCH) LOAF DRY FRENCH BREAD	4	EGGS
6	CUPS HEAVY CREAM	15	EGG YOLKS
2	CUPS MILK	½	CUP HEAVY CREAM
1	CUP SUGAR	8	OUNCES WHITE CHOCOLATE, BROKEN INTO SMALL PIECES
20	OUNCES WHITE CHOCOLATE, BROKEN INTO SMALL PIECES	1	OUNCE DARK CHOCOLATE, GRATED

Slice the bread and arrange the slices in a 9x13-inch baking pan. Heat 6 cups cream, milk and sugar in a large saucepan over medium heat until hot. Remove from the heat and add 20 ounces white chocolate. Stir until the chocolate is melted. Beat the eggs and egg yolks in a large bowl. Whisk a small amount of the hot cream mixture into the eggs; whisk the eggs into the hot cream mixture. Pour ½ of the custard over the bread slices. Press the bread down until it becomes saturated. Pour in the remaining custard. Cover the pan with foil. Bake at 350 degrees for 1 hour. Remove the foil and bake for 30 minutes or until set and golden brown. Remove to a wire rack to cool slightly. Bring ½ cup cream to a boil in a small saucepan. Remove from the heat and add 8 ounces white chocolate. Stir until the chocolate is melted and the sauce is smooth. Spoon the warm bread pudding onto serving plates and top with the sauce. Sprinkle with the grated dark chocolate. Note: The baked pudding can be chilled for 6 to 8 hours or until firm. Loosen the sides with a sharp knife and invert the pan onto a cutting board. Cut the pudding into six 4x4½-inch squares. Cut each square diagonally to make 2 triangles. Place the triangles on a baking sheet and bake at 275 degrees for 15 minutes. Place the triangles on serving plates and top with the warm sauce and grated dark chocolate.

Recipe provided by Dickie Brennan's Palace Café

Sugar

Sugar cane cuttings from the French West Indies were introduced to Louisiana by Iberville. Some growers, including the Jesuits, produced small quantities of *tafia* (rum) from their crops as early as 1751. However, it was not until 1796, following a failed indigo crop, that Etienne de Bore, a planter, and Antoine Morin, a sugar-maker from Sainte-Domingue, collaborated to raise and granulate sugar cane for sale commercially in Louisiana. Their success occurred on de Bore's plantation near the site of Audubon Park and was based on lessons learned from earlier attempts. By the 1840s, Norbert Rillieux, a free man of color, had patented a vacuum-pan process that enhanced the sugar's quality and increased its yield. Prior to the Civil War, Louisiana supplied 95 percent of sugar for the United States. The industry thrives today.

Bananas Foster

Yield: 6 servings

6	TABLESPOONS (3/4 STICK) BUTTER	1	TEASPOON GROUND CINNAMON
3/4	CUP PACKED BROWN SUGAR	6	TABLESPOONS BANANA LIQUEUR
6	RIPE BANANAS, SLICED LENGTHWISE	3/4	CUP WHITE RUM
		6	CUPS VANILLA ICE CREAM

Melt the butter in a chafing dish. Add the brown sugar and heat until the brown sugar dissolves, stirring constantly. Add the bananas and sauté until heated through. Sprinkle with the cinnamon. Add the banana liqueur and rum and ignite immediately. Baste the bananas with the flaming sauce until the flames die out. Spoon the ice cream into serving bowls and top with the bananas and sauce.

Applesauce Brûlée

Yield: 6 servings

3	POUNDS GRANNY SMITH APPLES, PEELED, CORED, SLICED		SALT TO TASTE
1/2	TO 1 CUP PACKED BROWN SUGAR	6	(3-INCH) TART SHELLS (SEE PAGE 240)
2	TABLESPOONS BUTTER	2	CUPS SOUR CREAM
2	TEASPOONS GROUND CINNAMON		BROWN SUGAR
1	TEASPOON FRESHLY GRATED NUTMEG		

Place the apples in a large saucepan. Add enough water to cover the bottom. Cook over medium heat until the apples are soft but not mushy. Stir in 1/2 cup to 1 cup brown sugar (adjusting for apple tartness), butter, cinnamon and nutmeg. Season with salt. Cook for 3 minutes. Divide the applesauce among the 6 tart shells. Top with the sour cream and sprinkle with brown sugar. Place the tarts on a baking sheet and broil until the brown sugar caramelizes. Watch closely to avoid burning.

Black-and-White Crème Brûlée

Yield: 6 servings

½	CUP HEAVY CREAM	6	EGG YOLKS
5	OUNCES SEMISWEET CHOCOLATE, CUT	½	CUP SUGAR
	INTO 1-OUNCE PIECES	1	TEASPOON VANILLA EXTRACT
2	CUPS HEAVY CREAM	6	TABLESPOONS LIGHT BROWN SUGAR

Combine ½ cup cream and the chocolate in a heavy saucepan. Cook over low heat until the chocolate is melted and the mixture is smooth, stirring constantly. Pour into a large bowl. Whisk 2 cups cream, egg yolks, sugar and vanilla in a bowl until the sugar is dissolved and the mixture is smooth. Whisk 1 cup of the egg mixture into the chocolate mixture. Cover and chill the remaining egg mixture. Divide the chocolate mixture among six 1-cup custard cups. Place the cups in a 9x13-inch baking pan. Pour hot water into the pan to come ½ inch up the sides of the cups. Bake at 325 degrees for 30 minutes or until the custards are almost set but the centers are still soft. Pour the remaining egg mixture carefully over the custards. Bake for 20 to 25 minutes longer or until the custards are set. Remove the custards from the baking pan to a wire rack to cool. Cover and chill for 8 hours or longer. Place the custards on a baking sheet and sprinkle each with 1 tablespoon brown sugar. Broil 5½ inches from the heat source for 2 minutes or until the brown sugar melts. Watch closely to avoid burning. Let stand for 5 minutes for the brown sugar to harden.

Pineapple Brûlée

YIELD: 4 SERVINGS

1	(3-POUND) PINEAPPLE		1	TABLESPOON WATER
1	TABLESPOON BUTTER		½	TEASPOON GROUND CINNAMON
⅓	CUP PACKED LIGHT BROWN SUGAR		2	TABLESPOONS DARK RUM

Place the pineapple on a cutting board. Quarter the pineapple lengthwise with a large sharp knife, cutting down through the leaves to leave them attached. Core each wedge. Cut the pulp from the peel of each wedge, leaving 4 wedges and 4 shells. Cover the wedges and set aside. Place the shells on a baking sheet covered with foil. Cover the shells and leaves with foil to prevent browning. Melt the butter in a large heavy skillet over medium heat. Add the brown sugar, water and cinnamon. Bring to a boil. Cook until the brown sugar is dissolved, stirring constantly. Remove from the heat. Add the rum and ignite immediately. Add the pineapple wedges when the flames die out. Cook over medium heat for 4 minutes or until the pineapple is heated through, turning to coat. Remove from the heat and remove the wedges to a cutting board. Cut each wedge crosswise into ½-inch slices, cutting to but not through the bottom. Arrange in the shells. Bring the sauce to a boil over medium heat. Boil for 2 minutes or until thick. Spoon the sauce over the pineapple. Broil for 3 minutes or until the sauce is bubbly and slightly browned. Transfer the wedges to serving plates. Note: The sauce can be made 1 day ahead. Cover and chill. Reheat to a simmer before adding the pineapple wedges.

Double-Chocolate Soufflé

Yield: 4 to 6 servings

1	CUP MILK	3	TABLESPOONS SUGAR
½	VANILLA BEAN, OR 1 TEASPOON	¼	TEASPOON SALT
	VANILLA EXTRACT	2	EGG YOLKS, SLIGHTLY BEATEN
2	TABLESPOONS UNSALTED BUTTER	5	EGG WHITES
2	TABLESPOONS FLOUR		CONFECTIONERS' SUGAR
4	OUNCES UNSWEETENED		HOT CHOCOLATE SAUCE
	CHOCOLATE, GRATED		WHIPPED CREAM FOR GARNISH
⅓	CUP HOT WATER		

Scald the milk with the vanilla bean in a small saucepan. (If using vanilla extract, do not add now.) Remove from the heat and set aside. Melt the butter in a heavy saucepan over medium heat. Add the flour. Cook for 3 minutes or until opaque but not browned, stirring constantly. Remove the vanilla bean from the milk and discard. Whisk the milk into the flour mixture. Cook for 5 minutes or until thick and smooth, whisking occasionally. Add the chocolate and cook until melted and smooth, stirring constantly. Remove from the heat and add the vanilla if using extract. Whisk in the hot water, sugar and salt. Add in the egg yolks gradually, whisking until the mixture is smooth. Pour into a bowl and press waxed paper directly onto the surface. Set aside in a warm place. Beat the egg whites in a medium bowl until stiff but not dry. Remove the waxed paper from the chocolate mixture and fold in a small amount of the beaten egg whites. Fold in the remaining beaten egg whites. Spoon the mixture gently into a 2-quart soufflé dish or four to six 1-cup ramekins. The dishes should be ¾ full. Bake at 450 degrees in the center of the oven for 20 to 25 minutes for a large soufflé or 12 to 13 minutes for individual soufflés. The soufflé should be puffed and browned when done. Sprinkle with confectioners' sugar and spoon onto serving plates. Top with Hot Chocolate Sauce (at right) and garnish with whipped cream.

HOT CHOCOLATE SAUCE

1½ OUNCES UNSWEETENED
CHOCOLATE, GRATED
1 CUP WATER
2 TABLESPOONS SUGAR
SMALL PIECE OF VANILLA
BEAN, OR ½ TEASPOON
VANILLA EXTRACT

COMBINE THE CHOCOLATE, WATER, SUGAR AND VANILLA BEAN IN A SMALL HEAVY SAUCEPAN. (IF USING VANILLA EXTRACT, DO NOT ADD NOW.) SIMMER FOR 15 TO 20 MINUTES, STIRRING OCCASIONALLY. REMOVE FROM THE HEAT AND REMOVE AND DISCARD THE VANILLA BEAN. STIR IN THE VANILLA IF USING EXTRACT. SERVE HOT.
YIELD: ABOUT 1½ CUPS

Spicy Pecan Ice Cream

Yield: 3 cups

5	EGG YOLKS	1/4	CUP SUGAR
1/2	CUP SUGAR	1/4	CUP (1/2 STICK) UNSALTED BUTTER
1 1/2	CUPS HEAVY CREAM	1/2	CUP PECAN HALVES (ABOUT 2 OUNCES)
1/2	CUP HALF-AND-HALF	1/4	TEASPOON CAYENNE PEPPER
1/2	VANILLA BEAN, SPLIT LENGTHWISE	1/8	TEASPOON SALT
2	TABLESPOONS DARK RUM		

Whisk the egg yolks with 1/2 cup sugar in a bowl. Set aside. Combine the cream and half-and-half in a medium saucepan. Scrape the seeds from the vanilla bean into the saucepan and add the bean. Heat over medium-high heat just until simmering. Whisk a small amount of the hot cream into the egg mixture; whisk the egg mixture into the hot cream. Cook over medium-high heat for 5 minutes or until thick, stirring constantly. Strain into a bowl; let cool. Stir in the rum. Cook 1/4 cup sugar in a skillet over medium-high heat for 5 minutes or until melted and golden brown, stirring constantly. Add the butter and pecans. Cook until the pecans are thoroughly coated, stirring constantly. Spread the pecans on a plate; let cool. Sprinkle with the cayenne pepper and salt. Break the pecans into small pieces and stir into the custard. Freeze the mixture in an ice cream maker according to the manufacturer's directions. Transfer the ice cream to a chilled container. Freeze, covered, for up to 3 days.

Mint Julep Sorbet

Yield: 4 servings

1 1/2	CUPS WATER	1	TABLESPOON GREEN CRÈME DE MENTHE
3/4	CUP LIGHTLY PACKED FRESH MINT	1	TEASPOON MINCED FRESH MINT
1/2	CUP SUGAR	4	FRESH MINT SPRIGS FOR GARNISH
3	TABLESPOONS BOURBON		

Cook the first 3 ingredients in a heavy saucepan over medium heat until the sugar is dissolved, stirring constantly. Increase heat; bring to a boil. Pour into a bowl. Cover and chill for 2 hours. Strain into a bowl. Press the leaves to extract all liquid. Discard the mint. Stir the bourbon, crème de menthe and 1 teaspoon minced mint into the syrup. Freeze in an ice cream maker using the manufacturer's directions. Spoon into a chilled container. Freeze, covered, for 2 hours or until firm. Place 4 parfait glasses in the freezer for 1 hour. Scoop the sorbet into the frozen glasses. Garnish with mint.

Raspberry and Rose Petal Parfaits

Yield: 4 servings

3	CUPS DRY CHAMPAGNE	1	TABLESPOON SUGAR
½	TEASPOON UNFLAVORED GELATIN	1	CUP CHILLED WHIPPING CREAM
1	CUP SUGAR		FRESH MINT SPRIGS AND ROSE PETALS
6	EGG YOLKS		FOR GARNISH
1	PINT RASPBERRIES		

Pour 1 tablespoon of the Champagne into a small bowl. Sprinkle with the gelatin and let stand for 10 minutes or until softened. Combine the remaining Champagne and 1 cup sugar in a medium saucepan. Cook over medium heat until the sugar is dissolved, stirring constantly. Increase the heat and bring to a boil. Boil for 15 minutes or until the mixture is reduced to 1⅓ cups. Whisk the egg yolks in a medium bowl. Whisk in the hot Champagne mixture gradually. Return to the saucepan. Cook over medium heat for 4 minutes or until a candy thermometer registers 175 degrees, stirring constantly. Remove from the heat and add the softened gelatin. Whisk until the gelatin is dissolved. Pour into a bowl and chill for 1 hour or until the mixture is thickened but not set, stirring occasionally. Set aside several of the raspberries for garnish. Stir the remaining raspberries and 1 tablespoon sugar in a bowl. Let stand for 10 minutes. Whip the cream in a bowl until stiff peaks form. Fold the cream into the chilled Champagne custard. Place ¼ cup raspberries in each of four 12 to 16-ounce balloon-shaped goblets. Spoon ½ cup of the custard over each. Repeat the layers until all ingredients are used. Cover and chill for 6 hours or longer. Garnish with the reserved raspberries, mint and rose petals.

Praline Sauce

YIELD: 3 (8-OUNCE) JARS

1   (1-POUND) PACKAGE LIGHT
    BROWN SUGAR
¼   CUP LIGHT CORN SYRUP
¾   CUP WATER
¼   TEASPOON SALT
1   CUP CHOPPED PECANS

2   TABLESPOONS BUTTER
1   TEASPOON VANILLA EXTRACT
2   TABLESPOONS PRALINE LIQUEUR
    (OPTIONAL)

Combine the brown sugar, corn syrup, water, salt and pecans in a saucepan. Bring to a boil and boil for 3 to 4 minutes, stirring frequently. Remove from the heat and add the butter, vanilla and liqueur. Stir until the butter is melted. Let cool. Pour into sterilized jars and screw on the caps. Chill until serving time. Serve over ice cream or bread pudding.

Hot Fudge Drizzle

YIELD: ABOUT 3 CUPS

4   OUNCES UNSWEETENED CHOCOLATE
½   CUP (1 STICK) BUTTER
3   CUPS SUGAR

1   (12-OUNCE) CAN EVAPORATED MILK
1   TEASPOON VANILLA EXTRACT

Melt the chocolate and butter in a saucepan. Stir in the sugar and evaporated milk. Cook for 30 minutes or until thick, stirring often. Remove from the heat and let cool. Stir in the vanilla. Serve hot over ice cream. Note: This sauce can be made several weeks ahead. Store, covered, in the refrigerator.

Strawberries au Poivre

Yield: 6 servings

1	CUP CABERNET SAUVIGNON		4	CUPS WHOLE STRAWBERRIES, HULLED
7	TABLESPOONS SUGAR			AND QUARTERED LENGTHWISE
¼	TEASPOON PEPPER		⅛	TEASPOON PEPPER, OR TO TASTE
1	(2-INCH) VANILLA BEAN, SPLIT			VANILLA ICE CREAM
	LENGTHWISE		2	TABLESPOONS GREEN PEPPERCORNS IN
1	TABLESPOON CORNSTARCH			BRINE, DRAINED
¼	CUP CABERNET SAUVIGNON		6	FRESH MINT SPRIGS FOR GARNISH
2	TABLESPOONS UNSALTED BUTTER			

Combine 1 cup wine, sugar and ¼ teaspoon pepper in a medium heavy saucepan. Scrape the seeds from the vanilla bean into the saucepan and add the bean. Cook over medium heat until the sugar is dissolved, stirring constantly. Whisk the cornstarch with ¼ cup wine in a bowl. Add to the saucepan. Cook for 2 minutes or until the mixture boils and thickens, whisking constantly. Remove from the heat and remove and discard the vanilla bean. Melt the butter in a large skillet over high heat. Add the berries and sauté for 1 minute. Add the wine sauce and ⅛ teaspoon pepper and heat through; remove from the heat. Divide the berries and half the sauce among 6 martini glasses. Top each with a scoop of ice cream. Top with the remaining sauce. Sprinkle with the peppercorns and garnish with mint. Note: The wine sauce can be made 1 day ahead. Let cool. Store, covered, in the refrigerator. Reheat gently before using.

Strawberry Tiramisu

Yield: 4 to 6 servings

1	PINT STRAWBERRIES, HULLED	2	TABLESPOONS SUGAR
12	OUNCES LIGHT CREAM CHEESE, SOFTENED	2½	TEASPOONS INSTANT ESPRESSO POWDER
¾	CUP CONFECTIONERS' SUGAR	2	TABLESPOONS MARSALA
5	TABLESPOONS MARSALA	2¼	(3½-OUNCE) PACKAGES LADYFINGERS
½	CUP SOUR CREAM	1	OUNCE BITTERSWEET OR SEMISWEET CHOCOLATE, GRATED
¾	CUP BOILING WATER		

Slice half the strawberries into a bowl. Cut the remaining strawberries into halves and place in another bowl. Set aside. Process the cream cheese, confectioners' sugar and 5 tablespoons marsala in a food processor until smooth. Add the sour cream and process until blended. Combine the boiling water, sugar and espresso powder in a small bowl. Stir until the sugar and powder are dissolved. Stir in 2 tablespoons marsala. Dip 1 ladyfinger briefly into the coffee mixture, turning to coat. Place the ladyfinger flat side up in the bottom of an 8-inch glass dish. Repeat the process with the ladyfingers until the bottom of the dish is covered. Trim the ladyfingers to fit the dish if necessary. Spread ⅔ of the cream cheese mixture over the ladyfingers. Cover with the sliced strawberries. Dip more ladyfingers in the coffee and arrange another layer over the strawberries. Spread the remaining cream cheese mixture on top. Sprinkle with the grated chocolate. Arrange the strawberry halves around the top edge. Cover and chill for 4 hours or until set. Cut into squares and serve.

Crescent Cheesecake

Yield: 10 servings

1/3	CUP PACKED DARK BROWN SUGAR
2	TABLESPOONS FLOUR
1	TABLESPOON CHILLED UNSALTED BUTTER, CUT INTO PIECES
1	CUP FINELY CHOPPED TOASTED PECANS
32	OUNCES CREAM CHEESE, SOFTENED
3/4	CUP PACKED DARK BROWN SUGAR
2	TABLESPOONS CORNSTARCH
6	EGGS, AT ROOM TEMPERATURE
1/4	CUP HEAVY CREAM, AT ROOM TEMPERATURE
1/4	CUP BOURBON
1	RECIPE PECAN CRUST (BELOW)
	CHOPPED TOASTED PECANS FOR GARNISH

Mix 1/3 cup brown sugar and the flour in a bowl. Cut in the butter until it is the consistency of coarse meal. Stir in the pecans and set the streusel aside. Beat the cream cheese and 3/4 cup brown sugar in a bowl with an electric mixer until smooth. Beat in the cornstarch. Beat in the eggs 1 at a time. Stir in the cream and bourbon. Pour half the filling into the Pecan Crust (below). Sprinkle with the streusel. Cover with the remaining filling. Run a knife through the filling to swirl the streusel. Bake at 425 degrees for 15 minutes. Reduce the oven temperature to 225 degrees and bake for 45 minutes or until the center is firm. (The top of the cheesecake may crack during baking.) Remove to a wire rack and let cool completely. Cover and chill overnight. Place the cheesecake on a large plate. Loosen from the side of the pan with a sharp knife and remove the side of the pan. Slice into wedges and place on serving plates. Garnish with chopped pecans. Note: This cheesecake may be served with Bourbon Sauce (page 214).

Pecan Crust

Yield: 1 crust

3/4	CUP GRAHAM CRACKER CRUMBS
1/3	CUP FINELY CHOPPED TOASTED PECANS
5	TABLESPOONS UNSALTED BUTTER, MELTED
3	TABLESPOONS PACKED DARK BROWN SUGAR

Combine the crumbs, pecans, butter and brown sugar in a bowl. Stir until well mixed. Press the mixture over the bottom of a 10-inch springform pan. Set aside until needed.

Café Brûlot

¼ CUP CHILLED HEAVY CREAM
8 (½X2-INCH) STRIPS LEMON
PEEL (YELLOW PART ONLY)
8 (½X-INCH) STRIPS ORANGE
PEEL (ORANGE PART ONLY)
2 CINNAMON STICKS,
BROKEN INTO HALVES
24 WHOLE CLOVES
⅔ CUP BRANDY
3 CUPS VERY STRONG FRESHLY
BREWED HOT COFFEE

BRING THE CREAM, LEMON PEEL,
ORANGE PEEL, CINNAMON AND
CLOVES TO A SIMMER IN A
HEAVY SKILLET OVER MEDIUM
HEAT, STIRRING CONSTANTLY.
SIMMER FOR 3 MINUTES.
REMOVE FROM THE HEAT AND
LET STAND FOR 30 MINUTES.
RETURN TO A SIMMER OVER
MEDIUM HEAT. POUR INTO A
LARGE HEATPROOF BOWL.
WARM THE BRANDY IN A
HEAVY SAUCEPAN OVER MEDIUM
HEAT. REMOVE FROM THE HEAT.
IGNITE WITH A LONG MATCH.
POUR THE BRANDY OVER THE
CITRUS MIXTURE. POUR THE
COFFEE DOWN THE INSIDE OF
THE BOWL GRADUALLY. BRING
TO THE TABLE WHEN THE
FLAMES DIE OUT. LADLE THE
COFFEE INTO MUGS. DISCARD
THE PEEL AND SPICES.
YIELD: 3 TO 4 SERVINGS

Chocolate Bourbon Pecan Torte

YIELD: 12 SERVINGS

1	CUP (2 STICKS) UNSALTED BUTTER	½	CUP HEAVY CREAM
8	OUNCES BITTERSWEET OR SEMISWEET CHOCOLATE, CHOPPED	¼	CUP (½ STICK) UNSALTED BUTTER
1	CUP SIFTED BAKING COCOA	10	OUNCES BITTERSWEET OR SEMISWEET CHOCOLATE, CHOPPED
6	EGGS		
1½	CUPS SUGAR	1	CUP CHOPPED TOASTED PECANS
1½	CUPS TOASTED PECAN HALVES	12	PECAN HALVES
⅓	CUP BOURBON		

Butter a 9-inch springform pan with 2¾-inch side. Line the bottom with parchment paper. Dust the side of the pan with flour and tap out any excess. Melt 1 cup butter in a heavy medium saucepan over low heat. Add 8 ounces chocolate and heat until melted, stirring until smooth. Stir in the baking cocoa and remove from the heat. Whisk the eggs and sugar in a large bowl just until blended. Add the chocolate mixture and whisk until blended. Grind 1½ cups pecans finely in a food processor and stir into the chocolate mixture. Stir in the bourbon.

Pour the batter into the prepared pan. Bake at 350 degrees for 45 minutes or until the edges are set but the middle moves slightly when the pan is shaken. Remove to a wire rack and cool completely. Bring the cream and ¼ cup butter to a simmer in a heavy medium saucepan. Add 10 ounces chocolate and heat until melted, stirring until smooth. Remove from the heat and let stand for 5 minutes or until slightly cooled and pourable. Loosen the torte from the side of the pan with a sharp knife and remove the side of the pan. Invert the torte onto an 8-inch round piece of cardboard. Remove the parchment paper. Set the torte with the cardboard onto a baking sheet. Pour the chocolate glaze over the top and side of the torte. Chill for 15 minutes or until the glaze is partially set but still sticky. Press 1 cup chopped pecans onto the side of the torte. Arrange the pecan halves around the top edge of the torte. Remove the torte and cardboard base to a cake plate and chill, covered, overnight. Cut into slices and serve cold.

Southern Decadence Cake

YIELD: 12 SERVINGS

1	CUP HEAVY CREAM	1	CUP PLUS 2 TABLESPOONS MILK
8	OUNCES BITTERSWEET	1	TABLESPOON VANILLA EXTRACT
	CHOCOLATE, CHOPPED	1/2	CUP (1 STICK) UNSALTED BUTTER,
1/4	CUP (1/2 STICK) BUTTER,		SOFTENED
	SOFTENED	2	CUPS SUGAR
2	CUPS CAKE FLOUR	4	EGGS
1	CUP ALL-PURPOSE FLOUR		COCONUT PECAN FILLING
1	TABLESPOON PLUS 1 TEASPOON		(AT RIGHT)
	BAKING POWDER		CHOCOLATE CURLS
1/2	TEASPOON SALT		FOR GARNISH

For the chocolate ganache, heat the cream in a medium saucepan until bubbles form around the edge. Remove from the heat. Add the chocolate, stirring until melted. Add the butter, stirring until smooth. Let cool for 3 hours. Beat with a wooden spoon until slightly thickened; set aside. Mix the cake flour, all-purpose flour, baking powder and salt in a bowl. Mix the milk and vanilla in a small bowl. Cream the butter in a bowl with an electric mixer at medium speed. Add the sugar; beat for 3 minutes. Add the dry ingredients 1/3 at a time alternately with the milk mixture, beating at low speed after each addition. Increase the speed to medium. Beat in the eggs 1 at a time. Divide the batter among 3 parchment paper-lined 9-inch cake pans. Bake at 350 degrees for 25 minutes or until light golden brown and a wooden pick inserted in the center comes out clean. Cool in the pans for 10 minutes. Invert the layers onto wire racks. Peel off the parchment paper; let cool completely. Place 1 layer on a cake plate; spread with 1/3 of the Coconut Pecan Filling (at right), leaving a 1/2-inch border around the edge. Add another layer; spread with 1/3 of the filling, leaving a 1/2-inch border. Top with the third layer. Spread the top and side of the cake with the chocolate ganache. Spread the remaining filling on top of the ganache. Garnish with chocolate curls.

COCONUT PECAN FILLING

6 EGG YOLKS
1/2 CUP EACH SUGAR AND PACKED DARK BROWN SUGAR
1 CUP EVAPORATED MILK
2 TABLESPOONS CORNSTARCH
1/8 TEASPOON SALT
1 2/3 CUPS TOASTED SWEETENED COCONUT
1 TEASPOON VANILLA EXTRACT
3/4 CUP WHIPPING CREAM, WHIPPED
2/3 CUP COARSELY CHOPPED SEMISWEET CHOCOLATE
2/3 CUP TOASTED CHOPPED PECANS

WHISK THE FIRST 3 INGREDIENTS IN A HEAVY SAUCEPAN. STIR IN THE EVAPORATED MILK, CORNSTARCH, SALT AND 1 CUP OF THE COCONUT. COOK OVER MEDIUM HEAT FOR 6 MINUTES OR UNTIL VERY THICK, STIRRING CONSTANTLY. STRAIN INTO A BOWL; PRESS ON THE COCONUT TO REMOVE ALL LIQUID. DISCARD THE COCONUT. LET THE CUSTARD COOL. STIR IN THE VANILLA. CHILL UNTIL COLD. FOLD THE WHIPPED CREAM INTO THE CUSTARD. FOLD IN THE CHOCOLATE, PECANS AND REMAINING COCONUT.
YIELD: 3 CUPS

Daisy Cake

Yield: 12 servings

6	EGG YOLKS	3/4	TEASPOON SALT
1/4	CUP MILK	3/4	CUP (1½ STICKS) UNSALTED BUTTER,
2¼	TEASPOONS VANILLA EXTRACT		SOFTENED
3	CUPS SIFTED CAKE FLOUR	3/4	CUP MILK
1½	CUPS SUGAR	2½	CUPS CAROLINE FROSTING
1	TABLESPOON PLUS 1 TEASPOON		
	BAKING POWDER		

Grease two 9-inch cake pans. Line the bottoms with parchment paper. Grease the parchment paper and sprinkle with flour. Dust the sides with flour and tap out any excess. Mix the egg yolks, ¼ cup milk and vanilla in a medium bowl. Set aside. Beat the flour, sugar, baking powder and salt in a large bowl with an electric mixer at low speed for 30 seconds. Add the butter and ¾ cup milk and beat until evenly moistened. Increase the speed to medium and beat for 90 seconds. Scrape down the sides of the bowl as needed while beating. Beat in the egg mixture ⅓ at a time, beating for 20 seconds after each addition. Pour the batter into the prepared pans and smooth the tops. Bake at 350 degrees for 25 to 35 minutes or until a wooden pick inserted in the center comes out clean and the cake springs back when lightly pressed. Cool in the pans for 10 minutes. Invert the layers onto greased wire racks. Peel off the parchment paper. Reinvert the layers to prevent the tops from splitting and let cool completely. Spread Caroline Frosting (below) between the layers and over the top and side of the cake.

Caroline Frosting

Yield: 2½ cups

16	OUNCES CREAM CHEESE, SOFTENED	1	TEASPOON LEMON JUICE
1/4	CUP (½ STICK) BUTTER, SOFTENED	1/2	CUP SEEDLESS RASPBERRY JAM
3/4	CUP CONFECTIONERS' SUGAR	2	DROPS OF RED FOOD COLORING
1	TEASPOON VANILLA EXTRACT		

Beat the cream cheese and butter in a bowl until smooth. Add the confectioners' sugar, vanilla, lemon juice, jam and food coloring and beat for 5 minutes or until smooth.

French King Cake

11	OUNCES ALMOND PASTE	2	TABLESPOONS DARK RUM
3/4	CUP (1½ STICKS) BUTTER, SOFTENED	2	(⅛-INCH-THICK) SHEETS PUFF PASTRY
3/4	CUP SUGAR	1	EGG
1½	CUPS FLOUR	2	TEASPOONS WATER
6	EGGS	½	CUP PREPARED APRICOT GLAZE

Process the almond paste, butter and sugar in a food processor until smooth. Add the flour and process until blended. Add 6 eggs 1 at a time and process until mixed. Add the rum and process until blended. Set aside. Place the puff pastry sheets on a work surface and cut two 12-inch circles. Place 1 circle on a baking sheet. Spread with the almond mixture, leaving a 1½-inch border. Mix 1 egg with the water in a small bowl. Brush some of the egg mixture on the border. Top with the other circle of puff pastry. Press the edges with a fork to seal. Brush the remaining egg mixture over the pastry. Bake at 400 degrees for 15 minutes. Reduce the heat to 350 degrees and bake for 35 to 40 minutes or until golden brown. Remove to a wire rack to cool slightly. Warm the apricot glaze in a small saucepan. Spread the glaze over the top of the cake. Transfer the cake to a cake plate. Serve warm or at room temperature.

Recipe provided by Jean-Luc Albin, Maurice French Pastries

KING CAKE

FRANCE HAS CELEBRATED EPIPHANY, OR TWELFTH NIGHT, SINCE THE SIXTEENTH CENTURY WITH A *GÂTEAU DES ROIS* (KING CAKE). FRENCH VERSIONS INCLUDE THE *COURONNE* (CROWN), A BRIOCHE DOUGH DECORATED WITH A SUGAR GLAZE AND FRUIT, AND A MORE ELABORATE CAKE FILLED WITH ALMOND CREAM PASTE. NEW ORLEANS' TRADITIONAL KING CAKE, EVOLVED FROM THE *COURONNE*, IS A CINNAMON-FLAVORED BRIOCHE BRAIDED INTO AN OVAL SHAPE. ITS COLORED SUGAR TOPPING DONS THE MARDI GRAS HUES: PURPLE FOR JUSTICE, GREEN FOR FAITH, AND GOLD FOR POWER. THE CAKES CONTAIN HIDDEN PLASTIC FIGURES, FORMERLY A BEAN OR CERAMIC TOY, NOW A PLASTIC BABY. A NEW ORLEANIAN WHO FINDS THE PLASTIC BABY IN HIS SLICE MUST BUY THE NEXT KING CAKE OR HOST THE NEXT PARTY.

AN OLD ADAGE:
NOIR COMME LE DIABLE (BLACK
AS THE DEVIL)/FORT COMME
LA MORT (STRONG AS DEATH)/
DOUX COMME L'AMOUR (SWEET
AS LOVE)/CHAUD COMME
L'ENFER! (HOT AS HELL)!
FROM A CHILD'S CUP OF MILK
LACED WITH A FEW DROPS OF
COFFEE TO A STEAMING CUP OF
CAFÉ AU LAIT AS AN ADULT,
NEW ORLEANIANS HAVE HAD
A LIFELONG LOVE AFFAIR WITH
THIS BEVERAGE. A SYRUPY,
STRONG BREW, A CREOLE
TRADITION, IS STILL THE
PREFERRED WAKE-UP CALL FOR
LOCALS, WHO ALSO HAVE AN
AFFINITY FOR CHICORY. THIS
PERENNIAL HERB, WHOSE ROOT
IS ROASTED AND GROUND TO
BLEND WITH COFFEE, CREATES
A RICH, BITTER TASTE THAT IS
THE CHOICE OF MANY. ROSE
NICAUD, A FREE WOMAN OF
COLOR, BROUGHT PUBLIC
COFFEEHOUSES TO THE
COMMUNITY IN THE EARLY
1800S, BEGINNING WITH
A PORTABLE STAND AND,
EVENTUALLY, A PERMANENT ONE
IN THE FRENCH MARKET.
COFFEEHOUSES NOW SUFFUSE
THE NEIGHBORHOODS OF THE
CRESCENT CITY.

Praline Gâteau au Café

YIELD: 12 SERVINGS

5	EGG YOLKS, AT ROOM TEMPERATURE	8	OUNCES TOASTED PECANS, FINELY GROUND
1	CUP PACKED LIGHT BROWN SUGAR	¼	TEASPOON GROUND CINNAMON
1	TEASPOON VANILLA EXTRACT (OPTIONAL)	¼	CUP PACKED BROWN SUGAR
6	EGG WHITES, AT ROOM TEMPERATURE	1	TEASPOON POTATO STARCH
		1½	TEASPOONS INSTANT COFFEE POWDER
¼	TEASPOON SALT	1	TABLESPOON HOT WATER
			GLAZED PECANS (PAGE 231)

Grease a 9-inch square cake pan. Line the bottom with parchment paper and grease the paper. Beat the egg yolks, 1 cup brown sugar and vanilla in a bowl with an electric mixer until pale yellow and very thick. Wash and dry the beaters well. Beat the egg whites and salt in a bowl with an electric mixer until stiff but not dry. Fold the pecans, cinnamon and ⅓ of the beaten egg whites gently into the egg yolk mixture. Fold the egg yolk mixture into the remaining beaten egg whites. Spoon the batter into the prepared pan; smooth the top. Bake at 325 degrees for 35 to 40 minutes or until a wooden pick inserted in the center comes out clean. Turn off the oven. Remove the cake to a wire rack; run a knife around the edge to loosen. Return the cake to the oven; leave the door ajar. Let stand in the oven for 15 minutes. Remove to a wire rack; let cool completely in the pan. Invert the cake onto a wire rack. Peel off the parchment paper. Reinvert the cake onto a plate. For the glaze, mix ¼ cup brown sugar and cornstarch in a small heavy saucepan. Dissolve the coffee powder in the hot water; pour into the saucepan. Simmer over medium-low heat for 2 minutes or until thick, stirring constantly. Remove from the heat and stir to dissipate foam. Spread over the top of the cake. Let stand until the glaze is firm. Cut the cake into 12 pieces and place on serving plates. Top each piece with 1 of the Glazed Pecans.

Red Wine Cake with Cherry Sauce

YIELD: 8 SERVINGS

2	CUPS FLOUR	1	CUP SUGAR
1½	TEASPOONS BAKING POWDER	14	TABLESPOONS (1¾ STICKS)
1	TABLESPOON GROUND CINNAMON		UNSALTED BUTTER
4	TEASPOONS BAKING COCOA	4	EGGS
3	OUNCES DARK CHOCOLATE,	½	CUP RED WINE
	SHAVED	2	TEASPOONS VANILLA EXTRACT

Sift the flour, baking powder, cinnamon and cocoa into a bowl. Stir in the chocolate. Cream the sugar and butter in a bowl with an electric mixer. Beat in the eggs 1 at a time. Beat in the wine and vanilla. Set the mixer speed to slow and beat for 30 seconds. Fold in the dry ingredients. Pour the batter into a greased 9-inch cake pan. Bake at 325 degrees for 1¼ hours or until a wooden pick inserted in the center comes out clean; let cool in the pan for 10 minutes. Invert the cake onto a wire rack; let cool completely. Reinvert the cake onto a plate. Cut into 8 slices; place on serving plates. Top with the Cherry Sauce (below) and serve with a scoop of vanilla ice cream.

Recipe provided by Klaus Hasmueller, New Orleans Marriott

Cherry Sauce

YIELD: 2 CUPS

1	POUND FRESH SWEET CHERRIES,	½	CUP CANNED CHERRY JUICE
	PITTED	1	CINNAMON STICK
½	CUP SUGAR	3	TABLESPOONS CORNSTARCH
½	CUP RED WINE	3	TABLESPOONS COLD WATER

Combine the first 5 ingredients in a saucepan. Bring to a boil. Add a mixture of the cornstarch and cold water to the boiling cherry mixture. Boil for 1 minute, stirring constantly. Remove from the heat and allow to cool. Remove the cinnamon stick before serving.

GLAZED PECANS

¼ CUP SUGAR
12 PECAN HALVES

HEAT THE SUGAR IN A SMALL HEAVY SAUCEPAN OVER LOW HEAT UNTIL THE SUGAR IS DISSOLVED, STIRRING FREQUENTLY. INCREASE THE HEAT TO MEDIUM-LOW AND COOK UNTIL THE SYRUP IS GOLDEN BROWN. ADD THE PECANS AND STIR UNTIL COATED. SPREAD THE PECANS ON A GREASED BAKING SHEET, USING A FORK TO SEPARATE THEM. ARRANGE THE PECANS ROUNDED SIDE UP AND LET COOL COMPLETELY.
YIELD: 1 DOZEN

Pralines

Yield: 3 dozen

2	CUPS SUGAR	2	TABLESPOONS LIGHT CORN SYRUP
1	CUP PACKED BROWN SUGAR	2	CUPS PECAN HALVES
½	CUP (1 STICK) BUTTER	2	CUPS CHOPPED PECANS
1	CUP HEAVY CREAM		

Bring the sugar, brown sugar, butter, cream and corn syrup to a boil in a 3-quart saucepan. Reduce the heat. Simmer for 10 minutes, stirring occasionally. Stir in the pecan halves and chopped pecans. Cook until a candy thermometer registers 234 degrees, soft-ball stage. Remove from the heat and beat well. Drop by tablespoonfuls onto a baking sheet covered with waxed paper. Remove the pralines from the waxed paper when cool. Store in an airtight container. Note: If the pralines start to harden in the saucepan before all have been spooned out, add 1 tablespoon heavy cream and mix well.

Almond Biscotti

Yield: 40 servings

2	CUPS FLOUR	2	TEASPOONS GRATED LEMON ZEST
1	TEASPOON BAKING POWDER	1	TABLESPOON PLUS 2 TEASPOONS
¼	TEASPOON SALT		ALMOND EXTRACT
1	CUP SUGAR	2	CUPS COARSELY CHOPPED TOASTED
3	EGGS		ALMONDS
1	TABLESPOON FRESH LEMON JUICE	1	EGG, BEATEN

Sift the flour, baking powder and salt together. Beat the sugar and 3 eggs in a large bowl with an electric mixer for 3 minutes or until thick and pale yellow. Beat in the lemon juice, lemon zest and almond extract. Add the dry ingredients and beat well. Stir in the almonds. The dough will be quite sticky. Drop the dough by spoonfuls onto a baking sheet sprayed with nonstick cooking spray, forming two 14-inch-long strips. Shape each strip with floured hands into a 2½-inch-wide log. Brush the logs with the beaten egg. Bake at 350 degrees for 30 minutes or until golden brown and firm. Remove the logs to a work surface. Cut diagonally into ¼-inch slices with a serrated knife. Arrange the slices cut side down on the baking sheet. Bake at 350 degrees for 6 minutes or until crisp and golden brown, turning once. Remove to a wire rack to cool.

Basil Lime Cookies

Yield: 3 dozen

2	CUPS SIFTED FLOUR	1	EGG
1½	TEASPOONS BAKING POWDER	1	TEASPOON VANILLA EXTRACT
½	TEASPOON SALT	3	TABLESPOONS CHOPPED FRESH
⅔	CUP BUTTER OR MARGARINE, SOFTENED		CINNAMON BASIL OR SWEET BASIL
1	CUP SUGAR	1	TABLESPOON FINELY CHOPPED LIME ZEST

Sift the flour, baking powder and salt together. Set aside. Cream the butter in a large
bowl with an electric mixer. Beat in the sugar gradually. Add the egg, vanilla, basil and lime
zest. Beat until light and fluffy. Reduce the mixer speed to low. Beat in the dry ingredients ⅓ at
a time. Turn the dough onto a lightly floured surface. Divide the dough in half; shape each
half into a 6- to 7-inch long roll. Wrap in plastic wrap; chill for 8 hours or longer. Cut the rolls
into ⅛-inch slices. Place 2 inches apart on ungreased cookie sheets. Bake at 375 degrees
for 8 to 10 minutes or until lightly browned. Remove the cookies to a wire rack to cool.
Note: The dough can be frozen. Thaw in the refrigerator before slicing and baking.

Double-Chocolate Pecan Brownies

Yield: 32 brownies

3	OUNCES UNSWEETENED CHOCOLATE, CHOPPED	3	EGGS
¾	CUP (1½ STICKS) UNSALTED BUTTER, SOFTENED	¾	CUP FLOUR
		6	OUNCES WHITE CHOCOLATE, CUT INTO ¾-INCH PIECES
½	CUP PACKED LIGHT BROWN SUGAR	1	CUP COARSELY CHOPPED PECANS
½	CUP SUGAR		CONFECTIONERS' SUGAR

Line the bottom of a 9x13-inch baking pan with foil. Butter and flour the foil and sides
of the pan. Heat the unsweetened chocolate in a double boiler over simmering water until
melted, stirring constantly. Remove from over the water; let cool. Beat the butter in a
large bowl with an electric mixer until light and fluffy. Beat in the brown sugar and sugar
gradually. Beat in the melted chocolate. Beat in the eggs 1 at a time. Add the flour and mix well.
Fold in the white chocolate and pecans. Spoon into the prepared pan. Bake at 350 degrees
for 20 minutes or until a wooden pick inserted in the center comes out clean. Cool in the
pan on a wire rack. Dust with confectioners' sugar and cut into squares.

Melpomene Molasses Cookies

YIELD: 16 COOKIES

1½	CUPS FLOUR	½	CUP VEGETABLE SHORTENING,
1	CUP SUGAR		MELTED, COOLED
1	TEASPOON BAKING SODA	1	EGG
½	TEASPOON SALT	½	CUP UNSULFURED MOLASSES
1	TEASPOON GROUND GINGER	¾	CUP ROLLED OATS
½	TEASPOON GROUND CLOVES	¼	CUP SUGAR

*L*ine 2 cookie sheets with silpat mats and set aside. (Silpat mats are flexible nonstick baking sheet liners.) Sift the flour, 1 cup sugar, baking soda, salt, ginger and cloves into a large bowl. Add the shortening, egg and molasses and mix until smooth. Add the oats and stir until mixed. Scoop out the dough with a 1-ounce ice cream scoop and place 3 inches apart on the prepared cookie sheets. Place ¼ cup sugar in a small shallow bowl. Press the bottom of a glass lightly onto a scoop of dough to dampen the glass. Dip the glass into the sugar and then press down on a scoop of dough to flatten ¼-inch thick. Repeat the process with the remaining cookies, dipping the glass in the sugar each time. Bake the cookies at 375 degrees for 12 minutes or until browned and crisp. Transfer the cookie sheets to a wire rack and let the cookies cool on the cookie sheets. Remove the cookies when cool.

Pistachio Baklava

Yield: 2 dozen pieces

1	POUND SHELLED UNSALTED PISTACHIOS (ABOUT 3⅓ CUPS)		½	CUP (1 STICK) UNSALTED BUTTER, MELTED
½	CUP SUGAR		1	CUP SUGAR
½	CUP (1 STICK) UNSALTED BUTTER, MELTED		½	CUP WATER
12	SHEETS PHYLLO DOUGH (ABOUT ½ POUND)		½	CUP HONEY
			½	TEASPOON GROUND CINNAMON

Combine the pistachios and ½ cup sugar in a food processor, pulsing just until the nuts are finely ground. Transfer to a medium bowl and stir in ½ cup melted butter. Stack the phyllo sheets on a cutting board and cut into halves crosswise. Set 1 half sheet in a buttered 9x13-inch baking dish. Brush with some of the melted ½ cup butter. Top with another half sheet and brush with butter. Repeat the process with 10 more half sheets. Spread the pistachio mixture evenly over the phyllo in the baking dish. Top with the remaining half sheets of phyllo, brushing with butter between each sheet. Drizzle any remaining butter over the top. Slice through the baklava diagonally 1½ inches apart with a sharp knife. Slice through in the opposite direction to make a diamond pattern. Bake at 400 degrees for 20 minutes or until golden brown. Remove to a wire rack. Combine 1 cup sugar and the water in a saucepan. Bring to a boil over medium heat and stir to dissolve the sugar. Remove from the heat and stir in the honey and cinnamon. Pour the syrup evenly over the baklava and let cool completely before serving. Note: The baklava can be made up to 3 days ahead. Cover and chill.

Pear Napoleon

YIELD: 5 SERVINGS

3	TABLESPOONS BUTTER		2	TABLESPOONS POIRE WILLIAM
3	TABLESPOONS SUGAR			PHYLLO SQUARES (BELOW)
8	PEARS, PEELED, CORED, QUARTERED			PASTRY CREAM (PAGE 237)
	LENGTHWISE			CONFECTIONERS' SUGAR
2	CUPS SIMPLE SYRUP			FRESH RASPBERRIES, WHIPPED CREAM
	(SEE NOTE, PAGE 184)			AND FRESH MINT SPRIGS FOR GARNISH
1	VANILLA BEAN, SPLIT LENGTHWISE			

Melt the butter and sugar in a large skillet over low heat, stirring occasionally. Add the pears. Cook for 3 minutes or until slightly softened. Increase the heat to medium-high. Sauté until golden brown. Remove the pears to a platter; keep warm. Pour the simple syrup into a saucepan. Scrape the seeds from the vanilla bean into the saucepan and add the bean. Cook until slightly thickened. Remove from the heat. Stir in the Poire William. Let cool slightly. Discard the vanilla bean. Pour the syrup into a squeeze bottle. Arrange 1 Phyllo Square (below) on each of 5 serving plates. Pipe some of the Pastry Cream on each square. Top each with 3 pear slices. Cover with a Phyllo Square. Pipe the remaining Pastry Cream on top of the squares. Place 3 or 4 pear slices on top of each. Top with the remaining Phyllo Squares. Dust with confectioners' sugar; drizzle with the syrup. Garnish with raspberries, whipped cream and mint.

Recipe provided by Lisa Liggett, Windsor Court Hotel

Phyllo Squares

YIELD: 5 SERVINGS

4	SHEETS PHYLLO DOUGH		½	CUP (1 STICK) CLARIFIED BUTTER
½	CUP HONEY			

Place 1 sheet of phyllo on a cutting board. Brush with a mixture of honey and butter. Top with another sheet of phyllo. Brush with the honey mixture. Repeat the stacking and brushing process. Cut the stack into 2½-inch squares. Place on a parchment paper-lined baking sheet. Bake at 350 degrees for 10 minutes or until golden brown. Remove the squares to a wire rack to cool.

White Chocolate Banana Cream Pie

Yield: 8 servings

3	EGG YOLKS	4	BANANAS, SLICED
⅓	CUP SUGAR	1	TABLESPOON FRESH LEMON JUICE
2	TABLESPOONS CORNSTARCH	4½	TEASPOONS BANANA LIQUEUR
1	CUP MILK	4½	TEASPOONS WHITE CRÈME
½	VANILLA BEAN, SPLIT		DE CACAO
	LENGTHWISE	1	CUP CHILLED WHIPPING CREAM,
1	TABLESPOON CHILLED UNSALTED		WHIPPED
	BUTTER, CUT INTO PIECES	1	TART CRUST (PAGE 240), BAKED
3	OUNCES IMPORTED WHITE		WHITE CHOCOLATE CURLS
	CHOCOLATE, FINELY CHOPPED		BAKING COCOA

Whisk the egg yolks and sugar in a bowl until pale yellow and thick. Whisk in the cornstarch. Bring the milk and vanilla bean to a boil in a heavy medium saucepan. Whisk 1 cup of the hot milk into the egg yolk mixture. Whisk the egg yolk mixture back into the hot milk. Cook for 30 seconds or until the custard boils and thickens, whisking constantly. Pour into a bowl. Whisk in the butter. Add the chocolate, whisking until melted. Discard the vanilla bean. Press plastic wrap onto the surface of the pastry cream. Chill until cold or for up to 2 days. Toss the bananas with the lemon juice in a bowl. Fold in the pastry cream. Fold in the banana liqueur and crème de cacao. Fold the whipped cream into the banana mixture. Spoon the filling into the baked pastry crust. Cover completely with white chocolate curls. Sift baking cocoa over the top.

PASTRY CREAM

4 EGG YOLKS
¼ CUP SUGAR
¼ CUP FLOUR
1½ CUPS MILK
¼ CUP SUGAR
⅛ TEASPOON SALT
1½ TEASPOONS VANILLA
EXTRACT
POIRE WILLIAM TO TASTE

WHISK THE EGG YOLKS AND ¼ CUP SUGAR IN A BOWL. SIFT THE FLOUR OVER THE EGG YOLK MIXTURE AND WHISK TO MIX. BRING THE MILK AND ¼ CUP SUGAR TO A BOIL IN A SAUCEPAN. WHISK ⅓ OF THE HOT MILK MIXTURE INTO THE EGG YOLK MIXTURE. WHISK THE EGG YOLK MIXTURE BACK INTO THE HOT MILK AND CONTINUE WHISKING UNTIL THE MIXTURE BEGINS TO BOIL. REMOVE FROM THE HEAT AND WHISK IN THE VANILLA AND POIRE WILLIAM. POUR THE PASTRY CREAM INTO A BOWL. PRESS PLASTIC WRAP ONTO THE SURFACE OF THE PASTRY CREAM. SET ASIDE TO COOL. USE FOR PEAR NAPOLEON (PAGE 236) OR OTHER DESSERTS. YIELD: ABOUT 2 CUPS

Citrus Trio Tart

YIELD: 6 SERVINGS

½	CUP FLOUR	2	TABLESPOONS FRESH ORANGE
2	TABLESPOONS SUGAR		JUICE
2	TABLESPOONS UNSALTED BUTTER,	¾	TEASPOON GRATED ORANGE ZEST
	MELTED	2	TABLESPOONS FRESH LIME JUICE
¼	CUP SUGAR	¾	TEASPOON GRATED LIME ZEST
4½	TEASPOONS FLOUR	2	EGG WHITES
½	TEASPOON BAKING POWDER	⅛	TEASPOON CREAM OF TARTAR
¼	TEASPOON SALT	2	TABLESPOONS SUGAR
3	EGG WHITES	¼	TEASPOON GRATED LEMON ZEST
1	EGG	¼	TEASPOON GRATED ORANGE ZEST
2	TABLESPOONS FRESH LEMON JUICE	¼	TEASPOON GRATED LIME ZEST
¾	TEASPOON GRATED LEMON ZEST		

Combine ½ cup flour and 2 tablespoons sugar in a large bowl. Add the melted butter and stir with a fork until the mixture is crumbly. Press the crumbs over the bottom of an 8-inch square baking pan coated with nonstick cooking spray. Bake at 350 degrees for 20 minutes or until the crust is set and golden brown. Remove to a wire rack to cool. Combine ¼ cup sugar, 4½ teaspoons flour, baking powder and salt in a small bowl. Whisk the 3 egg whites, egg, lemon juice and ¾ teaspoon zest, orange juice and ¾ teaspoon zest and lime juice and ¾ teaspoon zest in a medium bowl. Add the flour mixture and whisk until well mixed. Pour into the baked crust. Bake at 350 degrees for 18 minutes or until the filling is set. Remove to a wire rack to cool completely. Beat 2 egg whites and the cream of tartar in a large bowl until soft peaks form. Add 2 tablespoons sugar 1 tablespoon at a time and beat until stiff peaks form. Spread the meringue over the cooled filling. Sprinkle with ¼ teaspoon lemon zest, ¼ teaspoon orange zest and ¼ teaspoon lime zest. Bake at 350 degrees for 10 minutes or until the meringue tips begin to brown. Remove to a wire rack to cool completely. Cut into 6 squares. Note: The crust and filling can be baked 1 day ahead. Cover and chill. Warm to room temperature before topping with the meringue.

WHIPPING EGG WHITES

To attain stiff, shining peaks with egg whites, one must use a stabilizer. This is true even if you use a copper bowl. Pour one tablespoon vinegar and one teaspoon salt into the bowl. Rub the bowl with a paper towel, but do not wash the bowl. The vinegar and salt act as the stabilizer. Pour room-temperature egg whites into the prepared bowl and beat with a balloon whisk or electric mixer. Beat at low speed for 2 minutes or until the whites are foaming. Add a pinch of salt and ¼ teaspoon cream of tartar for every 4 eggs. Increase the mixer speed to high gradually, beating until stiff shining peaks form.

Cherry and Apple Galette

Yield: 8 servings

1½	CUPS FLOUR		1½	POUNDS GRANNY SMITH APPLES
½	TEASPOON SALT			(ABOUT 5)
½	CUP (1 STICK) CHILLED UNSALTED		3	TABLESPOONS SUGAR
	BUTTER, CUT INTO ½-INCH PIECES		⅓	CUP DRIED TART CHERRIES
4	TABLESPOONS ICE WATER		¼	TEASPOON GROUND CINNAMON
1	TABLESPOON UNSALTED		1	TABLESPOON SUGAR
	BUTTER			CRÈME FRAÎCHE
			1⅔	CUPS CARAMEL SAUCE

For the dough, blend the flour and salt in a food processor. Add ½ cup butter; pulse until crumbly. Add 3 tablespoons of the ice water; process until moist clumps form. Add the remaining water gradually if needed. Gather the dough into a ball; pat into a 6-inch disk. Wrap in plastic wrap; chill for 30 minutes. For the filling, melt 1 tablespoon butter in a skillet over medium heat. Peel, core and cut each apple into 8 wedges. Add the apples to the skillet. Sprinkle with 3 tablespoons sugar. Sauté for 8 minutes or until the apples are beginning to soften. Add the dried cherries and cinnamon. Sauté for 30 seconds. Remove from the heat; cool completely. Roll the dough on a floured surface into a 12-inch circle. Place on a baking sheet. Arrange the apple filling on top of the dough. Pinch up the edge of the dough to form a shallow rim to contain the filling. Sprinkle 1 tablespoon sugar over the apple filling and dough. Bake at 350 degrees for 15 minutes. Increase the oven temperature to 375 degrees. Bake for 35 minutes or until the crust is golden brown. Remove the baking sheet to a wire rack and let cool for 15 minutes. Serve warm with the Caramel Sauce (at right) and crème fraîche.

CARAMEL SAUCE

1½ CUPS SUGAR
½ CUP WATER
3 TABLESPOONS UNSALTED
BUTTER
1 CUP HEAVY CREAM

COMBINE THE SUGAR AND WATER IN A HEAVY SAUCEPAN. COOK OVER MEDIUM-LOW HEAT UNTIL THE SUGAR IS DISSOLVED, STIRRING CONSTANTLY. INCREASE THE HEAT AND BRING TO A BOIL. BOIL WITHOUT STIRRING FOR 12 MINUTES OR UNTIL THE SYRUP TURNS A DEEP AMBER COLOR. BRUSH DOWN THE SIDES WITH A PASTRY BRUSH DURING BOILING. REMOVE FROM THE HEAT AND WHISK IN THE BUTTER. WHISK IN THE CREAM GRADUALLY. COOK OVER LOW HEAT UNTIL SMOOTH, STIRRING CONSTANTLY. NOTE: THIS SAUCE CAN BE MADE UP TO 2 DAYS AHEAD. COVER AND CHILL. REWARM OVER LOW HEAT BEFORE SERVING.
YIELD: 1⅔ CUPS

TART CRUST

1½ CUPS UNBLEACHED
ALL-PURPOSE FLOUR
½ CUP CAKE FLOUR
1 TEASPOON SALT
¾ CUP (1½ STICKS) CHILLED
UNSALTED BUTTER,
CUT INTO PIECES
¼ CUP CHILLED SHORTENING
½ CUP ICE WATER

PULSE ALL THE FLOUR, SALT AND
BUTTER IN A FOOD PROCESSOR
TO BREAK UP THE BUTTER. ADD
THE SHORTENING AND PULSE
SEVERAL TIMES. ADD THE ICE
WATER GRADUALLY, PULSING
UNTIL CRUMBLY. KNEAD THE
DOUGH ON A FLOURED SURFACE
SEVERAL TIMES; SHAPE INTO A
DISK. WRAP IN PLASTIC WRAP.
CHILL FOR 2 HOURS. ROLL ON A
FLOURED SURFACE INTO A 12-
INCH CIRCLE. FIT INTO A 9-INCH
TART PAN. FIT A LARGE PIECE
OF BUTTERED FOIL BUTTER SIDE
DOWN ON THE DOUGH. FILL
WITH DRIED BEANS OR PIE
WEIGHTS. BAKE AT 450
DEGREES FOR 15 MINUTES OR
UNTIL THE EDGE IS LIGHTLY
BROWNED. REMOVE TO A WIRE
RACK. REMOVE THE FOIL AND
WEIGHTS. LET COOL COMPLETELY.
YIELD: 1 (9-INCH) TART CRUST

Coconut Custard Tart with Roasted Bananas

YIELD: 8 SERVINGS

½ CUP PLUS ⅓ CUP HEAVY CREAM
½ CUP CANNED UNSWEETENED
COCONUT MILK
½ CUP SUGAR
3 EGGS
1 TEASPOON VANILLA EXTRACT
¼ TEASPOON GROUND CARDAMOM
⅛ TEASPOON GROUND NUTMEG
⅛ TEASPOON SALT
1 BAKED (9-INCH) TART CRUST
(AT LEFT)

2 TABLESPOONS UNSALTED BUTTER
2 TABLESPOONS DARK BROWN
SUGAR
1 TABLESPOON DARK RUM
1 TABLESPOON ORANGE JUICE
3 MEDIUM BANANAS, CUT INTO
¾-INCH SLICES
½ CUP SWEETENED SHREDDED
COCONUT, LIGHTLY TOASTED

Whisk the cream, coconut milk, sugar, eggs, vanilla, cardamom, nutmeg and salt in a large bowl. Pour into the baked tart crust. Bake at 350 degrees for 20 minutes or until the filling is barely set. Remove to a wire rack to cool. Melt the butter in a large ovenproof skillet over medium heat. Add the brown sugar, rum and orange juice. Cook until the brown sugar is melted and the mixture is bubbling, stirring constantly. Add the bananas and toss to coat. Place the skillet in a 350-degree oven. Bake for 5 minutes or until the bananas are tender. Remove to a wire rack and let cool slightly.

Sprinkle the toasted coconut over the baked tart. Slice the tart and serve with the warm bananas. Note: This tart can be made up to 5 hours ahead. Cover and let stand at room temperature.

Cookbook Marketing Committee

Chair: Lyn Hallaron
Vice-Chair: Michelle Dodenhoff
Vice-Chair: Liz Goliwas

Treasurer: Lynden Swayze
Executive Liaison: Melanee Usdin
Executive Liaison: Eileen Gambel

Committee

Karyn Bewley
Carolyn Blaine
Caroline Blitzer
Barbara Bossier
Rae Bryan
Julie Buhrer
Patricia Charles
Kendall Gensler
Lynne Gibbons
Sarah Hoffman
Jami Kampen
Jane Landry
Evelyn Liberto

Ashley Longwell
Jennifer Mattingly
Margaret Mauté
Courtney Murphy
Ashley Nelson
Lesley Paxton
Nancy Plough
Stephanie Sherling
Michelle Slatten
Helen Smith
Laine Thomas
Lynne Tutt

JLNO Marketing Committee

Co-Chair: Carolyn Fitzpatrick
Co-Chair: Terri Havens
Cookbook Liaison: Melissa Rufty

Special Thanks

Jean Luc Albin (Maurice French Pastries)
Alliance Francaise
Joan Allison
Nina Austin
Rene Bajeaux (Windsor Court Hotel)
Ina and Randy Barlow (Kelsey's Restaurant)
Avery Bassich
Emily Becker
Judy Belsome
Pam Bennett
Donna Bologna
Denise Boudreaux
Gene Bourg
Betsy Bowman
Mr. and Mrs. Hjlmar E. Breit, Jr.
Dickie Brennan (Palace Café)
Ralph Brennan (Red Fish Grill and Bacco)
Mrs. Harold Brennand
Vanessa Brown
BeBe Guste Bruno
Mr. & Mrs. Joseph Bruno
Benny Burst
Stacy Day Burst
Cajun Injector
Robert J. Cangelosi, Jr., A.I.A.
Becky Chittal
Mr. and Mrs. Robert E. Cockrum
Patti Constantin
Frank Davis

Mark DeFelice (Pascal's Manale Restaurant)
Bill Dodenhoff
Laurie Doyle
Ann Dunbar (Anna Banana)
Nanci Easterling (Food Art)
Mr. and Mrs. Walter Flower
Ben Frank, Sr.
Ben Frank
Catherine Frank
Mrs. Richard Freeman
Haley Gabel (Bacco)
Dawn Gallo
John Gallo
Adolfo Garcia (Lucky Cheng's)
David Gooch (Galatoire's Restaurant)
Bernard Guste (Antoine's)
Jocelyn K. Hallaron
Susan Hamshire
John Harris (Gautreau's)
Klaus Hasmueller (Marriott Hotel)
Eades Hogue
Barbara Hogue
Patsy Hunter
Dennis Hutley (Le Parvenu)
Haley Gabel (Bacco)
Scott Gensler
Historic New Orleans Collection
Anne Kearney (Peristyle)
Mr. and Mrs. Peter Koeppel

Emeril Lagasse
(Delmonico Restaurant and Bar)
Benjamin Lazich (The Wine Seller)
Lisa Liggett (Windsor Court Hotel)
Betty Lyons (Ikebana International)
Joey Marcotte
Sr. Shirley Miller, RCSJ
(Academy of the Sacred Heart)
Devon Mohr (Planet Xeno)
L. W. Paxton
Elizabeth Perino (Perino's Garden Center)
Mr. and Mrs. David G. Perlis
Greg Piccolo (Bistro at the Maison de Ville)
Jerry Plough
Carol Pointer
Ann Preaus
Mr. and Mrs. Gothard J. Reck
Sally K. Reeves
Susan Ridgeway (Best of Susan)
Maureen and Billy Roberts
(The Gumbo Shop)
Mr. and Mrs. Charlie Rollins

Devlin Roussel (Red Fish Grill)
Mike Roussel (Brennan's Restaurant)
Jane Rubenstein
Hubert Sandot (Martinique Bistro)
Jackie Shreeves
(Academy of the Sacred Heart)
Jamie Shannon (Commander's Palace)
Patrick Singley (Gautreau's)
Mr. and Mrs. Eric F. Skrmetta
(House of Windsor)
Smith and Wollensky
Mary and Greg Sonnier
(Gabrielle Restaurant)
David G. Spielman
Muffin Spielman
Susan Spicer (Bayona)
Lynne Tutt
Glenn Vesh (Perfect Presentations)
Kevin Vizard
Elizabeth Walden
Mr. and Mrs. Thomas Westfeldt
Phyllis Waring

Recipe Contributors

Stacey Adams
Jean Luc Albin
Dia Allman
Tiffany Alexander
Cinny Anderson
Carol Appel
Maria Argote
Kimberly Armatis
Bruce Ashley
Rene Bajeaux
Colleen Barber
Randy Barlow
Colleen Barringer
Patricia Beeker
Margaret Bell
Pam Bennett
Ana Berry
Jackie Boh
Barbara Bossier
Dickie Brennan
Ralph Brennan
Ashley Bright
Aimee Brignac
Jata Brown
Margie Brown
BeBe Guste Bruno
Helen Burdin
Ed Burke
Gina Burke
Ann Burnside
Benny Burst
Stacy Day Burst
Helen Butcher
Anne Cain
Mary Capouch
Anne Chaffe

Nancy Chaffe
Mollee Clark
Mickey Cockrum
Ellen Coleman
Grant Coleman
Patti Constantin
Kimberly Conway
Pamela Cooper
Jeanne Couret
Katie Crosby
Cathy Daigle
Jennifer Daly
Karen Danna
Frank Davis
Kim Davis
Mark DeFelice
Rose Anne DeRussy
Eleanor Dodenhoff
Michelle Dodenhoff
Catherine Downs
Priscilla Duffy
Ann Dunbar
Nanci Easterling
Anne Eckert
Louise Erwin
Mary Eymard
Janet Favrot
Joan Ferrara
Donna Flower
Priestley Frank
Jan Friend
Kirsti Friend
Nina Friend
Haley Gabel
Millie Gaines
Adolfo Garcia

Katherine Gelderman
Betty Gensler
Kendall Gensler
Phil Gensler
Scott Gensler
Gwathmey Gomila
David Gooch
Elizabeth Goodyear
Lori Graves
Sanda Groome
Cynthia Guice
Bernard Guste
Lyn Hallaron
Marla Hamilton
Susan Hardy
John Harris
Lisa Hart
Klaus Hasmueller
Stacy Head
Mimi Heebe
Odom Heebe
Christina Hellmich
Debbie Hill
Sarah Hoffman
Valerie Howard
Billie Hultgren
Dennis Hutley
Anne Kearney
Flora Kelly
Gretchen Kemp
Cynthia Kessler
Joal B. Kuebel
Peggy Laborde
Emeril Lagasse
Elizabeth Landry
Jane Landry

Reece Lanier
Lisa Lapeyre
Lisa Liggett
JoAnn Lignon
Jamie Lindler
Mary Kate Lo Conte
Deeda Luke
Martiel Luther
Betty Lyons
Pamela Lyons
Elizabeth Macdiarmid
Meredith Macdiarmid
Beth Magee
Rhonda Magee
Melinda Mallery
Amy Marzullo
Jennifer Mattingly
Nisey Mayeaux
Elizabeth McAloon
Monique McCleskey
Carolyn McGavock
Maude McGuire
Ann McLeod
Laura McNeal
Kay Mettz
Sally Mettz
Ann Middleton
Mary Montague
Dee Moody
Ann Morton
Michelle Moulis
Cathy Myers
Lorri Murray
Holly Nalty
Jill Nalty
Kim Navarre

Trudy Nelson
Missie Noel
Robin O'Bannon
Jeanne Ogden
Elaine Olivier
Ashley Paxton
L.W. Paxton
Lesley Paxton
Lynsey Paxton
Greg Piccolo
Sheila Plater
Nancy Plough
Cissy Poindexter
Carol Pointer
Elizabeth Reed
Stephanie Reed
Mrs. H.E. Reily
Barbara Renaudin
Maury Rendeiro
Susan Ridgeway
Claire Riviere
Maureen and Billy Roberts
Lisa Rollins
Ellen Roniger
Alma Roohi
Debra Ropp
Devlin Roussel
Mike Roussel
Hubert Sandot
Gabriella St. Amant
Jennifer Schaumburg
Linda Schroeder
Jamie Shannon
Mary Grace Sellars
Elizabeth Sewell
Debbie Skrmetta

Eric Skrmetta
Jennifer Smith
Katherine Smith
K.T. Snyder
Mary and Greg Sonnier
Susan Spicer
Ann Stewart
Ebie Strauss
Marie Summitt
Marianne Swanson
Debbie Tabb
Virginia Taylor
Martha Thayer
Lucie Thornton
Ellen Tombaugh
Jennifer Tompkins
Elizabeth Truett
Ashbrooke Tullis
Melanee Usdin
Micheline Vandenburgh
Marcia Verret
Kevin Vizard
Peggy Waechter
Nicole Waguespack
Cynthia Wakefield
KK Walk
Phyllis Waring
Shannon Webre
Joan Wetzel
Leah Whann
Marilyn White
Maria Wisdom
Kathy Youngberg
Heather Zimmer

Resource Guide

Anna Banana
2916 Cleary Ave.
Metairie, LA 70001
504-887-2664

Antoine's Restaurant
713 St. Louis St.
New Orleans, LA 70130
504-581-4422

Bacco
310 Chartres St.
New Orleans, LA 70130
504-522-2426

Bayona
430 Dauphine St.
New Orleans, LA 70112
504-525-4455

Best of Susan
5145 General DeGaulle Blvd.
New Orleans, LA 70131
504-394-5640

Bistro at the Maison de Ville
733 Toulouse St.
New Orleans, LA 70130
504-528-9206

Gene Bourg
Independent Journalist
1227 Royal St., No. 5
New Orleans, LA 70116
504-525-9532

Brennan's Restaurant
417 Royal St.
New Orleans, LA 70130
504-525-9711

Cajun Injector
By Chef Williams
P.O. Box 97
Clinton, LA 70722
800-221-8060

Robert J. Cangelosi, Jr., A.I.A.
Restoration Architect
Koch and Wilson Architects
1100 Jackson Ave.
New Orleans, LA 70130
504-581-7023

Patti Constantin
131 Nursery Ave.
Metairie, LA 70005
504-835-5552

Commander's Palace
1413 Washington Ave.
New Orleans, LA 70130
504-899-8221

Delcambre Interior Design
Tom Delcambre
936 Valence St.
New Orleans, LA 70118
504-896-2318

Delmonico Restaurant and Bar
Emeril Lagasse
1300 St. Charles Ave.
New Orleans, LA 70130
504-523-9307
504-525-4937

Food Art
801 Carondelet St.
New Orleans, LA 70130
504-524-2381

Bruce Givens Foreman, Inc.
Bruce Givens Foreman, ASID
6262 Highland Rd.
Baton Rouge, LA 70808
225-769-3745

Gabrielle Restaurant
3201 Esplanade Ave.
New Orleans, LA 70119
504-948-6233

Galatoire's Restaurant
209 Bourbon St.
New Orleans, LA 70116
504-525-2021

Gautreau's Restaurant
1728 Soniat St.
New Orleans, LA 70115
504-899-7397

The Gumbo Shop
630 St. Peter
New Orleans, LA 70116
504-525-1486

Historic New Orleans
   Collection
533 Royal St.
New Orleans, LA 70130

Home Hook and Ladder
   Antiques
Sandra Freeman, Owner
4100 Magazine St.
New Orleans, LA 70115
504-895-4480

House of Windsor
    Gourmet Products
501 Destrehan Ave.
Harvey, LA 70058
504-341-5631

Ikebana International
Betty Lyons
6323 West End Blvd.
New Orleans, LA 70124
504-486-2658

Kelsey's Restaurant
3923 Magazine St.
New Orleans, LA 70115
504-897-6722

Lucky Cheng's Restaurant
720 St. Louis St.
New Orleans, LA 70130
504-529-2045

Anne McGee, Inc.
Interior Design
Anne McGee, Owner
940 Royal St., Suite 347
New Orleans, LA 70116
504-430-2858

Marriott Hotel
555 Canal St.
New Orleans, LA 70130
504-581-1000

Martinique Bistro
5908 Magazine St.
New Orleans, LA 70115
504-891-8495

Maurice French Pastries
3501 Hessmer Ave.
Metairie, LA 70002
504-885-1526

Dan Merrell Painting
Dan and Judy Merrell, Designers
265 Hord St.
New Orleans, LA 70123
504-733-3122

Paint Works
Julie Neill
6378 Louis XIV St.
New Orleans, LA 70124

Palace Café Restaurant
605 Canal St.
New Orleans, LA 70130
504-523-1661

Le Parvenu
509 Williams Blvd.
Metairie, LA 70062
504-471-0534

Pascal's Manale Restaurant
1838 Napoleon Ave.
New Orleans, LA 70115
504-895-4877

Perfect Presentations
Floral Design and Event Planning
810 Fulton St.
New Orleans, LA 70130
504-522-7442

Perino's Garden Center
3100 Veterans Memorial Hwy.
Metairie, LA 70002
504-834-7888

Peristyle
1041 Dumaine St.
New Orleans, LA 70114
504-593-9535

Planet Xeno
3818 Magazine St.
New Orleans, LA 70115
504-895-3828

Red Fish Grill
115 Bourbon St.
New Orleans, LA 70130
504-598-1200

David G. Spielman
Photography
The Spielman Company
P.O. Box 15741
New Orleans, LA 70175
504-899-7670

Elizabeth Walden Floral Design
4401 Camp St.
New Orleans, LA 70115
504-899-2794

Windsor Court Hotel
300 Gravier St.
New Orleans, LA 70130
504-523-6000

The Wine Seller
5000 Prytania St.
New Orleans, LA 70115
504-895-3828

Index

Crescent City Collection

A TASTE OF NEW ORLEANS

Junior League of New Orleans, Inc.
4319 Carondelet Street
New Orleans, Louisiana 70115
504-895-6653
www.jlno.org

Please send _____ copies of *Crescent City Collection* @ $26.95 each $ _____

New Orleans residents add sales tax @ $2.43 each $ _____

Louisiana residents add sales tax @ $1.08 each $ _____

Postage and handling @ $5.00 each $ _____

Total $ _____

_____
Name

_____
Address

_____
City   State   Zip

Method of Payment: [   ] MasterCard   [   ] VISA
                     [   ] Check payable to Junior League of New Orleans

_____
Account Number   Expiration Date

_____
Signature

Photocopies will be accepted.